The Culture of Urban Control

The Culture of Urban Control

*Jail Overcrowding in the
Crime Control Era*

John P. Walsh

LEXINGTON BOOKS
Lanham • Boulder • New York • Toronto • Plymouth, UK

Published by Lexington Books
A wholly owned subsidiary of The Rowman & Littlefield Publishing Group, Inc.
4501 Forbes Boulevard, Suite 200, Lanham, Maryland 20706
www.rowman.com

10 Thornbury Road, Plymouth PL6 7PP, United Kingdom

British Library Cataloguing in Publication Information Available

Library of Congress Cataloging-in-Publication Data

Walsh, John P., 1966–
The culture of urban control : jail overcrowding in the crime control era / John P. Walsh.
p. cm.
Includes bibliographical references and index.
ISBN 978-0-7391-7464-7 (cloth : alk. paper)—ISBN 978-0-7391-7465-4 (ebook)
ISBN 978-1-4985-1138-4 (pbk : alk. paper)
1. Jails—Overcrowding—United States. 2. Corrections—United States. I. Title.
HV9471.W334 2013
365'.34--dc23
2013012293

Printed in the United States of America

For Thomas "Nino" Castellano (1955–2009), a friend, a mentor, and a consistent supporter of the need for humane criminal justice policy.

Contents

List of Tables and Figures

Acknowledgments

I am fortunate to have benefited from the insight, advice and support of numerous mentors, friends and colleagues during differing stages of this project. In its earliest stages the critical comments and suggestions of criminologists Arvind Verma, Steven Chermak, Jody Sundt, William Pridemore and political scientist Mary Lee Luskin created an environment that substantively shaped my approach to investigating this subject matter. In addition many thanks for the support and perspective of fellow colleagues Gregg Barak, Thomas Castellano, James "Chip" Coldron, Douglas Thomson, Joseph Trotter and Kevin Whiteacre, who weighed in at differing points during the development of this project and provided avenues of understanding as I traveled through this process. In addition, I would like to thank my current colleagues within the School of Criminal Justice and the College of Community and Public Service at Grand Valley State University, who continue to provide me with an environment of intellectual growth and compassion.

Many thanks to the Cook County Sheriff's Office and the John Howard Association for access to the data used within this research and for the encouragement and support to document this important policy narrative. Specifically, I would like to thank Michael Sheahan, Thomas Dart, David Devane, William Wallace, Charles Fasano and Dan Hoffman. Thanks also to Anne Schaffer of the Office of the Secretary of the Cook County Board of Commissioners, CaTrice Monik and Scott Erdman of the Office of the County Clerk, and Kevin Byrnes for research and structural support at differing stages of this endeavor.

As a first-time author this volume would not have come to fruition without the support faith and patience of a select group at Lexington Books including my editor Jana Hodges-Kluck, editorial assistant Eric Wrona and a group of excellent anonymous reviewers. I am continually grateful for their time and effort.

Finally and most importantly, I would like to thank my family, who have continued to believe in me and support my interest in this venture and the multiple trajectories involved with pursuing this project: specifically, my father, Michael Walsh, and my partner and love, Maureen Morrissey Walsh. It is through their support and trust that this project was possible.

Introduction

The purpose of this book is to expand upon the literature and research associated with large urban jail systems within the United States. Historically, jails have been given very little attention in the criminal justice literature when compared with the research and literature associated with prison systems and more recently post-conviction community corrections initiatives. The *Jail*, written by the late John Irwin, published over twenty-five years ago, continues to provide students and scholars alike with their general initiation and many times conclusion of local level incarceration perspectives.[1] This void in the literature is problematic on many fronts. First and foremost, it seems quite obvious that every individual who ends up within a state prison system spends a period of time incarcerated within a local jail system. Second, local jail systems have been an instrumental criminal justice decision point connecting enforcement policies of the crime control era with the outcome now commonly referred to as the prison industrial complex. Third, pretrial defendants incarcerated and processed through a county jail system, who do not end up within their state prison systems, perceive the process of justice based upon experiences within the local incarcerated setting. Finally, jails differ from prisons in that they are shaped by the complexities of local criminal justice agencies, local government politics, local courts and their communities. How federal judicial intervention affects local jail settings and the political actors within those settings is an issue that has received limited attention within the criminal justice literature.[2]

SETTING AND BACKGROUND

The area of study focused on inmate overcrowding and conditions of confinement within large urban jail settings and the subsequent dispute arising from federal judiciary oversight within the Cook County Department of Corrections. In 1974, pretrial detainees filed a class action suit protesting the conditions of confinement, citing them as violations of their constitutional rights. The suit, *Duran v. Elrod*, led to a federal consent decree[3] handed down in 1982 that stated each pretrial detainee is entitled to a permanent bed in a cell.[4] Twenty-seven years later the ongoing consent decree and litigation now known as *Duran v. Brown* continues to address overcrowding problems at the Cook County Jail. Currently the jail consists of eleven divisions with 9,798 beds. According to an April 2002 population and capacity summary the jail had an average daily population of 11,142 persons. The daily average of overflow population between January and April 2002 was at 1,621 persons.[5] By mid-year 2003, the capacity rate at Cook County Jail was at 109 percent with an average daily population of 10,864 inmates relegated to 9,798 beds.[6]

In response to the filed class action lawsuit and the subsequent ongoing federal consent decree, numerous stakeholders have contributed to the shaping of Cook County Jail policy through negotiation, mediation, and oversight committees. These actions or disputes have included the Cook County Sheriff's Department and the Cook County Department of Corrections who operate the jail, the Cook County State's Attorney who legally represents the county, the Cook County Board of Commissioners who allocate the jail budget, local and federal judiciary members, the Cook County Judiciary Advisory Council, the John Howard Association (an NGO prison watchdog group providing oversight and analysis for the federal judiciary), community activists, the media and litigants' legal representatives.

The time period between 1993 and 2003 was chosen as the focus of this study due to the fact that by the early 1990s the rights of prisoners in relation to incarceration were firmly established in the federal courts. A basic blueprint of rights and amenities established in other jurisdictions (which will be further elucidated upon in chapter 1) were processually being transferred to the Cook County Department of Corrections. Yet in Chicago, in the 1990s, specific historical incidents placed a new stress on the Cook County Department of Corrections and in turn changed a static and straightforward consent decree, focusing on established national standards of incarceration, to a consent decree whereby individuals were thrust into reacting to a crack epidemic and the associated incarceration binge of the war on drugs. By 1992, the Cook County Department of Corrections had reached record heights of occupancy. In addition by 1993, numerous internal and external evaluation reports had been disseminated among the disputants; and the Department of Community Supervision and Intervention, an alternative to jail incarceration, had been formed. These historical incidents and the subsequent political metaphors, policies, and rhetoric associated with these events served to place strain on the consent decree and create a dynamic disputing process. Subsequently, the qualitative data associated with the framing dialectic between 1993 and 2003 is not only richer in context; it also reveals the dynamic political and social landscape of punishment and its relation to federal oversight within a large urban jail setting.

Historical Background of the Research Setting

Prior to the beginning of the Duran federal consent decree, Cook County approached growing inmate populations through policy rooted in new construction. In 1928, construction began on a new county jail, Division I, at 26th Street and California Avenue in Chicago. The new jail had a designed capacity of approximately 1,275 small (4' x 8') single bed cells.[7] Coupled with the already existing House of Corrections, the two facilities had a combined daily population of over 3,200 individuals. By the mid-1950s, Division I had a daily population of approximately 2,400 inmates. During this time period the existing single bed cells in Division I had been double bunked, and inmates were sleeping on floors, tables and homemade hammocks suspended from the bars in dayroom areas.[8] The population was increased by the presence of convicted inmates serving up to five-year sentences in the jail, as well as the presence of a death row for condemned inmates awaiting executions.

In 1955, Division II was constructed. This building had a designed capacity of 1,396 inmates. By 1967, a special grand jury investigating conditions at the jail, which was dominated by a barn boss system, led to the firing of the jail warden.[9] [10] In the 1970s, Cook County Jail capacity increased by approximately 70 percent with the construction of four new divisions housing approximately 3,000 more inmates. In 1976, the successor to the previously fired warden was also fired after scandalous conditions were highlighted by another special grand jury.[11] In addition and most importantly in 1974, an inmate named Dan Duran filed a section 1983 federal lawsuit against the Cook County Sheriff and the Cook County Board of Commissioners. The lawsuit *Duran v. Elrod* (74 C 2949) alleged inadequate and inhumane living conditions, which violated Duran's constitutional rights. The suit was subsequently transformed into a class action suit on behalf of all pretrial detainees (approximately 85 percent of the total population) housed at the Cook County Jail.

Prior to the *Duran v. Elrod* case being filed in 1974, Cook County had already begun construction on the aforementioned new four divisions totaling approximately 3,000 beds. In addition to overcrowding, *Duran v. Elrod* focused attention on qualitative issues such as sanitation, discipline, classification, food, law library use, telephone privileges, and staffing patterns, among other issues. Besides overcrowding and the subsequent qualitative issues associated with overcrowding conditions and confinement, another lawsuit was filed under 42 U.S.C. section 1983 alleging that Cook County and the Illinois Department of Mental Health failed to provide necessary mental health care in the Cook County Department of Corrections (CCDOC).[12] By 1982, with the additional bed space created by new construction and initial improvements to jail conditions brought about by *Duran v. Elrod*, CCDOC was accredited by the American Correctional Association.

Between 1982 and 1993, Cook County continued to address jail crowding concerns with a strong focus on building. In 1985, the addition of a 520-bed facility for inmates with medical and psychiatric problems was opened. By 1993, 1,750 new beds were made available with the construction of two new divisions. Yet, these beds were filled immediately and merely lowered the number of individuals sleeping on floors each night from a peak of 2,750 in late 1992 to an average of 1,500 during 1993.[13]

Concurrently with the building impetus during the period of 1982–1993, the plaintiffs and defendants of the *Duran v. Elrod* case entered into a consent decree. In 1983, the Duran plaintiffs charged the defendants with violating the consent decree by allowing inmates to sleep on floors. While the court maintained that jail population should be managed by the relevant branches of local government, it ordered that CCDOC administrators were to begin releasing inmates on their own recognizance. During the last five months of 1983, more than 6,500 inmates were released on jail I-bonds.[14] In 1984, more than 15,000 individuals were released on I-bonds by CCDOC. During this time period local judges and media focused attention on individuals released on I-bond who failed to appear or occasionally committed new crimes while on bond. In addition, local judges who believed their bail-setting authority was being threatened began raising bail amounts, marking arrest reports with "no I-bond" and threatening to hold sheriff's officials in contempt.[15] These judicial and media pressures reduced CCDOC I-bonds to 7,483 in 1985 and 1,450 in 1986. Increased jail populations resulted in a return to the recognizance bond policy with an increase of I-bonds in 1987 to 12,000.[16]

In spite of increased I-bond use jail overcrowding continued to intensify. By 1989, with I-bonds reaching over 35,000 and the development of an electronic monitoring program instituted as an early-release mechanism, U.S. District Judge Milton Shadur held Sheriff James O'Grady (1986–1990) and Cook County Commissioners in contempt of court imposing fines of $1,000 a day for inadequate efforts to relieve crowding. When county commissioners appropriated $365,000 to cover the cost of fines, Judge Shadur threatened jailing county officials for contempt.

As overcrowding, as well as the overcrowding dispute, continued to worsen, Judge Shadur directed the John Howard Association to compile a comprehensive report on jail overcrowding and conditions with short-term and long-term recommendations. In addition, the jail population was also being investigated by the Bureau of Justice Assistance through the Adjudication Technical Assistance Project (ATAP). ATAP analyzed felony court processing within Cook County and its relation to jail overcrowding.[17] The John Howard Association report to Judge Shadur recommended eleven major changes including: development of long-term and short-term plans for compliance, creation of a criminal justice coordinating council and an expanded range of mechanisms for supervised release.[18] The ATAP analysis specified over seventy recommendations related to court processing and length of stay for individuals incarcerated in the jail. Included in these recommendations was the implementation of pretrial services, specialty courts, increased felony review screening, as well as a countywide criminal justice coordinating council.[19]

In 1990, a consulting consortium of criminal justice planners, architects, engineers, and other experts including the National Council on Crime and Delinquency (NCCD) developed the Cook County Long-Range Master Plan.[20] The master plan provided population analysis and projections, evaluation of existing jail space, and future construction and space needs. In 1992, the Illinois Criminal Justice Information Authority (ICJIA) published an evaluation of Cook County pretrial release mechanisms that focused on the use of I-bonds. The study revealed that the increased use of I-bonds by CCDOC resulted in high rates of failure to appear, delays in case processing, higher instances of arrests for new crimes, and frequent reincarceration.[21] As mentioned previously, 1992 to 1993 also brought about the opening of 1,750 new beds at CCDOC. In 1992, CCDOC occupancy levels reached a high of 133 percent of bed space used.[22]

It is within the aforementioned historical context that this research begins. While this is a snapshot of a larger struggle surrounding overcrowding and conditions of confinement at CCDOC, the time period being studied provides an avenue to examine public service, judicial decision making, and correctional management within the political complexity of a large urban criminal justice system. The role of the researcher in regard to this project began in June 2002. The researcher met with Cook County Sheriff Michael F. Sheahan to discuss research and policy evaluation possibilities within the Cook County Sheriff's Department. During the initial meeting Sheriff Sheahan remarked that the vast majority of time and energy associated with criminal justice policy at the county level was focused within the Cook County Department of Corrections. Having already served as sheriff, beginning with his first county-wide election in 1990, twelve years later he remarked that "if I knew of all the problems embedded within the jail I may have never run for this position." This particular statement was the beginning of my research into this topic. The researcher was aware that Sheriff Sheahan was not an experiential novice within the criminal justice system of Cook County. Prior to his position as Cook County sheriff (1990–2006) he was a city of Chicago alderman who chaired the police and fire commission. Prior to his political career he was a Chicago police officer and high school teacher. After a lifetime of public service positions, the majority within the criminal justice realm, and after twelve years as sheriff there was specific exasperation to his remark regarding the Cook County Department of Corrections as an endless public policy problem.

INVESTIGATIVE RESEARCH PLAN

Many of the overcrowding and conditions of confinement consent decrees within the United States have been settled, vacated, or resolved in some manner over the last several years.[23] Within Cook County, the Duran consent decree dispute continues into its twenty-seventh year. During this time period numerous building projects, oversight reports, internal and external analysis projects have facilitated changes within the Cook County Department of Corrections. The consent decree surrounding overcrowding and conditions of confinement at CCDOC provides an opportunity to analyze the function, structure and process of disputing within the criminal justice system at the local level. Within this dispute numerous claims have been made by differing claims-makers regarding conditions of confinement and jail overcrowding. Through frame analysis this research will examine the differing claims posited between the years of 1993 and 2003.

Frame Theory and Claims-Making Research

Claims-making research analyzes the presentation of crime, fear of crime, and media representations of crime as socially constructed events.[24] At its extreme, the constructive paradigm argues a methodology based on rejection of belief in an external reality; it emphasizes the importance of exploring the way in which different stakeholders in a social setting construct their beliefs. "Thus, we define social problems as the activities of groups making assertions of grievances and claims with respect to some putative condition."[25] As Best argues, "Our sense of what is or is not a social problem is a product, something that has been produced or constructed through social activities."[26] Within constructionist perspectives of the presentation of crime, fear of crime, and media representation of crime there is a lineage of literature investigating the interaction between political actors, media representatives, subsequent public fear, and the shaping of criminal justice policy.[27]

The exploration of a constructed reality by way of stakeholders' presentations is rooted in interpretivism. The primary task of researchers using an interpretive framework is to present the interpretations of reality that are being presented by the people they are studying. As Rubin and Rubin point out, events are understood differently by different people.[28] There is a rich history of interpretivism not only within the constructionist-based literature of sociology and criminology but also within the fields of anthropology, as well as cultural studies.[29]

Within the field of cultural anthropology the study of how reality, ideas, depictions, and occurrences are framed at the local level is based within the interpretivist construct. As Geertz points out, "Frameworks are the very stuff of cultural anthropology, which is mostly engaged in trying to determine what this people or that take to be the point of what they are doing."[30] Within the field of cultural studies, interpretivism is used to understand the collective ways the group understands experience. In addition, cultural theorists argue that the ideology of a group is produced and reproduced within the interpretive practices of the individuals within these groups. From a cultural studies standpoint ideology is a general process of the production of meanings and ideas. Cultural studies theorists argue that a differing number of ideologies compete for preeminence. Within this competition, dominant features of an ideology are challenged and shaped by emergent features while continuing to reflect residual features.[31] In other words, the production of meaning is narrowed and expanded as former or residual perspectives fall by the wayside and newer emergent perspectives are promulgated. This dynamic interrelation, or as Hall argues "an untidy but characteristic unevenness of development," are what interpretivist methodologies seeks to document and understand.[32]

> What is important are the significant breaks where old lines of thought are disrupted, older constellations displaced, and elements, old and new, are regrouped around a different set of premises and themes.[33]

Within the field of cultural anthropology interpretivist frameworks are predominantly examined through differing levels of participant observation and/or ethnography. Within cultural studies interpretive frameworks are routinely examined through evaluation of social texts. Regardless, both disciplines are applying interpretivism in an attempt to describe and understand phenomena from a comprehensive perspective.

> As Frow points out, cultural studies' starting point is an inclusive conception of culture which it derives indirectly from anthropology and which it understands to cover the whole range of practices and representations through which a social group's reality (or realities) is constructed and maintained.[34]

From an anthropological explanation of interpretivist frameworks we can come to an understanding on the previous points of reference that Frow is explaining in his conception of cultural studies and its relation to cultural anthropology.[35]

> The figurative nature of social theory, the moral interplay of contrasting mentalities, the practical difficulties in seeing things as others see them, the epistemological status of common sense, the revelatory power of art, the symbolic construction of authority, the clattering variousness of modern intellectual life, and the relationship between what people take as fact and what they regard as justice are treated, one after the other, in an attempt somehow to understand how it is we understand understandings not our own.[36]

The application of interpretivist frameworks serves to reveal representation, reproduction and transformation from the particular unit of analysis of study. Mather and Yngvesson point out that transformation of a dispute occurs when a change in its content results from interaction and involvement of the participants.[37] These changes occur through processes of narrowing and expanding the discourse surrounding a dispute. In addition, the ability of supporters and audience members to effect narrowing and expansion is also a consideration. Through case study examples, these authors explore the transformative aspects of narrowing and expansion across disputes. Mather and Yngvesson conclude that "transformations tend to be dominated by the powerful, and since those in power typically have a vested interest in the existing social order, most disputes will be transformed by narrowing."[38]

The exploration of social texts or the exploration of communicative interaction within social texts is rooted within the methodology of frame analysis. The theoretical precursor to the framework methodology was initially explicated within Erving Goffman's *Frame Analysis: An Essay on the Organization of Experience*, which explores how concepts are used in organizing individual as well as institutional experience. The premises of Goffman's approach follow the philosophical tenets put forth by William James in his phenomenological exploration of how individuals come to understand things as "real."[39] Goffman argues that activity and interaction operate within what are considered appropriate or acceptable frames.[40] From an institutional perspective we may see competing frames emerging in opposition to dominant frames. As emergent frames, or aspects of these frames, become acceptable or appropriate the dominant frame is incrementally changed. This change in the dominant frame is also shaped by residual frames from previously acceptable or appropriate dominant frames of the past.

Goffman looks toward the frame dispute as a unit of analysis when attempting to explain institutional differences and the subsequent differing realities considered appropriate or acceptable in the field of justice.[41] By frame dispute Goffman is referring to how opposing versions of events differentially define what has been or is happening.

> Similarly, there are disputes—not uncommonly heated—in the matter of whether or not to see a particular act as a symptom of some kind, to be viewed in a natural framework, or as a culpable guided doing. Theories of crime, for example, provide no agreement on this matter, tending to fall into two camps, depending on which analysis is put forward. Obviously, viewing a criminal as sick leads to one remedial ideal, viewing him within a moralistic framework, another. Indeed there are criminal offenses that one jurisdiction will see primarily as expressions of psychological disorder and another jurisdiction as a question of responsible bad behavior. (And moreover, if there is institutional machinery for dealing with cases defined in both of the two ways, and if,

in addition, there are professionals occupationally committed to the
two different approaches, then an institutional basis for frame disputes
is to be found.[42]

It is clear Goffman is pointing out that frame analysis can be applied to
institutions involved in disputing such as the courts and the criminal
justice system. Previously, researchers positing analytical frame perspectives have focused on how the media has presented crime to the public
and in turn how the public perception of crime is shaped by these
frames.[43] Chermak argues that stakeholders within criminal justice institutions have a financial and ideological stake in how social problems are
presented to the public.[44] These institutional presentations result from
behind-the-scenes disputes, negotiations and mediations, which many
times result in a combination of coherent agreed-upon presentations, as
well as competing presentations to the media and subsequently to the
public. In essence, competing discourse is meted out within and between
institutional actors prior to presentation to the media and subsequent
public. Many times public policy issues such as crime and punishment
are ideologically and politically negotiated prior to media presentation.
While there may be specific disagreements between institutional agencies
and actors that are presented to the media, much of the dispute is infor-
mally negotiated to acceptance prior to media and public presentation.

The process by which these disputes are negotiated takes place
through symbolic discourse into what Gamson refers to as interpretive
packages. These interpretive packages pay attention to specific worldviews and assumptions held by institutions and actors involved in the
dispute, as well as media outlets and the public who may eventually be
presented with these packages.[45]

> Each policy issue has a relevant public discourse—a particular set of
> ideas and symbols that are used in various public forums to construct
> meaning about it. This discourse evolves over time, providing interpre-
> tations and meanings for newly occurring events.[46]

The interpretive packages use metaphors, visuals, stories and numbers in
what are referred to as "condensing symbols" to present core frames on a
specific issue.[47] Beckett applied this method in an analysis examining
how the media frames crime and drug issues.[48] In her methodology she
outlines core frames for differing interpretive packages. These packages
display rhetorical devices (i.e., exemplars, catchphrases, depictions, principles and motifs) which suggest particular frames and courses of policy
appropriate to address the issue.[49]

The differing interpretive packages and the underlying ideological
and political policy implications that are eventually presented to the media and the public are sponsored by particular agencies, groups and individuals involved within the ongoing dispute. Beckett's (1995) analysis of
drug crime in the news, categorizes interpretive packages as state spon-

sored or nonstate sponsored.[50] Chermak's analysis of drugs in the news argues that over 50 percent of source attribution to the media is reliant upon official sources such as police and court officials and that this source documentation serves to protect and benefit the sponsor of the information.[51] Analyzing the interpretive packaging of issues prior to a coherent state sponsorship or prior to official source presentation to the media or public provides a unique insight into the development of policy, as well as how official agencies and their representatives shape an ongoing ideological dispute to their benefit.

The Cook County Jail Consent Decree Dispute

The complexity of the ongoing conflict is clarified through the development of a process model of the consent decree dispute. The model provided in figure 1 conceptualizes claims-making and framing as a continuous process where outcomes of certain processes serve as inputs for subsequent processes. The process model provides the linkage between key stakeholders and breaks those links down into inputs, processes, and outcomes. The dispute is examined through four processes: frame building, frame setting, individual-level effects of framing and a link between individual-level frames and the originators' susceptibility to framing.[52]

As the feedback loop returns, the primary claims-maker reanalyzes judgment based on the new frames produced at the individual level and reframes their original claims. For example, the John Howard Association as a primary claims-maker within the model may build a frame based on the presentation of data indicating overcrowding within a specific division within the jail. The frame-setting process may consist of particular rhetoric focusing on drug defendants as nonviolent offenders who do not need to be incarcerated. This frame is presented to secondary claims-makers such as the Cook County State's Attorney who then re-frames the originally posited frame to include rhetoric regarding previous violent convictions by particular drug defendants. This process continues indefinitely during the course of the consent decree, continually changing or reinforcing the dominant framing of the jail overcrowding dispute, as well as expanding and narrowing residual and emergent frames within the dispute.[53]

Within a large urban jail setting such as Cook County, critiques of arrest policy, bail/bond processing, civil rights/due process issues, and infrastructure shortfalls combined with external economic developments of dwindling social safety nets, structural inequality, and local community needs provide a micro-level stage to examine the dialectic surrounding incarceration and punishment. Using a frame analysis approach to investigate these communicative interactions at the local level in regard to the *Duran v. Sheahan* consent decree is the script that defines this political theater production.

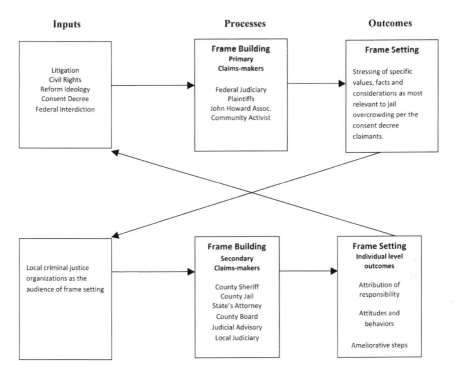

Figure Intro 1. Consent Decree Dispute Process Model. *As the dispute moves from individual level outcome frame setting a feedback loop occurs whereby the dispute is reframed.*

The importance of examining stakeholder claims is that it provides a systematic avenue to expose the narrative emanating from the consent decree between 1993 and 2003. This narrative provides the reader with a comprehensive account of local level incarceration within a large urban jail. The dominant frames reveal the concepts and arguments that have taken priority within the overcrowding and conditions of confinement dispute. Residual frames are the lingering or the remainder of previous arguments and concepts related to the dispute and emergent frames are the concepts and arguments that are coming into existence within the dispute. Two groups of stakeholders influence the aforementioned frames: first, the primary stakeholders, who are positing ameliorative changes within the Cook County Department of Corrections; alternately, the secondary stakeholders are reacting to these claims through a process of reframing. The primary stakeholders consist of the federal judiciary, plaintiffs, the John Howard Association, and community activists. Secondary stakeholders consist of the Cook County Sheriff's Office, the Cook County Department of Corrections, the Cook County State's Attorney's

Office, the Cook County Board of Commissioners, local judicial advisory, and the local judiciary.

PLAN OF THE BOOK

Examining how the culture of local punishment is structured, functions, reproduces, and expands within Cook County's local jail setting requires a methodological approach that assesses the ongoing communicative interaction between the differing stakeholders that shape county level correctional policy. Examining the themes and frames produced from a qualitative perspective through the analysis of differing claims-maker documents demonstrates how the discourse over disputes about over-crowding are embedded in the broader cultural context of justice and punishment. The unit of analysis within the stakeholder textual data is the claims-makers. How jail overcrowding is related to politics, bureau-cratic-administrative concerns, punishment perspectives, community ideals, and judicial priorities is embedded within the claims-maker dis-course and subsequent frames emanating from the discourse. In addition, shared meaning and negotiation as to what are the most important con-siderations in addressing the overcrowding dispute across all claims-makers emerged. As Chermak argues, "Claims-makers work to sponsor and then promote preferred meanings."[54] These preferred meanings pos-ited by differing claims-makers were not entirely static over the course of the dispute.

The use of frame analysis applied to textual communication was uti-lized to capture individual level and organizational level interaction within the ongoing jail dispute. Frame theory is rooted in linguistic stud-ies of interaction, and points to the way shared assumptions and mean-ings shape the interpretation of any particular event.[55]

The population of documents and textual sources for the study in-cluded federal court documents, oversight monitoring reports, county board hearing transcripts, correspondence between disputants, budget and planning documents, previous consultant-based research on the dis-pute and newspaper media articles surrounding Cook County Jail over-crowding.

Two levels of analysis occurred within this research. First, primary claims-making within the decree by the federal judiciary, litigants, John Howard Association, media, and community activists served to indicate changes over time within the dominant frames presented to the Cook County criminal justice system and county-level agencies involved in the jail overcrowding dispute. Dominant frames are defined as the issue or central organizing idea that is of the most prominence surrounding the social issue of jail overcrowding during the particular time period of measurement.[56] In addition, secondary claims-makers (i.e., individual level county agencies and their representatives within the system) were assessed in their reframing, over time, of the dominant frames originally supplanted by the primary claims-makers. At each stage within this analysis residual and emergent properties were identified and analyzed (refer to figure 1). Residual frames refer to those central organizing ideas that fade from prominence over time, and emergent frames refer to those central organizing ideas that gain prominence over time.[57] These analytical approaches draw attention toward the complexity of this particular dispute, its relation to a loosely coupled criminal justice system and how the discourse on local level jail overcrowding is embedded in the broader cultural context of justice, punishment and the growth of the penal industrial complex.

Data Collection

The population of stakeholder textual data used for this research included 2,410 pages of documents produced between 1993 and 2003 from the federal judiciary, the John Howard Association, litigants and their attorneys, the county sheriff, state's attorney, CCDOC, the County Board of Commissioners, the County Judicial Advisory Council, local judiciary, and consultants involved with the dispute. The completeness and accuracy of this population of documents provides a dense amount of textual data representing all of the disputants involved with the consent decree between 1993 and 2003. The John Howard Association and the Cook County Sheriff's Office were contacted by the researcher, and each organization provided access to its library holdings of all documents produced during the time period of the study.[58] Primary claims-makers included the federal judiciary, plaintiffs within the lawsuit, the John Howard Association (a nongovernmental prison watchdog group providing oversight for the federal judiciary), and community activists. Secondary claims-makers included the county sheriff, county state's attorney, the Judicial Advisory Council of Cook County, Cook County Board members, and local judiciary.

Table: Intro. 1. Stakeholder Textual Data Population Stratified by Claims-maker and Year between 1993 and 2003

	1993	1994	1995	1996	1997	1998	1999	2000	2001	2002	2003	Total
Primary Claims-makers	N=21	N=132	N=174	N=160	N=263	N=171	N=170	N=30	N=166	N=102	N=168	N=1557 64.6%
Secondary Claims-makers	N=14	N=47	N=86	N=104	N=120	N=99	N=52	N=57	N=76	N=48	N=150	N=853 35.4%
Total	N=35 1.4.5%	N=179 7.43%	N=260 10.80%	N=264 10.96%	N=383 15.90%	N=270 11.20%	N=222 9.21%	N=87 3.60%	N=242 10.04%	N=150 6.22%	N=318 13.19%	N=2410 100%

Table 1 reflects that almost two-thirds of the stakeholder text data population was produced by primary claims-makers and just over one-third of the documents were produced by secondary claims-makers. In addition, stratifying the text population by year reveals the time periods with the most active dialectic regarding the ongoing dispute.

Also included in the data population were 334 newspaper media articles from the *Chicago Sun-Times* and the *Chicago Tribune* that were published between 1993 and 2003 focusing on the Cook County Jail and conditions of confinement at the jail. The *Sun-Times* and the *Tribune* are the two major print media sources within Chicago and Cook County. The newspaper media article population was generated using two different library database search tools. Using Boolean searching across the Lexis-Nexis and Newsbank database systems, the terms "Cook County Jail" and "jail overcrowding," as well as "conditions of confinement" within headings and narratives, were searched across the years 1993 and 2003 for the *Chicago Sun-Times* and *Chicago Tribune*. This media text acquisition process is well recognized within content analysis research.[59]

Beginning in the late 1980s CCDOC data revealed a sharp increase in the number of inmates incarcerated, as well as a sharp increase in the inmate average overflow population. By 1992, CCDOC was experiencing an overflow population rate that was increasing at a much faster rate than the daily population. Between 1992 and 2003 the average daily population continued to increase while the average overflow population began a decline. The inverse relationship as exhibited in figure 2 provides a clear demarcation whereby the public policy agenda regarding jail overcrowding and conditions of confinement began to change. The context of those changes was embedded within the two different textual data populations.

The defined population of documents between 1993 and 2003 provided a ten-year era of disputing whereby the disputants have all become increasingly knowledgeable and educated on the issues surrounding jail overcrowding and conditions of confinement. In addition, the increased occupancy rates created a dialectical dynamic whereby the disputants were forced to interact and address this policy concern in a public arena producing documented textual data.

Data Analysis

The stakeholder textual data population was subjected to theoretical sampling. This nonprobability approach to sampling provided a systematic avenue to view the large amount of data without being as rigid as probability-based sampling techniques. Probability sampling techniques were considered to be too rigid in analyzing the vast array of documents of differing lengths produced by the stakeholders over the ten-year period. Choosing preset categories or randomly selected pages of documents

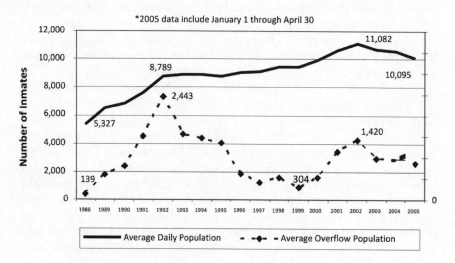

Figure Intro.2. CCDOC Institutional Growth, 1988–2005. *Source: John Howard Association, 2005.*

would have resulted in the possibility of excluding particular themes and messages presented by the differing stakeholders. A progressive theoretical sampling approach ensued based on an emerging understanding of the jail overcrowding dispute as the entire stakeholder text population was read. Using a critical case sample design the researcher selected a number of documents that logic and prior experience allowed generalization to the entire population of documents.[60] The benefit to this approach is that it allows an orientation toward discovery and comparison of the relevant meaning attached to the overcrowding dispute by differing stakeholders.

The sampling method employed resulted in the creation of three broad categories or parameters of discourse emanating from the progressive theoretical sampling approach of primary source documents. The categories of population and space, conditions within CCDOC and expansion beyond the jail walls served to classify and make sense of the vast amount of stakeholder data originating from the dispute. As stipulated in figure 3, within these three parameters further delineation evolved as reoccurring themes were identified and the frames within those themes surfaced. This two-tier process is analogous to the grounded theory approach of inductive analysis employed within qualitative narrative research.[61]

The broad parameter or topic categories were categorized into subgroups as the data was read, reread and reflected upon over time. Through this analytical coding approach all the data fit within one of the

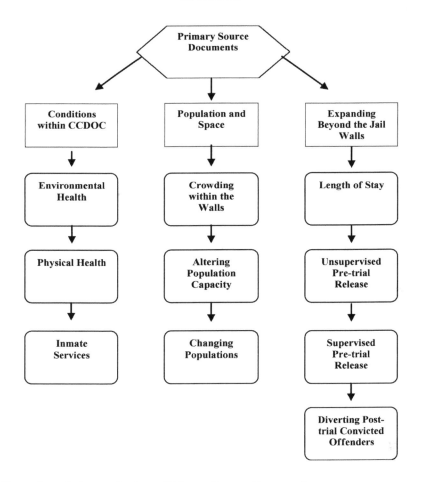

Figure Intro.3. Categorization of Primary Source Documents

ten subcategories. The primary source documents and emanating parameters encompass chapters 2 through 4 of the book.

Qualitatively, the official source data created by differing claims-makers was subjected to an interpretive analysis. While parameters of discourse refers to the relevant meaning that particular stakeholders use to talk about things, themes are the recurring typical theses, and frames are the issues discussed, how they are discussed and how they are not discussed.[62] Application of the discourse, theme and frame concepts were applied to examine the meaning and emphasis that differing claims-makers attached to the overcrowding dispute between 1993 and 2003. The official source data provided a further understanding of the organizational routines employed by differing claims-makers. Through this analysis, ideological conceptions related to politics, bureaucratic-administrative concerns, humanist ideals, and judicial priorities were identified and explored. In addition to the themes and frames manifestly presented in the official source discourse, further language that delegitimizes opposing perspectives or frames was also distinguished and analyzed. These sub-categories or themes, and their emanating frames provide not only a description but the texture of the consent decree dispute and the texture of local level incarceration within Cook County. Description, explanation and examples of the broad parameters of discourse, the subcategories or themes and the emerging, dominant and residual frames within those themes are presented within chapters 2 through 4.

Chapter 5 provides a media analysis of local newsprint articles produced concerning jail overcrowding between 1993 and 2003. Methodologically this analysis differed from the previous sections in that the entire population of local print media data was analyzed as opposed to a sample. In addition, the coding scheme applied to this data proceeded deductively as theoretical constructs of punishment ideologies were used to code the data. The difference in analysis strategy within this section serves to examine how claims-makers promote preferred meanings to the general public. As the data was coded two new categories emerged inductively from the original four theoretical constructs postulated within the methodology. The analysis proceeded two-fold: first the news stories were analyzed across the frames presented and by year. Second, the media articles were attributed to the differing claims-makers within the consent decree dispute.

In conjunction with the stakeholder text analysis examined in chapters 2 through 4, the 334 media articles produced concerning jail overcrowding in Cook County between 1993 and 2003 also provided a representation of the various discourses and claims-makers involved in the overcrowding dispute.

The unit of analysis within the media text research consisted of two levels. First, the media articles themselves served as a unit of analysis. The media articles were coded for prominence of particular issue frames. The packages of issue frames and examples of the differing frames are provided in table 2. The operationalization of these frames into a coding scheme required the development of a table or matrix of jail overcrowding issue packages identifying and describing core frames.

This categorization approach applied a methodological technique whereby differing frames, positions, exemplars, catchphrases, depictions, roots, principles and motifs were identified and coded throughout the data.[63] These categories are philosophically linked to specific packages related to assumptions and worldviews of incarceration and corrections. Positions are the value assumptions indicated within the issue package. Exemplars are stories or incidents portraying the aforementioned positions. Catchphrases are slogans meant to attract attention, and depictions are characterizations of the individuals incarcerated. Roots identify the

Table Intro.2. Packages and Issue Frames Related to Jail Overcrowding

Packages	Issues
1. Order and Control	The issue is how to provide order, safety, control and respect for authority within the institution for all individuals incarcerated, working within and visiting the institution.
2. Rights of the Accused	The issue is how to address the rights of the accused under the mantra of due process and civil rights.
3. Root Causes of Arrest and Incarceration	The issue is social stratification and its relation to those individuals who are arrested and incarcerated.
4. Community Pursuit of Justice and Balanced Needs	The issue is the relationship between the community and the individuals who become incarcerated, those individuals imminent return to the community, victims' rights and restoration.

social problem creating the core frame, and principles are the propositions that need to be upheld within the issue package.

Examples of the coinciding positions, exemplars, catchphrases, depictions, roots, principles, and motifs of the different issue frames are numerous. For instance, within the order and control frame different catchphrases include: crime control, public and institutional safety, dangerous criminals, violent histories, gangs and gang members. These catchphrases are included within exemplars whereby data, incidents, and stories are presented within the media narrative that bolsters the frame of order and control. Depictions of violent gang members committing acts of violence within the institutional walls frames jail overcrowding as a social problem that is best addressed through increased control. This is substantively different than the root causes of arrest and incarceration frame. Within this frame catchphrases such as joblessness, homelessness, mental illness, poverty, and racism are visible. These catchphrases will be included within exemplars whereby data, incidents, and stories are focused on incarcerated populations existing as a consequence of social conditions. Policy solutions applying this frame are focused on obligations to address structural inequality rather than order and control. A full listing of the signature matrix with accompanying positions, exemplars, catchphrases, depictions, roots and principles is in the appendix.

After initial coding of the differing packages presented within the media articles, attributions were linked to the differing claims-makers through a second analysis. The approach of linking the frames to specific claims-makers as a second analysis was conducted in previous research by Chermak in his investigation of the construction of militias in the news.[64] The analytical purpose of this two-pronged approach provides an analysis that not only explores the frames being presented but which frames are presented by which claims-makers and to what extent.

Cook County Jail and the Penal Industrial Complex

Chapter 6 examines the role of local political actors and offices as willing participants in the expansion of local level incarceration and punishment and contextualizes these actions across other jurisdictions. Over 227,000 inmates are being held within the nation's fifty largest local jail jurisdictions. More than half of those inmates are minorities.[65] Individuals incarcerated within local jails increased from 182,000 in 1980 to almost 750,000 in 2005.[66] The three largest jail populations are located within New York City, Los Angeles County and Cook County.[67] In essence, local jail expansion and growth have mirrored similar punishment expansion within state and federal prison systems that has been documented across the criminal justice policy literature.[68]

Between 1993 and 2003 the average daily population incarcerated within the Cook County Jail was 9,640 inmates.[69] Placing this within a contextual perspective of the United States, the average state and federal prison population in Iowa was 8,813 inmates and in the state of Minnesota inmates averaged 9,986 at year-end 2009.[70] Arguably, the institutional challenges and industrial growth that are manifestly disputed within the Cook County Jail overcrowding consent decree are relevant not only to similar mega-jail systems such as New York City and Los Angeles County but also other burgeoning mega-jail systems in cities such as Houston, Phoenix and Philadelphia, to name a few. In addition, the nineteen states that have incarcerated populations fewer than 10,000 inmates are clearly struggling with some of the same penal industrial growth issues imbued within the Cook County dispute. Examining the interaction between disputants involved in these processes will provide other jurisdictions currently facing overcrowding problems, as well as growing jurisdictions that will inevitably face overcrowding problems, a greater understanding of the complexities surrounding federal judicial intervention and its subsequent results within their particular criminal justice systems.

While population comparisons between the Cook County Department of Corrections and smaller state prisons systems can be intuitive in helping understand the magnitude of a mega-urban jail complex, it is important to keep in mind the numerous differences between jails and prisons. In general, jails are the admittance point to the larger correctional system which includes prisons, probation and intermediate sanctions. Sentenced offenders, usually serving one year or less, are only one population within the jail system which also includes a majority of pretrial defendants. In addition, jail systems house sentenced felons who have been remanded back to local jurisdictions for ongoing trials and investigations, as well as those individuals sentenced and awaiting transport to state prison. Geographically, mega-urban jails make up a small portion of the number of jails but a large portion of those incarcerated in jails. Also, jails are administered at the local level, falling outside the purview of direct state control.

Finally, the ongoing federal consent decree offers an opportunity to examine disputing in a loosely coupled criminal justice setting. The perspective of a "loosely coupled" criminal justice system maintains that differing subsystems within the larger criminal justice system vary as to which aspects of the overall system should be of the most influence.[71] Therefore, while differing subsystems remain responsive to each other in general, their specific focus has the capacity to vary greatly. Among the disputants/claims-makers within the consent decree, discursive practices serve to reify the penal industrial complex at the local level. As Arrigo and Milovanovic argue in their theoretical conception of constitutive penology, "The productive content of discursive work in framing, describing, evaluating, and conceptualizing the penal is a crucial aspect of how prisons are maintained and how society conceives of itself as ordered."[72] Exploring the culture of urban control through the use of a federal consent decree as the unit of analysis provides an avenue of reflection for the reader to examine the politicizing aspects of criminalization, our connection to these control apparatus at the local level, and in turn our lack of responsiveness toward addressing a growth industry rooted in control and violence.

The analytic plan as outlined within the introductory chapter seeks to provide an encompassing view of how large urban jails systems and in particular the Cook County Department of Corrections fit within the broader correctional expansion occurring within the United States over the past twenty years. The role of the jail in linking specific neighborhoods and populations to the prison industrial complex begins at the local level. Examining conditions within CCDOC, alterations of populations and space within the institution, how local corrections expands beyond the jail walls and the role that politics and media play in shaping public perceptions of these issues all serve to reveal the complex nature of a fragmented criminal justice system, the current role of the large urban jail in our society and what it means to be a jail inmate during the era of crime control.

NOTES

1. John Irwin, *The Jail: Managing the Underclass in American Society* (Berkeley, CA: University of California Press, 1985).
2. Charles Fasano and Suzanne MacKinnon, "The Impact of Litigation on the Cook County Department of Corrections," *Corrections Management Quarterly* 3, no. 2 (1999):

35–41; Malcolm Feeley & Roger Hanson, "The Impact of Judicial Intervention on Prisons and Jails: A Framework for Analysis and Review of the Literature," in *Courts, Corrections, and the Constitution,* ed. John Dilulio, (New York: Oxford University Press, 1990); Malcolm Feeley and Edward Rubin, *Judicial Policymaking and the Modern State: How the Courts Reformed America's Prisons* (Cambridge: Cambridge University Press, 2000); Michael Welch, "Jail Overcrowding: Social Sanitation and Warehousing of the Urban Underclass," in *Crime and Justice in America,* ed. P. Cromwell & R. Dunham (Upper Saddle River, NJ: Prentice-Hall, 1997): 263–284; Wayne Welsh, *Counties in Court: Jail Overcrowding and Court-Ordered Reform* (Philadelphia: Temple University, 1995).

3. A consent decree is an agreement in the nature of a solemn contract under the sanction of the court whereby both parties agree that the decree is a just determination of their rights upon the real facts of the case, if such facts had been proved.

4. Welsh, "Jail Overcrowding," 278.

5. John Howard Association, *Court Monitoring Report for Duran v. Sheahan et. al. 74 C2949: Crowding and Conditions of Confinement at the Cook County Department of Corrections and Compliance with the Consent Decree,* (Chicago, 2004), 4.

6. Ibid..

7. Fasano and MacKinnon, "Impact of Litigation," 36.

8. Ibid..

9. The basis of a barn boss system relies on supervisory and disciplinary authority being given to peer members of a group. In the case of a correctional facility the supervisory and disciplinary control is given to fellow inmates over other inmates.

10. Fasano and MacKinnon, "Impact of Litigation," 36.

11. Ibid..

12. *Harrington v. Kiley et al.,* 74 C 3290, U.S. District Court, (N.D. Ill. 1983).

13. Fasano and MacKinnon, "Impact of Litigation," 37.

14. The term I-bond is synonymous with Administrative Mandatory Furlough or recognizance bond within the Cook County criminal justice system. These are signature bonds whereby the defendant is released based on a signed statement that they will appear in court.

15. Fasano and MacKinnon, "Impact of Litigation," 37.

16. John Howard Association, *Court Monitoring Report,* 2004, 4.

17. Charles Edelstein et al., *An Assessment of the Felony Case Process in Cook County, Illinois and Its Impact on Jail Crowding,* (Washington, DC: The American University, School of Public Affairs, 1989).

18. John Howard Association, *Court Monitoring Report for Duran v. Sheahan et al. 74 C 2949: Crowding and conditions of confinement at the Cook County Department of Corrections and compliance with the consent decree,* (Chicago, 1998).

19. Edelstein et al., *Assessment of the Felony Case.*

20. Fasano and MacKinnon, "Impact of Litigation," 38.

21. Christine Martin, *Cook County Pretrial Release Study,* (Chicago: Illinois Criminal Justice Information Authority, 1992).

22. John Howard Association, *Court Monitoring Report,* 2004, 4.

23. The majority of this legal resolution has been due to the Prison Litigation Reform Act (PRLA). This statute enacted in 1994 by Congress and signed into law by President Clinton in 1996 restricted the federal court in cases involving overcrowding of prisons. The rationale of the statute and subsequent law was to limit the ability of prisoners to complain about their conditions of confinement, reinstall managerial authority to states and local governments related to incarceration matters, and limit the federal judiciary in their management of these institutions. John Palmer, *Constitutional Rights of Prisoners,* 8th ed. (New York: Anderson Publishing, 2006).

24. Joel Best, "'Road Warriors' on 'Hair-Trigger Highways' cultural resources and media construction of the 1987 freeway shooting problem," *Sociological Inquiry* 61, no. 3 (1991); Joel Best and Mary Hutchinson, "The Gang Initiation Rite as a Motif in Contemporary Crime Discourse," *Justice Quarterly* 13, no. 3 (1996); Steven Chermak,

"The Presentation of Drugs in the News Media: The News Sources Involved in the Construction of Social Problems," *Justice Quarterly* 14, no. 4. (1997); Phillip Jenkins, "'The Ice Age' The Social Construction of a Drug Panic," *Justice Quarterly* 11, no.1 (1994).

25. John Kitsuse and Macolm Spector, "Toward a Sociology of Social Problems: Social Conditions, Value-Judgment and Social Problems," *Social Problems* 20, (1973): 415.

26. Joel Best, "Constructionism in Context," in *Images of Issues 2nd ed.,* (New York: Aldine DeGruyeter, 1995): 6.

27. Stuart Scheingold, *The Politics of Street Crime: Criminal Process Cultural Obsession,* (Philadelphia: Temple University Press, 1991); Michael Tonry, "Racial Politics, Racial Disparities, and War on Crime," *Crime and Delinquency* 40, (1994): 475–97.

28. Herbert Rubin and Irene Rubin, *Qualitative Interviewing: The Art of Hearing Data,* (Thousand Oaks, CA: Sage, 1995).

29. Clifford Geertz, "Deep Play: Notes on Balinese Cockfight" in *Interpretive Social Science: A Second Look,* eds. Paul Rainbow and William Sullivan (Berkeley, CA: University of California Press, 1987); Marshall Sahlins, *Historical Metaphors and Mythical Realities: Structure in the Early History of the Sandwich Islands Kingdom,* (Ann Arbor, MI: University of Michigan Press, 2000); Alison Young, *Imagining Crime,* (London: Sage, 1996).

30. Clifford Geertz, *Local Knowledge,* (New York: Basic Books, 1983): 4.

31. Raymond Williams, *Marxism and Literature* (New York: Oxford University Press, 1977).

32. Stuart Hall, "Cultural Studies: Two Paradigms," *Media Culture and Society* 2, no.1 (1980): 57.

33. Hall, "Cultural Studies: Two Paradigms," 57.

34. John Frow, *Cultural Studies and Cultural Value* (Oxford: Clarendon Press, 1995): 3.

35. Frow, *Cultural Studies and Cultural Value,* 3.

36. Geertz, *Local Knowledge,* 5.

37. Lynn Mather and Barbara Yngvesson, "Language, Audience, and the Transformation of Disputes," *Law and Society Review* 15, (1980–81): 777.

38. Mather and Yngvesson, "Language, Audience, Transformation," 818.

39. Erving Goffman, *Frame Analysis: An Essay on the Organization of Experience* (Cambridge: Harvard University Press, 1974).

40. Goffman, *Frame Analysis,* 27.

41. Ibid., 301–44.

42. Ibid., 325.

43. Katherine Beckett, *Making Crime Pay: Law and Order in Contemporary American Politics,* (New York: Oxford University Press, 1997).

44. Chermak, "Presentation of Drugs," 687.

45. William Gamson, *Talking Politics,* (Cambridge: Cambridge University Press, 1992).

46. Gamson, *Talking Politics,* 24.

47. Gamson, *Talking Politics,* 6–7, 198; William Gamson and David Stuart, "Media Discourse as a Symbolic Contest: The Bomb in Political Cartoons," *Sociological Forum* 7 (1992), no. 1, 59.

48. Beckett, *Making Crime Pay,* 65–74.

49. Ibid., 66.

50. Katherine Beckett, "Media Depictions of Drug Abuse: The Impact of Official Sources," *Research in Political Sociology* 7, (1995): 177.

51. Chermak, "Presentation of Drugs," 698.

52. Dietram Scheufele, "Framing as a Theory of Media Effects," *Journal of Communication* Winter, (1999): 115–16.

53. The process model concept was adapted from a process originally formulated by Scheufele in the exploration of frame theory and media effects. The model was

adapted by the author to fit the consent decree process and the local frame makers within the process in Cook County.

54. Steven Chermak, *Searching for a Demon: The Media Construction of the Militia Movement* (Boston: Northeastern University Press, 2002), 111.

55. Goffman, *Frame Analysis*, 301; Scheufele, "Framing as a Theory," 105.

56. Beckett, *Making Crime Pay*, 65; Gamson, *Talking Politics*, 197–98.

57. Gamson, *Talking Politics*, 6–8, 197–98; Williams, *Marxism and Literature*, 121–27.

58. These two organizations were used as a criterion to define the population of documents due to the fact that they are both the major initiators within the dispute. The Cook County Sheriff's Office provides administrative and budgetary control over CCDOC and is the leading named plaintiff in the consent decree. The John Howard Association is the assigned federal court monitor for the consent decree. The consent decree and subsequent suit *Duran v. Sheehan* which continues to be active in the federal court requires each of these parties to retain library holdings of all documents related to the ongoing case.

59. Kimberly Neuendorf, *The Content Analysis Guidebook,* (Thousand Oaks, CA: Sage Publications, 2002): 221–23.

60. Gary Henry, *Practical Samples* (Newbury Park, CA: Sage, 1990): 21.

61. Barney Glaser and Anslem Strauss, *The Discovery of Grounded Theory: Strategies for Qualitative Research* (Chicago: Aldine, 1967).

62. David Altheide, *Qualitative Media Analysis* (Thousand Oaks, CA: Sage, 1996): 31.

63. For an example of this operational scheme see Katherine Beckett's "Media Depictions," 161–182, and *Making Crime Pay*, 62–78. Beckett uses a signature matrix of crime issue packages to operationalize how drugs and crime are framed in the media.

64. Chermak, *Searching for a Demon*, 113–116.

65. William Sabol and Todd Minton, *Jail Inmates at Midyear 2007* (Washington, DC: U.S. Department of Justice, Office of Justice Programs, 2008), NCJ Publication No. 22–1945.

66. Ibid..

67. Ibid..

68. Alfred Blumstein and Joel Wallman. *The Crime Drop in America* (New York: Cambridge Press, 2000); Elliot Currie, *Crime and Punishment in America* (New York: Holt Publishing, 1998); John Irwin and James Austin, *It's About Time: America's Imprisonment Binge* (Belmont, CA: Wadsworth Publishing,1994); Mark Kleiman, *When Brute Force Fails: How to Have Less Crime and Less Punishment,* (Princeton, NJ: Princeton University Press, 2009); Marc Mauer, *Race to Incarcerate* (New York: The New Press, 2006); Franklin Zimring, *The Great American Crime Decline,* (New York, NY: Oxford University Press, 2007).

69. John Howard Association, *Court Monitoring Report*, 4.

70. Heather West, William Sabol, and Sarah Greenman, *Prisoners in 2009* (NCJ Publication No.23–1675). Washington, DC: U.S. Department of Justice, Office of Justice Programs, 2010.

71. John Hagan, "Why is There So Little Criminal Justice Theory? Neglected Macro- and Micro-Level Links Between Organization and Power," *Journal of Research in Crime and Delinquency* 26, no. 2 (1989): 118.

72. Bruce Arrigo and Dragon Milovanovic. *Revolution in Penology: Rethinking the Society of Captives.* Lanham, MD: Rowman & Littlefield Press, 2009: 9.

ONE

From Past to Present

Correctional System Overcrowding and Institutional Reform

The fact is true all over the world that in hard times more people go to jail than in good times, and in winter more people go to jail than in summer. Of course it is pretty hard times for people who go to jail at any time. The people who go to jail are almost always poor people— people who have no other place to live first and last.[1]
—Clarence Darrow, *Address to the Prisoners in the Cook County Jail*, 1902

The research and writings surrounding overcrowding and conditions of confinement within local jail settings can be categorized within three separate areas of literature. While these areas are not necessarily mutually exclusive of one another, they provide a framework that illustrates the context of the differing perspectives which shape the public policy issues surrounding overcrowding and conditions of confinement. First, jail overcrowding and conditions of confinement will be reviewed historically through the institutional reform literature emanating from the federal courts as a public policy problem of national scope. Second, the literature review will hone the unit of analysis to review overcrowding and conditions of confinement from the state and local perspective through the case study literature. Third, the criminal justice administration literature will be reviewed as to system-wide understandings, responses, reactions, and attempts at ameliorating overcrowding and poor confinement conditions.

CORRECTIONAL SYSTEM OVERCROWDING
AND INSTITUTIONAL REFORM

Research and analysis on correctional system overcrowding within the United States has been sporadic. While there is no specific history of correctional overcrowding within the United States, numerous historical accounts of the criminal justice system in general provide a cursory overview of correctional development and reform.[2] In addition, classics in the field of correctional policy and practice illustrate the tenacity of punishment and imprisonment reform issues throughout the history of corrections. Beaumont and Tocqueville's study of the developing United States penitentiary system illustrates the consistent flux that defined correctional policy in early America. Opposing perspectives of the religious and philosophical basis for punishment and its relation to burgeoning reform movements is a persistent theme within the correctional literature. What is considered humane, appropriate, or necessary within a correctional environment develops concurrently with changing public perceptions on punishment.[3]

The Historical Eras of Judicial Intervention in Prisons and Jails

Feeley and Rubin's *Judicial Policymaking and the Modern State: How the Courts Reformed America's Prisons* provides a useful timeline and synopsis of changing legal perceptions of punishment in the United States and its affected change within prisons and jails.[4] While the focus of this analysis centers on judicial decision-making processes that address overcrowding and conditions of confinement within prisons and jails, the authors use case studies of particular prisons and jails to exemplify the complexity of developing policy changes.

> Instead of being decided at a single moment in time, they extend over periods ranging from five to twenty years. Instead of being contained within the conceptual framework of the law, they involve bargains, negotiations, appeals to public opinion, and a variety of quasi-legal threats and counter threats.[5]

While the case studies outlined within this work provide an indication as to the local complexity of the reform movement, the judicial decisions illustrate the changing legal guidelines which initiated reform and drove the disputing processes in different locales. Feeley and Rubin categorize judicial and legislative decision making into the four eras of hands-off, emergence, dominance, and retreat.[6] Through these four eras, Feeley and Rubin provide an organized description of the rise and decline of judicial activism as it relates to correctional reform. The opposing arguments that define the differing eras are based in a traditional view versus a structural reform view of the role of the judiciary. According to Fuller, a "traditional view" of the judiciary is as dispute resolver focusing on established rules and the presentation of proofs and arguments on one's own behalf which the judiciary uses to make rational, impartial decisions.[7] In contrast to this Fiss explains that the idea of structural reform within an adjudicative framework argues that the courts have a responsibility to effectuate basic changes in the structure of organizations in an effort to fully realize Constitutional values.[8] The struggle between these two polemics is evident within the history of judicial intervention and correctional policy making.

The Hands-Off Era of Judicial Intervention

The hands-off era of judicial intervention within prisons and jails (1776–1960) is illustrated by decisions revolving around substantive as well as procedural arguments against expanding the rights of prisoners. A clear indication of these decisions can be found in the complaints of George Atterbury, incarcerated in Statesville prison, who made claims of physical beatings and poor conditions of confinement.[9] From a substantive perspective, the 7th circuit court of appeals affirmed in *Atterbury v. Ragen* that in spite of general assertions that prison officials and guards were acting under the color of state law that there is not a claim upon which relief can be granted under the civil rights act.[10] In essence, regardless of the fact that prison guards were physically abusing an inmate as part of their employment, the court ruled that the inmate could not seek a remedy through the civil rights act. In addition, from a procedural standpoint, the federal courts ruled that habeas corpus[11] was only relevant to the process by which prisoners had been convicted and not to subsequent conditions of confinement.[12] The affirming decision within *Atterbury v. Ragen* on substantive and procedural grounds is indicative of the general tone and approach that the federal judiciary applied prior to 1961.

The Emergence Era of Judicial Intervention

Between 1960 and 1965, Feeley and Rubin highlight the emergence of the prison reform era.[13] In 1961, *Monroe v. Pape* held that police officers on duty, regardless of the illegality of their actions, were acting under the color of state law. The significance of this decision is that the actions of the individual government agent were now attributable to the state. Thus, prisoners could now seek relief under the civil rights act in regard to physical abuse carried out by prison guards. In addition, in a summary decision, the Supreme Court reversed *Johnson v. Dye*, which stated that a prisoner must exhaust state remedies prior to pursuing their claim in federal court.[14] These two legal instances mark the erosion of the judicial thinking on which *Atterbury v. Ragen* was based. Also, during this time period numerous Supreme Court decisions outside the realm of prisons were injecting the basis for judicial activism that would subsequently set the stage for the Civil Rights Act of 1964.[15] In addition, the early 1960s produced specific prisoner's rights cases such as *Cooper v. Pate* in which prisoner Thomas Cooper argued that his civil rights were being violated based on religious beliefs.[16] In essence, all the aforementioned cases, as well as numerous others, had a cumulative effect of dismantling the hands-off doctrine and creating a fertile legal landscape to address prison confinement and condition issues at the federal level.

The Reform Era of Judicial Intervention

Feeley and Rubin argue that the correctional reform movement was in full stride beginning in 1965 through 1986.[17] Beginning in 1965, the Arkansas prison system came under judicial scrutiny. By 1970, the federal judiciary ruled that the Arkansas prison system in its entirety was in violation of the Eighth Amendment. Within a five-year period following the Arkansas case, the federal courts declared prisons in Mississippi, Oklahoma, Florida, Louisiana and Alabama to be unconstitutional in whole or in part based on conditions of confinement.[18] The courts reaffirmed religious liberty decisions, expanded First Amendment rights to receive mail, enforced the equal protection clause forbidding segregated facilities, applied the due process clause requiring hearings prior to the imposition of discipline and initiated extensive prison management regulatory codes.[19] As Feeley and Hanson argue, "The extent of this involvement by the federal judiciary in overseeing major changes in the nation's jails and prisons is perhaps second in breadth and detail only to the courts' earlier role in dismantling segregation in the nation's public schools."[20] The prominent issue that drove the courts toward examining the conditions of confinement in many of these state prison systems, federal detention centers and local jails was overcrowding.[21] The importance of this era, as outlined by Feeley and Rubin, is that during the time period of 1965–1986 the rationale of the hands-off doctrine was completely abandoned in favor of an interventionist approach by the federal judiciary.[22] As Supreme Court Justice White stated in *Wolff v. McDonald* (1977), a case which related to correctional disciplinary procedure, "There is no iron curtain drawn between the constitution and the prisons of this country."[23]

The Retreat Era of Judicial Intervention

The era beginning in the late 1980s witnessed a decline in federal intervention as the pendulum began to swing away from structural reform. Feeley and Rubin point out that many judges perceived "the worst conditions have been eliminated and the challenge has shifted to administrative efforts, not test-case litigation."[24] For example, *Rhodes v. Chap-*

man concluded that double celling of prisoners did not necessarily constitute a violation of the Eighth Amendment and that harsh conditions are part of a criminal offender's penalty. In addition, *Wilson v. Seiter* concluded that Eighth Amendment suits based on conditions of confinement could be precluded based on insufficiently trained staff, operations budgets and physical plant constraints. Also, in *Rufo v. Inmates of the Suffolk County Jail*, the U.S. Supreme Court held that a flexible standard of review should apply to requests to modify consent decrees stemming from institutional reform litigation.[25]

Since 1991, within the federal legislative branch of government, the Violent Crime Control and Enforcement Act of 1994 codified that an individual prisoner must prove that crowding constitutes cruel and unusual punishment. In addition, the Prison Reform Litigation Act applies this barrier to all condition and confinement claims, as well as allowing government agencies to reopen previously agreed upon consent decrees.[26] Finally, the Anti-Terrorism and Effective Death Penalty Act limits the ability of prisoners to file habeas corpus petitions. In essence, recent judicial decision making, legislative action, as well as the executive branch's ability to terminate judicial jurisdiction by closing cases has removed the federal judiciary from direct oversight of prisons and jails in many locations. This judicial and legislative trend marks a philosophical detachment from the ideals of structural reform.

The philosophical debate as to the role of the judiciary as merely dispute resolvers or structural reformers is an underlying current within overcrowding and confinement judicial decision making. Depending upon the degree to which philosophical premise a particular individual administers credence, an assessment of legitimacy surrounding judicial policymaking within prisons and jails will undoubtedly follow. In the cases highlighted during the hands-off era (1776–1960) an extremely traditional view of adjudication relying on a judicial intervention strategy focusing on a strictly dispute-resolving philosophy was applied. In the cases highlighted during the reform era the federal courts made public policy by imposing national standards on state prisons and local jail through administrative action and new legal doctrine.[27] This particular era marks the height of a judicial philosophy focused on structural reform. The retreat era of prison reform, in which we are currently enmeshed, has clearly moved back toward a traditional view of dispute resolving, while at the same time retaining many of the administrative changes spurred during the structural reform era.

The accomplishments of the structural reform era which continue to shape prison and jail policies include: recognized constitutional rights to prisoners, the emergence of a national corrections profession, the formulation of national standards of corrections, the bureaucratization of prisons and jails, as well as an end to the South's plantation model of prisonization.[28] Unfortunately, the accomplishments of the structural reform era are many times overshadowed by issues that were not addressed through structural reform. Included among these ongoing problems are the incarceration explosion beginning in the 1980s and early 1990s as a result of drug policies,[29] the growth of special needs populations within prisons and jails,[30] violence within correctional facilities,[31] the rise of prison gangs, the creation of novel approaches to incarceration, population management strategies (intake and length of stay, speeding up arraignment) and budgetary constraints on capital projects and services.

The four differing eras of hands-off, emergence, dominance and retreat provide a national level view of the rise and decline of judicial activism within prisons and jails in the United States. Specific judicial, legislative and executive branch decisions within the differing eras served to nationalize the conceptual thinking of the purpose and administration of incarceration within each of the differing eras. Yet, from regional and local perspectives, these overarching decisions were met with differing amounts of acceptance and repudiation.

CASE STUDY RESEARCH AND INSTITUTIONAL REFORM

As the reform era emerged and took hold within judiciary mandates related to overcrowding and conditions of confinement decisions were passed down from the federal level to state and local governments and correctional administrations. Through case study analysis, regional and local actions toward institutional reform mandates have been contextualized. These case studies provide a multitude of narratives exemplifying the complexity involved as jurisdictions began to mete out federally mandated change at the state and local level.

Case Studies of State Prison Reform Litigation

The early prison reform litigation literature is largely constructed of descriptive and analytic case studies exploring particular court cases that shaped state prison policy and practice. The majority of this literature focused on the geography of the South. Prisons in southern states had long been considered the most brutal and atavistic in the nation, and judicial intervention and the subsequent analysis of judicial intervention focused mainly within this geography.

In particular and most cited among these case studies is the *Ruiz v. Estelle* litigation in Texas. Feeley and Rubin describe the *Ruiz* proceedings, which began in 1972, as the largest, longest, and most acrimonious in the history of prison reform.[32] Claims included a breadth of constitutional violation and complaint based on inmate space, medical access, safety, security, supervision and discipline.[33] In addition, case study analysis revealed legal and political attempts to stall and thwart changes emanating from the Texas Department of Corrections and state level politicians.[34] Eventually, inmate profit-making labor was transformed to vocational training, and the building tender system was dismantled; living conditions and medical access were improved. The changes were grudgingly accepted over time as new leadership within the Texas Department of Corrections and the broader Texas government emerged.[35] Marquart and Crouch summarized the outcome of changes in policy and procedure after the *Ruiz* case as an organizational movement from decentralized decision making to centralized decision making lacking flexibility.[36] In addition, staff-inmate relationships changed from paternalistic toward combative with a distanced relationship that hampered communication between the captives and the officers. According to Marquart and Crouch, less discretion by staff and lower communication between staff and inmate added to an environment prone to violence as evident in the increased stabbings and racial tension in the post-*Ruiz* era.[37] This summation was echoed by John Dilulio in his analysis of the *Ruiz* litigation.[38] The judicial litigation and subsequent organizational change modified the culture of the Texas prison system. While acknowledging the manifest violence occurring in Texas prisons post *Ruiz*, Ekland-Olson and Martin argued that the lengthy denial of the social and policy change required by prison administrators in Texas created a disorganized environment and increased opportunities for violence among inmates.[39] In essence, according to these authors recalcitrant administrators created an environment leading to increases in violence. As Feeley and Rubin summarized, "The court had won a decisive, if potentially unstable victory."[40]

In addition to the *Ruiz*-based research other case studies focusing on prison reform litigation within southern states include Yackle's focus on Alabama prison reform, Anderson's perspective of prison reform in Kentucky, Feeley and Rubin's analysis of Arkansas' prison system, Chilton and Chilton and Talarico's examination of Georgia's prisons system and Useem's description of West Virginia's prison and institutional litigation.[41] All of these analyses were descriptive in nature, identifying relationships between the key players within the litigation, local politics, implementation strategies, and expansive financial spending and system pressure associated with mandated organizational change.[42] Each of these case studies, except Anderson, focused predominantly on the litigation process and incremental outcome change in prison conditions from a legal standpoint as opposed to the day-to-day living conditions of prisoners within the institutions.[43] Anderson's application of the prisoner-litigant experience added a thick description element that included prisoner perspectives of conditions of confinement.

Perception of success or lack of success of the prison reform litigation process within these southern states was shaped by the authors' definition of success. In the case of Georgia, Chilton defined the litigation as successful in that incremental change for the better was achieved.[44] Contrary to this perception Yackle regarded success and change as superficial in his analysis of Alabama prisons.[45] As Smith points out, conclusions of success within the case study research of prison reform litigation spanned from the realist perception of incrementalism to that of the idealists who were looking for wholesale change.[46] Yet, as pointed out by Feeley and Rubin, who posited the incremental success perspective of Chilton in their analysis of Arkansas' prisons, the main emphasis and result of the southern prison reform litigation was the further dismantling of the southern plantation model of prisonization.[47]

Case study research of prison reform litigation outside of the southern states has been limited in number and scope. Edward Rhine's analysis of the New Jersey Rahway State prison focused on prison disciplinary procedures and due process in the aftermath of reform litigation.[48] Rhine argued that due process was compromised by the perception of a lack of credibility by the accused inmate and inmate witnesses within disciplinary processes. He further argued that prison officials provide a sense of fair play in the disciplinary hearing process by allowing prisoners an opportunity to establish their innocence. Yet, he argued this is not the same as prison officials establishing guilt. A more robust case study conducted by Carroll examined the role of the special master as a conduit for professionalization between unmotivated Rhode Island correctional officials and other jurisdictions implementing reform.[49] Carroll's conclusions noted a similar destabilizing effect of violence analogous to Marquart and Crouch's conclusions in Texas. Feeley and Rubin's case study of the "Old Max" maximum security prison in Colorado followed the litigation analysis perspective of many of the early case studies focusing on the incremental change possible through judicial reform in the areas of building conditions and health services policies and practices as this particular Colorado prison expanded to three new facilities in place of a crumbling century-old building.[50]

Case Studies of Federal Prison Reform Litigation

Feeley and Rubin's case study of litigation surrounding the increased security initiatives in Marion federal super-max penitentiary highlight the polemic approaches to litigation style that many of the state level prison reform case studies captured in a less defined manner.[51] The strategy of the ACLU lawyers representing plaintiffs in the Marion case approached the judiciary with claims focusing on inhumane conditions and overt suppression of the human spirit within this super-max federal penitentiary. In contrast, the defendants applied an approach based on what Feeley and Rubin suggest was "great respect" and an opportunity to "validate" their programs.[52] According to the authors, the success of this approach by the defendants created a long-standing legal strategy that has been used in subsequent litigation regarding conditions of confinement within super-max facilities at the state level throughout the country.

Case Studies of Jail Reform Litigation

Case studies focused on local level jail reform litigation have been less numerous than those at the state level.[53] The majority of these case studies have examined jail facilities within the state of California. The most developed research concerning jail reform litigation was produced by Wayne Welsh in his analysis of thirty-five counties facing court order in California.[54] Within this analysis Welsh conducted three case studies of jail reform litigation within Contra Costa County, Santa Clara County, and Orange County, California.[55] Feeley and Rubin also conducted a local level case study within Santa Clara County, California.[56] Outside of California, Storey produced a case study examining New York City jails.[57] As Welsh argued, analysis of jails and jail reform litigation is distinct from prison analysis.[58] First, the large amount of inmate turnover, average length of stay for inmates, and broad array of inmate offenses processed is much different than within the prison setting.[59] Second, the administrative, bureaucratic, and local political structures at the county level create different and many times more pronounced problems than what occurs at the state or federal level.[60]

Welsh's analysis attributed a vast array of factors that influence variation and outcome within local level jail reform litigation.[61] Broad categories included the environment, the judge, special masters, plaintiffs, defendants, and interagency relations. Within each of these broad categories, Welsh identified specific factors that influence and differentiate the process and outcome of litigation across local geographies.[62] Depending upon how these categories and factors interact with one another impact in regard to institutional conditions, structure and organization, correctional expenditures, local justice policy, and interagency coordination differs by locality.[63] Welsh categorized these interactions and outcomes within a process model of five different stages of litigation. The stages include the trigger stage, liability stage, remedy stage, post-decree stage, and impact stage.[64] Welsh applied this research model in his case study analysis of three California counties involved in jail reform litigation.

According to Welsh, Contra Costa County revealed the least amount of resistance and more proactive interagency activity than Santa Clara and Orange County. Welsh attributed this difference to preexisting interagency coordination and a smaller county population. He concluded that tighter coupling due to the difference in scale, budgetary allocation, punishment practices, and the behavior of key actors led to a shorter duration of litigation. The Contra Costa County litigation case lasted from 1984 through 1986.[65]

Within Santa Clara County the duration of the litigation was much longer, beginning in 1971 and lasting into 1989. Within the larger populated Santa Clara County, disagreement and resentment between county and jail administrators, partisan politics at the local level, and a special master beholden to county politics led to a passivity of action even as judicial orders mounted.[66] The federal judge overseeing Santa Clara County litigation began micromanaging daily jail operations from the bench, county supervisors challenged court orders at the appellate level, contempt threats were levied against county administrators, the federal judge as well as a subsequent local judge resigned from the case, and control of the jail was wrestled away from the local sheriff by county supervisors.[67] The conflict involving Santa Clara County litigation is analogous to much of the recalcitrant political action occurring within state level litigation cases.[68]

Welsh's case study of Orange County revealed violations of inmates' rights including inmates sleeping on jail cell floors.[69] The federal judge in this particular case held the sheriff and Board of Supervisors in contempt for intentionally violating his orders and fined the county $50,000 and $10 a day for each inmate whose mattress was on the floor. Population caps were introduced, and the federal judge released jurisdiction when he was satisfied the county was taking steps toward ameliorating the overcrowding problem. Judicial oversight related to this litigation lasted from 1975 through 1988.

Ted Storey's analysis of New York City pretrial detention facilities concluded that incremental changes for the better had been made in the areas of conditions, programs and services for inmates.[70] Storey stated that the litigating parties all agreed that changes would not have occurred without federal litigation and the firm control imposed over the litigants by federal Judge Morris E. Lasker.[71]

Methodology Considerations in Case Studies of Reform Litigation

Case studies of judicial intervention within correctional institutions are limited in their ability to generalize across jurisdictions. As Feeley and Hanson point out, the use of atypical cases is problematic in regard to generalizing across correctional facilities when addressing institutional reform.[72] Yet, the case studies referenced within this body of research serve to inform the reader of general commonalities within specific geographies. For example, the multitude of case studies focusing within the prison systems of southern states provide a repeated pattern of federal intervention addressing the southern plantation model of prisonization and issues of federalism that these particular states have historically imbedded themselves within before and after the Civil War.[73]

In addition to generalization as a methodological limitation of the case study approach, another criticism of this body of research is its overt focus on the judicial role as a protagonist within the institutional reform drama.[74] Smith categorizes institutional reform-based prison case studies as either descriptive or descriptive analytical.[75] He argues that the small amount of descriptive analytical case studies, Marquart and Crouch and Carroll are more complex in that they begin to address the larger research questions related to line level organizational change after litigation.[76] In essence, the focus on judicial frustration, judicial threat, the role of the judge as a coordinator of litigants, and the role of the judge as the intelligent problem solver has served to minimize analysis and discussion of the day-to-day context of prisoners' and correctional officers' institutional experiences prior to and as they have absorbed reform decisions.[77] General conclusions have been formed by differing authors suggesting incremental change or insufficient change within these particular prisons and jails.[78] Yet, the actual context of these changes has been limited within the case study research.

Integrated Studies of Prison and Jail Reform

Integrated studies of prison and jail reform have been few.[79] Yet, these approaches have increased understanding of the complexity of sociopolitical factors and philosophical legal trajectories within fragmented criminal justice systems. In addition these approaches have led to some basic generalizations in regard to judicial intervention within prisons and jails. Feeley and Rubin argue that as a whole judicial intervention reconceptualizes the social institution of the prison as morally and legally justifiable.[80] Through the emergence of a national corrections profession, the formulation of national standards and the bureaucratization of state prisons coordinating ideas promoted by the judiciary created new legal doctrine.[81] Welsh's integrated analysis applying qualitative and quantitative methods, cross-sectional and longitudinal data, historical documents, content analysis, interviews, and secondary statistical data across thirty-five California counties posits that differing sociopolitical and legal factors at the local level fashion jail reform differently by jurisdiction.[82] Welsh argued that the three case studies he presents illuminate these differences. As Welsh categorized legal disputes into the five stages of trigger, liability, remedy, post-decree, and impact, and analyzed the multitude of factors that shape these stages he concludes with institution specific and system-wide changes affecting local level institutions. Institution specific changes included significant improvements within the county jails analyzed. Yet, Welsh proceeds to argue that no one involved in these disputes was completely happy with the results of these improvements. In addition, structural and organizational changes included jail expansion, increased correctional expenditure and increased policy across all the jails studied.[83] As far as system-wide impact of judicial intervention at the local level, Welsh argued that there was increased pressure toward proactive criminal justice planning, yet the pressure and subsequent planning were unique to each legal and political environment.[84]

The case study research in relation to institutional reform within prisons and jails displays differing degrees of success and failure in addressing the system-wide conceptualization of the "justifiable" incarcerated setting. Through differing sociopolitical factors, state and local reform created structural and organizational change within the administration of criminal justice systems. Proactive criminal justice planning began to replace reactive functioning within jurisdictions where stakeholders were more galvanized toward resolution.

Criminal Justice Administration and Court-Ordered Reform

As the issue of overcrowding and conditions of confinement became a concept of management as opposed to solution, criminal justice system administrators and researchers undertook the task of operationalizing the concepts mandated within the reform era. Defining and measuring overcrowding, identifying who is overcrowded and how these conditions fluctuate, as well as the structural and organizational solutions that can be successfully implemented to address these sociolegal problems have been examined, expanded and integrated within criminal justice administration.

Overcrowding, Density and Capacity

Defining the main terms associated with the base argument surrounding institutional reform within local jails continues to be a frustrating if not problematic venture within the research. Agreement as to what constitutes crowding within a jail setting differs across localities.[85] Previous research on crowding suggests that the perception of being crowded is subjective and dependent upon individual perception.[86] As Bleich argues, crowding is a condition that is often defined by symptoms.[87] Focus group and survey research of jail administrators' definitions of crowding include identification of overcrowding dependent upon severity across variables including institutional violence, disciplinary problems, staff grievances, morale and turnover, inmate mental and physical health access, and decreased inmate recreation.[88] The fluid definition of overcrowding across setting and administrator has led to difficulty in providing comparative analysis of overcrowding across jurisdictions.

The use of density, an objective physical measure, has been used as a substitute to operationalize the conceptual term of overcrowding. Density can be categorized into spatial and social density.[89] Spatial density is defined as the amount of space that is available to inmates in a room or cell. Social density is defined as the number of people who sleep in a room or cell.[90] In addition to density, measures of capacity are also used to ascertain whether or not a facility is overcrowded. Design capacity refers to the architectural designer's conception of how many prisoners a facility can hold.[91] Rated capacity is defined by the highest number of prisoners a facility can hold while providing a proper amount of service and management.[92] The Bureau of Justice Statistics measures facility density by dividing the rated capacity into the average daily population for a year. This measure is multiplied by one hundred and provides a percent capacity comparable across jail facilities. Nationally, the percent capacity occupied within jails at midyear 2003 was 93 percent; within Cook County, Illinois, the percent of capacity was 109 percent.[93]

According to jail administrators queried by Klofas, Stojkovic and Kalinich, 80 percent capacity is the benchmark for identifying a facility as overcrowded.[94] Problematic is that a rated capacity approach for ascertaining if an institution is overcrowded is subject to manipulation on a system-wide level, as well as at an institutional level.[95] In addition, capacity-based measures do not provide a substantive indication of the severity of conditions within an institution.[96] As Klofas, Stojkovic and Kalinich argue, severity is determined by the interaction of population, the features of facilities and a range of administrative and management practices.[97]

Demographics of Jail Use

Jails have been categorized as either overcrowded or not overcrowded based upon capacity measures. In addition, research has also examined how jails are used and for whom jails are used. In its most common conception jails are perceived to be used for pretrial detainees awaiting adjudication on misdemeanor and felony charges. Bureau of Justice Statistics data reveal that 780,581 inmates were being held in local jails in 2007; over 38 percent of these inmates were convicted offenders.[98] Between 1995 and 2005, the female population within jails had grown 6.2 percent annually, and the male population within jails had grown 3.7 percent annually.[99] Women constitute approximately 12 percent of the nation's jail population while men constitute 88 percent of the population.[100] Minorities are disproportionately represented within the jail population. Over 54 percent of the individuals being held in jails are minorities.[101] At midyear 2005, African Americans made up over 38 percent of the national jail population.[102] In addition, jail inmates are relatively young in age with just over 28 percent between the ages of eighteen and twenty-four and 60 percent under the age of thirty-four.[103] Approximately 29 percent of the nation's inmates being held in jails are held in the nation's fifty largest local jail jurisdictions. Over 18 percent of the 227,626 inmates residing within the fifty largest local jail jurisdictions are housed within Los Angeles County, New York City, and Cook County.[104]

Understanding Increasing Jail Populations

A common public perception concerning increasing jail populations is that population growth and increased crime rates within communities and cities are attributable to increased jail populations. In a national comparative analysis using booking rates and jail population rates Klofas found meaningful differences in communities' use of their jails, yet population of the jurisdiction contributed little to explaining patterns.[105] Shelden and Brown's analysis of the Clark County (Las Vegas), Nevada, jail cited county officials' positing that county population growth and increased crime were related to increases in jail population.[106] Yet, UCR index crimes were decreasing in the 1980s in Clark County, and the population growth within the jail was double the growth of the population outside the jail walls.[107] Similar findings between increasing jail populations and community population and crime rates were also established in jail analysis within California. These authors went on to argue that the assumed causality fueled policy solutions that focused on building more jail space and limiting the consideration of other policy solutions.[108]

Building Space as a Solution

Establishing new jail construction as a solution to overcrowding has been perceived to be problematic for numerous reasons. First, citizens are reticent to accept the public spending necessary to construct new jail facilities.[109] Second, increases in funding through court mandate have not necessarily ensured a budgetary response at the local level.[110] Feeley argues in response to Taggart's findings that on a regional level judicial mandates have had a significant impact on prisons and jails in the South.[111] Duncombe and Straussman argue that "claims of positive and/or negative impact related to increase funding have rested on thin empirical grounds."[112] These authors further argue that local jurisdictions factor in jail age as well as size when assessing expansion and will invest in expansion if the resources are available regardless of court mandates.[113] Once capital development of new jail space is achieved the effect on overcrowding has been short term. In an analysis of jail capacity in Orange County, Florida, D'Alessio and Stolzenberg found a positive relationship between available capacity and increasing incarceration levels.[114] Similar conclusions of failing to build one's way out of overcrowding were captured in other local jurisdictions.[115]

Coupling and the Criminal Justice Nonsystem

As capital expansion of jails was found to actually increase the number of individuals incarcerated without providing long-term impact on overcrowded conditions, the processing of jail defendants at the front end of the system, as well as at the back end of the system, has been viewed as a solution to addressing overcrowded populations. Addressing the number of individuals arriving at the local jail, as well as how long these individuals reside within the jail, has been viewed as a processing issue malleable through adjustments within the wider criminal justice system. As Shelden and Brown observed in their analysis of overcrowding in Las Vegas, the increase in population was not due to a rise in crime but instead related to the kinds of crime that were receiving the most attention and the longer periods for which these defendants were being held in the local jail.[116]

The perspective of criminal justice as a nonsystem is rooted in the decentralized and fragmented nature of the police, courts and correctional relationship.[117] Yet, the decentralized and fragmented aspects of this nonsystem are not necessarily nonresponsive to one another between subsystems. As Hagan argues, responsiveness exists while the differing subsystems maintain their separate identities in regard to policy and operation.[118] This loosely coupled system provides an environment whereby general change can be adopted yet specific change or the degree of change can be selectively ignored. As Sullivan and Tift observed, correctional system changes influenced by court pressure are not rejected but tempered so as to maintain the correctional system's structure and independence from the other subsystems.[119] When challenged to change, such organizations can take on new appendages, while at the same time selectively ignoring the activities of these new appendages.[120]

Hagan argues that during sudden changes in sociopolitical landscapes loosely coupled systems become tightly coupled to address crisis situations.[121] Hagan provides Balbus's 1973 analysis of urban riots as an example of a tightly coupled system in action toward order maintenance whereby individual level decision making became less variable through cooperative decision making by police, prosecutors, and the judiciary. In recent years, organizational adaptations from reactive individualized decisions toward proactive uniformity based decisions have become quite common within policing and prosecution in regard to gun and violence crises in urban communities.[122] The perspective of creating tightly coupled relationships between subsystems to provide proactive uniformity in relation to jail overcrowding and court orders to address jail overcrowding is logical.[123]

The perspective of creating tightly coupled proactive problem solving coordination among local criminal justice subsystems that have the capacity to affect jail overcrowding has been promulgated by the United States Department of Justice in recent years.[124] Addressing population fluctuation through a coordinating systems perspective and focusing on jail population indicators, local criminal justice agencies are encouraged to track arrest data, jail bookings, inmate length of stay, court case filings and court sentencing through a nationalized forecasting structure. Data collection across local police, courts, and correctional subsystems inherently requires a loosely coupled nonsystem to move toward a tightly coupled system. This approach argues that through coordinated enhanced data collection, identification as to how and why jail populations are rising and falling can be addressed and subsequently local officials can manipulate admission and length of stay numbers through changes in local policy.[125] According to Allen Beck of the corrections statistics program at the Bureau of Justice Statistics, small changes in policy and practice can result in large impacts on populations.[126] Coordinating partnerships toward these goals requires commitment from a critical mass of key leaders and strong leadership from key individuals within the partnership.[127]

Changes in Processing through Tighter Coupling

Increased policing activity concerning homeless and drug-dependent citizens, as well as individuals apprehended under harsher DUI and domestic violence legislation, were found to increase the number of individuals entering local jails in Clark County, Nevada.[128] Overreliance on incarceration rooted in politically motivated crime control policies has been postulated as the producer of overcrowded correctional institutions.[129] The crime control era of corrections and criminal justice policy has developed through a combination of get-tough-on-crime policies, the war on drugs, changes in sentencing laws, limiting judicial discretion, and expansion of intermediate sanctions. The end result is a larger incarcerated population within jails and prisons.

Within the jail setting and in regard to jail overcrowding, Juszkiewicz argued that harsher penalties should be addressed through increasing the use of summonses and imposing alternative sentencing.[130] The use of summons or field citation by police officers for specific crimes as an avenue to reduce the intake numbers within overcrowded jails has been implemented within select jurisdictions. Wayne Welsh's analysis of arrest policy changes as a result of court order in California counties experiencing overcrowding revealed that while some police departments either reactively or proactively increased their use of citations for misdemeanor crimes, there were neither large-scale nor long-term changes in arrest policies as a result of court intervention.[131] More recent research by Baumer and Adams examined the use of judicially mandated summonses rather than arrest across seven misdemeanor offenses within a county suffering from overcrowded jail conditions.[132] These authors found a small but positive outcome in lowering jail intake numbers when using summonses in lieu of arrest.

According to Baumer and Adams, problematic was that impact was thwarted as eligibility for summons was restricted to individuals only charged with the specific misdemeanor offenses.[133] Individuals with multiple charges including the catchment offenses were not eligible for summons. The result was the reduction in the potential target population of defendants. In effect the discretionary decisions of police officers to file multiple charges limited judicial discretion to mandate a summons.[134] The filing of multiple charges was also found to be an influence on jail overcrowding within Clark County, Nevada.[135] The filing of multiple charges in Las Vegas mandated a higher bail amount, thereby increasing length of stay for defendants.[136] According to Welsh police officers were displeased when obligated to cite and release people who they believed should have been booked into the jail and detained.[137] The success of an expanded mandated summons policy is dependent upon the use of individual level discretion by line level agents. Tension between individualization and uniformity has the capacity to reveal itself within the actions of individual agents (i.e., arresting officers) in a hydraulic effect of discretion.[138] Judicially mandated summons and citation policies have the capacity to be selectively ignored through the individual level discretion of line level arresting officers who may either disagree with the mandated policy in general or disagree with its application to specific individuals who are perceived to be hostile to police.[139]

While summons and citation policies have a limited capacity to effect overcrowded jail populations, Baumer evaluated an expedited processing program initiated within a midsize midwestern county attempting to address length of stay for jail defendants.[140] This particular program was initiated after the arrest at the prosecutorial stage of process. The focus of this program was not the manipulation of the criminal justice process prior to individuals entering the jail, but manipulating the process to affect the amount of time individuals were residing in jail. Through the development of a new processing center this particular jurisdiction targeted misdemeanor and low-level felons for expedited screening around the clock seven days a week. Baumer found a significant reduction in screening length, time to initial court hearing, release on recognizance and the decision to drop charges on individuals.[141] In essence, bed space was saved by moving a vast majority of low-level defendants through a local criminal justice system faster. Problematic with this approach was that while saving limited bed space the county increased their custodial capacity through the development of a separate processing center.[142] In actuality the new processing center was a form of capital expansion under a new name or in other words, old wine in new bottles. In addition, probation officers were critical of the expedited processing program as an intrusion upon their individual-level discretion. As Baumer points out, probation officers relied on extended length of stay as a disciplinary tool to teach particular clients a lesson short of probation revocation.[143] The perspective of navigating criminal justice processing and associated temporary detention as a punitive measure for defendants charged with low-level offenses has been posited in other jurisdictions.[144]

In addition to front-end system processing changes such as summons and citation and expedited jail processing, pretrial diversion programs rooted in intermediate sanction-style programming have been implemented to reduce overcrowded jail populations in many jurisdictions. Community restraint-style programming such as day reporting and home confinement/electronic monitoring were implemented and expanded as alternative punishments for convicted individuals in the mid-1990s as a reaction to prison overcrowding.[145] Research of community restraint programs, specifically electronic monitoring, involving prison populations have shown a failure to reduce recidivism.[146]

Within jail settings, community restraint programming has been implemented yet rarely evaluated. The emphasis within evaluation research on this programming has been based on assessing failure-to-appear rates and subsequent arrests while on release. Austin, Krisberg and Litsky using an experimental design with random assignment across three cities found defendants who were initially denied pretrial release and later screened and released under close supervision were not likely to become arrested while on release or become fugitives.[147] More recent findings related to pretrial release and failure to appear has been contradictory. Cooprider and Kerby found lower rates of failure to appear, yet higher rates of technical violations for individuals placed on electronic monitoring.[148] Cadigan found higher rates of failure to appear with individuals released to electronic monitoring.[149]

Within Cook County, Illinois, evaluation of pretrial release to a day-reporting setting found predictors of recidivism such as high rates of illegal drug use, prior criminal histories and low levels of education and employment cannot be resolved in the short time period that pretrial defendants are involved in day reporting.[150] Yet, the longer individuals did participate in day-reporting programming, a lower rate of post-release arrest was found.[151] A consistent finding across intermediate sanction programming is that programs combining services related to addiction, education, and employment along with supervision have been found to have more successful outcomes than programming that relies on supervision alone.[152] In addition to receiving programming that includes treatment and supervision, the amount of time individuals receive these services is related to success.

While the goals of using intermediate sanctions within overcrowded correctional populations are to divert individual defendants and offenders away from incarceration thereby saving tax dollars and increasing bed space, a criticism of these sanctions is net-widening. In other words, the development of intermediate sanctions as an alternative to probation or incarceration has the capacity to expand the number of persons under correctional control, as well as the level of supervision applied to particular individuals under control. Within the realm of pretrial jail defendants, Pontell and Welsh argue that reliance on intermediate sanctions as a quick fix to reduce inmate population problems ignores the correctional policy that created the overcrowding problem in the first place.[153] Examination of net-widening as a consequence of intermediate sanctions has been limited in systematic evaluations across differing types of intermediate sanctions. Net-widening continues to remain as a general concern within the intermediate sanction literature.[154] Within more punitive and surveillance focused intermediate sanctions such as intensive supervision, increased technical violations have led evaluators to conclude net-widening does exist.[155] In a recent analysis of electronic monitoring of serious convicted offenders in Florida, Padget, Bales and Blomberg found "scant" support for a net-widening effect they argue should be weighed against effective reductions in the likelihood of reoffending and absconding while on home confinement.[156] Examination of net-widening in relation to pretrial defendants released on intermediate-style sanctions has been nonexistent.

Success of front-end programs such as citation and summons that attempt to limit the number of individuals entering the local jail setting and expedited processing programs that attempt to lower the length of stay of pretrial detainees are reliant on a tightly coupled criminal justice system for success. While tight coupling may be possible in the short term through firm judicial oversight either at the local or federal level, long-term achievement of a tightly coupled system across large geographies and long-term policy crises seems unlikely.[157] Criminal justice policy makers within police, courts, and corrections generally recognize the existence of jail overcrowding as a policy problem.[158] Yet, there is discord as to agency responsibility in addressing jail population problems.[159] Suggestions and arguments toward developing interagency coordination (i.e., tight coupling) have become a mainstay within the jail overcrowding literature from academic and government sources.[160] Success in implementing inter-agency coordination has been short-lived and has required a heavy handed judicial oversight.[161]

Loosely coupled local criminal justice systems provide agencies and policy makers protection against criticism.[162] Individual criminal justice agents and criminal justice agencies in general that hold crime control values are less likely to alter the routinization of their policies within a loosely coupled system.[163] Through a loosely coupled system, enforcement-oriented policy makers within policing and the courts can delay fully implementing pragmatic solutions to jail overcrowding, instead clinging to the symbolic politics of crime control and blame avoidance.[164] Bleich argues that political conditions drive the prison crowding debate and that all political players involved including legislators, administrators, reformers, lawyers and prisoners use overcrowding and conditions of confinement toward enhancing their respective political perspectives.[165] In essence, a loosely coupled criminal justice system rooted in blame avoidance and subsequent judicial oversight provides political players with leverage to obtain resources, exercise greater control over conditions and provides excuses for institutional shortcomings. [166]

The sporadic nature of research and analysis related to correctional system overcrowding requires a review of literature and research drawing from three areas of differing context. The institutional reform literature that is national in scope focuses on the judiciary as protagonists within an ongoing dispute attempting to define the conceptual thinking and purpose of incarceration. At the state and local level, the case study research explores the sociopolitical conflict associated with enacting institutional reform. Limited success, incremental change, failures and political maneuvering define institutional reform differently based upon local geography, history, and political relations. The criminal justice systems literature provides a contextual overview as to how the concepts of institutional reform posited through the judiciary are operationalized in the day-to-day administration of corrections. How a loosely coupled criminal justice system incorporates or fails to incorporate mandated change is the underlying theme of these analyses.

NOTES

1. Clarence Darrow, *Crime and Criminals: Address to the Prisoners in the Cook County Jail and Other Writings on Crime and Punishment* (Chicago, IL: Charles H. Kerr, 2000): 16.

2. Currie, *Crime and Punishment*; Lawrence Friedman, *Crime and Punishment in American History* (New York: Basic Books, 1993).

3. Todd Clear and George Cole, *History of Corrections in America* (Belmont, CA: Wadsworth, 1997); Michel Foucault, *Discipline and Punish: The Birth of the Prison* (New York: Vintage, 1977); David Rothman, *Conscience and Convenience: The Asylum and Its Alternatives in Progressive America* (Boston: Little Brown, 1980); David Rothman, *The Discovery of Asylum: Social Order and Disorder in the New Republic* (Boston: Little Brown, 1990).

4. Feeley and Rubin, *Judicial Policymaking*.

5. Ibid., 29.

6. Ibid., 30–50.

7. Lon Fuller, "The Forms and Limits of Adjudication," *Harvard Law Review* 92, (1978): 363–65.

8. Owen Fiss, "Foreword: The Forms of Justice," *Harvard Law Review* 93, (1979): 2.

9. James Jacobs, *Statesville: The Penitentiary in Mass Society* (Chicago: University of Chicago Press, 1977): 37.

10. Atterbury v. Ragen, 237 F.2d 953 (7th Cir. 1956); Feeley and Rubin, *Judicial Policymaking*, 30.

11. Habeas corpus is the name given to a variety of writs. The primary function of the writ is to release individuals from unlawful imprisonment.

12. Feeley and Rubin, *Judicial Policymaking*, 30.

13. Ibid., 39–46.

14. Johnson v. Dye, 338 U.S. 864 (1949).

15. Particular Supreme Court cases such as *Brown v. Allen* (1953), a case which broadened the writ of habeas corpus, *Monroe v. Pape* (1961), a Civil Rights Act case, and *Robinson v California* (1962), an Eighth Amendment incorporation case all served to open the arena of correctional reform at the federal judicial level. One may argue

that these cases are philosophically similar to other landmark civil rights decisions of the era including *Brown v. Board of Education* (1954).

16. Jacobs, *Statesville: The Penitentiary*, 64–67.

17. Feeley and Rubin, *Judicial Policymaking*, 39–46.

18. Ibid., 39–40.

19. Regulatory code decisions included such matters as the wattage of lightbulbs, frequency of showers, frequency of change in clothes, caloric content of meals, medical care, use of law libraries and staff hiring.

20. Malcolm Feeley & Roger Hanson, "The Impact of Judicial Intervention on Prisons and Jails: A Framework for Analysis and Review of the Literature," in *Courts, Corrections, and the Constitution*, ed. John Dilulio, (New York: Oxford University Press, 1990):13.

21. John Dilulio, "Conclusion: What Judges Can Do to Improve Prisons and Jails." 1990; in *Courts, Corrections, and the Constitution*, ed. John Dilulio, (New York: Oxford University Press, 1990):290–91; Feeley and Rubin, *Judicial Policymaking*, 40.

22. Feeley and Rubin, *Judicial Policymaking*, 43.

23. Wolff v. McDonald, 418 U.S. 539 (1974): 555–56.

24. Feeley and Rubin, *Judicial Policymaking*, 46.

25. Michael Fieweger, "Consent Decrees in Prison and Jail Reform: Relaxed Standard of Review for Government Motions to Modify Consent Decrees," *The Journal of Criminal Law and Criminology* 83, no. 4 (1993): 1026.

26. John Palmer, *Constitutional Rights of Prisoners* 8th ed. (New York: Anderson Publishing, 2006).

27. Feeley and Rubin, *Judicial Policymaking*, 46, 357.

28. Ibid., 366–74.

29. John Irwin and James Austin, *It's About Time: America's Imprisonment* Binge (Belmont, CA: Wadsworth Publishing, 1994); Marc Mauer, *Race to Incarcerate* (New York: The New Press, 2006); Franklin Zimring and Gordon Hawkins, *The Scale of Imprisonment* (Chicago: University of Chicago Press, 1991); Franklin Zimring and Gordon Hawkins, *The Search for Rational Drug Control* (Cambridge: University of Cambridge Press, 1992).

30. Barbara Zaitzow and Jim Thomas, *Women in Prison: Gender and Social Control* (Boulder, CO: Lynne Rienner Publishers, 2003).

31. James Byrne & Don Hummer, "The Nature and Extent of Prison Violence," in *The Culture of Prison Violence*, eds. James Byrne, Don Hummer, and Faye Taxman (Boston: Pearson Publishing, 2008).

32. Feeley and Rubin, *Judicial Policymaking*, 80.

33. Sheldon Ekland-Olson and Steve Martin, "Organizational Compliance with Court-Ordered Reform," *Law and Society Review* 22, (1988); Feeley and Rubin, *Judicial Policymaking*; Ben Crouch, and James Marquart, "Judicial Reform and Prisoner Control: The Impact of *Ruiz v. Estelle* on a Texas Penitentiary," *Law and Society Review* 19, (1985).

34. Ekland-Olson and Martin, "Organizational Compliance with Court–Ordered Reform," 360–63; Malcolm Feeley and Edward Rubin, *Judicial Policymaking and the Modern State: How the Courts Reformed America's Prisons*, 80–84; James Marquart and Ben Crouch, "Judicial Reform and Prisoner Control: The Impact of *Ruiz v. Estelle* on a Texas Penitentiary," 569.

35. Ekland-Olson and Martin, "Organizational Compliance," 374–75; Feeley and Rubin, *Judicial Policymaking*, 89; Marquardt and Crouch, "Judicial Reform," 583.

36. Marquart and Crouch, "Judicial Reform," 582.

37. Ibid.

38. John Dilulio, "The Old Regime and the *Ruiz* Revolution: The Impact of Judicial Intervention on Prisons and Jails on Texas Prisons," in *Courts, Corrections, and the Constitution*, ed. John Dilulio, (New York: Oxford University Press, 1990): 51–72.

39. Ekland-Olson and Martin, "Organizational Compliance," 378.

40. Feeley and Rubin, *Judicial Policymaking*, 95.

41. Lloyd Anderson, *Voices From a Southern Prison* (Athens, GA: University of Georgia Press, 2000); Bradley Chilton, *Prisons Under the Gavel: The Federal Takeover of Georgia Prisons* (Columbus: Ohio State University, 1991); Bradley Chilton & Susette Talarico, "Politics and Constitutional Interpretation in Prison Reform Litigation: The Case of *Guthrie v. Evans,*" in *Courts, Corrections, and the Constitution,* ed. John Dilulio, (New York: Oxford University Press, 1990); Feeley and Rubin, *Judicial Policymaking;* Bert Useem, "Crain: Non-Reformist Prison Reform," in *Courts, Corrections, and the Constitution,* ed. John Dilulio, (New York: Oxford University Press, 1990); Larry Yackle, *Reform and Regret: the Story of Federal Judicial Involvement in the Alabama Prison System* (New York: Oxford University Press, 1989).

42. Feeley and Hanson, "Impact of Judicial Intervention," 40–42.

43. Anderson, *Voices From a Southern Prison,* xviii.

44. Chilton, *Prisons Under the Gavel,* 107–9.

45. Yackle, *Reform and Regret,* 260.

46. Christopher Smith, "The Prison Reform Litigation Era: Book Length Studies and Lingering Research Issues," *The Prison Journal* 83, no.3 (2003): 352–53.

47. Feeley and Rubin, *Judicial Policymaking,* 79, 367.

48. Edward Rhine, "The Rule of Law, Disciplinary Practices, and Rahway State Prison: A Case Study in Judicial Intervention and Social Control," in *Courts, Corrections and the Constitution,* ed. John Dilulio, (New York: Oxford University Press, 1990): 203–205.

49. Leo Carroll, *Lawful Order: A Case Study of Correctional Crises and Reform* (New York: Garland Press, 1998).

50. Feeley and Rubin, *Judicial Policymaking,* 96–111.

51. Ibid., 142.

52. Ibid., 140.

53. Ted Storey, "When Intervention Works: Judge Morris E. Lasker and New York City Jails," in *Courts, Corrections and the Constitution,* ed. John Dilulio, (New York: Oxford University Press, 1990); Wayne Welsh, *Counties in Court: Jail Overcrowding and Court–Ordered Reform* (Philadelphia: Temple University, 1995).

54. Welsh, *Counties in Court.*

55. Welsh, *Counties in Court,* 228–29; Wayne Welsh & Henry Pontell, "Counties in Court: Interorganizational Adaptions to Jail Litigation in California," *Law and Society Review* 24, no.1 (1991):77.

56. Feeley and Rubin, *Judicial Policymaking,* 111–28.

57. Storey, "When Intervention Works," 138–72.

58. Welsh, *Counties in Court,* 5–7.

59. Ibid., 6.

60. Hans Mattick, "The Contemporary Jails of the United States: An Unknown and Neglected Area of Justice," in *Handbook of Criminology,* ed. Daniel Glaser, (Chicago: Rand McNally, 1974): 785–89; Welsh, *Counties in Court,* 6.

61. Welsh, *Counties in Court,* 25.

62. Ibid., 19.

63. Ibid., 198–99.

64. Ibid., 19.

65. Welsh, *Counties in Court;* Welsh and Pontell, "Counties in Court: Interorganizational," 79.

66. Feeley and Rubin, *Judicial Policymaking,* 125; Welsh, *Counties in Court,* 119–25; Welsh and Pontell, "Counties in Court: Interorganizational," 80–83.

67. Feeley and Rubin, *Judicial Policymaking,* 126; Welsh, *Counties in Court,* 211–13; Welsh and Pontell, "Counties in Court: Interorganizational," 82.

68. Ekland-Olson and Martin, "Organizational Compliance with Court-Ordered Reform," 376.

69. Welsh, *Counties in Court,* 122–23.

70. Storey, "When Intervention Works," 165.

71. Ibid., 166.

72. Feeley and Hanson, "Impact of Judicial Intervention," 40.

73. Feeley and Rubin, *Judicial Policymaking*, 200; David, Oshinsky, *Worse Than Slavery: Parchman Farm and the Ordeal of Jim Crow Justice* (New York: Simon and Schuster, 1997).

74. Margo Schlanger, "Beyond the Hero Judge: Institutional Reform Litigation as Litigation," *Michigan Law Review* 97, (1999): 2031.

75. Smith, "Prison Reform Litigation Era," 355.

76. Marquart and Crouch, "Judicial Reform," 572–73; Carroll, *Lawful Order*, 317–18.

77. Smith, "Prison Reform Litigation Era," 355.

78. Chilton, *Prisons Under the Gavel*, 107; Feeley and Rubin, *Judicial Policymaking*, 380–81; Welsh, *Counties in Court*, 215–19; Yackle, *Reform and Regret*, 256–60.

79. Feeley and Rubin, *Judicial Policymaking*; Welsh, *Counties in Court*.

80. Feeley and Rubin, *Judicial Policymaking*, 371.

81. Ibid., 38.

82. Welsh, *Counties in Court*, 227–31.

83. Ibid., 216–19.

84. Ibid., 222–23.

85. Ibid., 35–37.

86. Gerald Gaes, "The Effects of Overcrowding in Prison," *Crime and Justice* 6, (1985): 98; Daniel Stokols, "On the Distinction Between Density and Crowding: Some Implications for Future Research," *Psychological Review* 79, (1972): 275–76.

87. Jeff Bleich, "The Politics of Prison Crowding," *California Law Review* 77, (1989):1133.

88. Patrick Kinkade, Matthew Leone and Scott Semond, "The Consequences of Jail Crowding," *Crime and Delinquency* 41, no.1 (1995): 155; John Klofas, Stan Stojkovic and David Kalinich, "The Meaning of Correctional Crowding: Steps Toward an Index of Severity," *Crime and Delinquency* 38, no.2 (1992): 178.

89. Gerald Gaes, "Effects of Overcrowding in Prison," in *Crime and Justice an Annual Review of Research Vol. 6*, eds. Michael Tonry and Norval Morris, (Chicago: University of Chicago Press, 1985):136; Dale Sechrest, "The Effects of Density on Jail Assaults," *Journal of Criminal Justice* 19, (1991): 214.

90. Christine Tartaro, "The Impact of Density on Jail Violence," *Journal of Criminal Justice* 30, (2002): 500.

91. Bleich, "The Politics of Prison Crowding,"1138–1140; Christine Tartaro, "The Impact of Density on Jail Violence," 500.

92. Bleich, "Politics of Prison Crowding," 1140–43; Stan Stojkovich and John Klofas, "Crowding and Correctional Change," in *Turnstile Justice: Issues in American Corrections*, eds. Ted Alleman and Rosemary Gido (Upper Saddle River, NJ: Prentice Hall, 1997): 91; Tartaro, "Impact of Density," 500.

93. Paige Harrison and Jennifer Karberg, *Prison and Jail Inmates at Midyear 2003* (Washington, DC: U.S. Department of Justice, Office of Justice Programs, 2003), NCJ Publication No. 20–3947): 10.

94. Klofas, Stojkovic and Kalinich, "Meaning of Correctional Crowding," 178.

95. Bleich, "Politics of Prison Crowding,"1142.

96. Bleich, "Politics of Prison Crowding,"1143; Klofas, Stojkovic and Kalinich, "Meaning of Correctional Crowding," 186.

97. Klofas, Stojkovic and Kalinich, "Meaning of Correctional Crowding," 186.

98. Sabol and Minton, *Jail Inmates at Midyear 2007*.

99. Paige Harrison and Alan Beck, *Prison and Jail Inmates at Midyear 2005* (Washington, DC: U.S. Department of Justice, Office of Justice Programs, 2006), NCJ Publication No. 21–3133).

100. Sabol and Minton, *Jail Inmates at Midyear 2007*.

101. Ibid.

102. Harrison and Beck, *Inmates at Midyear 2005*.

103. Ibid.

104. Sabol and Minton, *Jail Inmates at Midyear 2007*.

105. John Klofas, "Measuring Jail Use: A Comparative Analysis of Local Corrections," *Journal of Research in Crime and Delinquency* 27, no.3 (1990a): 312.

106. Randall Shelden and William Brown, "Correlates of Jail Overcrowding," *Crime and Delinquency* 37, no.3 (1991): 351.

107. Ibid., 352.

108. Wayne Welsh, et al., "Jail Overcrowding: An Analysis of Policymakers' Perceptions," *Justice Quarterly* 7, no.2 (1990): 360–67.

109. Mark Pogrebin, "Scarce Resources and Jail Management," *International Journal of Offender Therapy and Comparative Criminology* 26, (1982): 270; Welsh, et al., "Jail Overcrowding: An Analysis," 351.

110. William Taggart, "Redefining the Power of the Federal Judiciary: The Impact of Court-Ordered Prison Reform on State Expenditures for Corrections," *Law and Society Review* 23, no.2 (1989): 249.

111. Malcolm Feeley, "The Significance of Prison Conditions Cases: Budgets and Reasons," *Law and Society Review* 23, no.2 (1989): 274.

112. William Duncombe and Jeffery Straussman, "Judicial Intervention and Local Spending," *Policy Studies Journal* 22, no.4 (1994): 610.

113. Ibid., 612.

114. Stewart D'Alessio and Lisa Stolzenberg, "The Effect of Available Capacity on Jail Incarceration: An Empirical Test of Parkinson's Law," *Journal of Criminal Justice* 25, no.4 (1997): 285.

115. Shelden and Brown, "Correlates of Jail Overcrowding," 360; Henry Pontell and Wayne Welsh, "Incarceration as a Deviant Form of Social Control: Jail Overcrowding in California," *Crime and Delinquency* 40, no.1 (1994): 32; Welsh, *Counties in Court: Jail Overcrowding and Court-Ordered Reform,* 165–70.

116. Shelden and Brown, "Correlates of Jail Overcrowding," 352–54.

117. David Duffee, *Explaining Criminal Justice: Community Theory and Criminal Justice Reform* (Cambridge, MA: Oelgeschlager, Gunn & Hain, 1980); James Eisenstein and Herbert Jacob, *Felony Justice: An Organizational Analysis of the Criminal Courts* (Boston: Little Brown Company, 1977); Pontell and Welsh, "Incarceration as a Deviant," 73.

118. Hagan, "Why is There So Little," 118 (see intro., n. 71).

119. Dennis Sullivan and Larry Tift, "Court Intervention in Corrections: Roots of Resistance and Problems of Compliance," *Crime and Delinquency* July, (1975): 219–20.

120. Hagan, "Why is There So Little," 119.

121. Ibid., 126.

122. Steven Chermak and Edmund McGarrell, "Problem Solving Approaches to Homicide: An Evaluation of the Indianapolis Violence Reduction Partnership," *Criminal Justice Policy Review* 15, no.2 (2004): 162.

123. Pontell and Welsh, "Incarceration as a Deviant Form," 33.

124. Mark Cunniff, *Jail Crowding: Understanding Jail Population Dynamics* (NIC Publication No. 017209). (Washington, DC: U.S. Department of Justice, National Institute of Corrections, 2002), Robert Cushman, *Preventing Jail Crowding: A Practical Guide* (Washington, DC: U.S. Department of Justice, 2002), National Institute of Corrections; Pretrial Services Resource Center, *A Second Look at Alleviating Jail Crowding: A Systems Perspective,* (Washington, DC: U.S. Department of Justice, Office of Justice Programs, Bureau of Justice Assistance, 2000), NCJ Publication No. 182507.

125. Cunniff, *Jail Crowding: Understanding Jail*; Cushman, *Preventing Jail Crowding*; Pretrial Services Resource Center, *Second Look at Alleviating*.

126. Allen Beck, *Jail Population Growth: Sources of Growth and Stability,* (Washington, DC: U.S. Department of Justice, Bureau of Justice Statistics, 2003):19.

127. Jane Sigmon, Elaine Nugent, John Goerdt and Scott Wallace, *Key Elements of Successful Adjudication Partnerships,* (Washington, DC: U.S., Department of Justice, Office of Justice Programs, Bureau of Justice Assistance, 1999). NCJ Publication No. 173949.

128. Shelden and Brown, "Correlates of Jail Overcrowding," 352–53.

129. Irwin and Austin, *It's About Time*, 5–8 (see intro., n. 68); Mauer, *Race to Incarcerate*, 55–91 (see intro., n. 68); Pontell and Welsh, "Incarceration as a Deviant Form," 32–34; William Selke, *Prisons in Crisis*, (Bloomington, IN: Indiana University Press, 1993): 27; Michael Tonry, *Thinking About Crime: Sense and Sensibility in American Penal Culture*, (Oxford; Oxford University Press, 2004): 21–61.

130. Jolanta Juszkiewicz, "Dealing Effectively with Crowded Jails: The Judge's Role," *Policy Studies Review* 7, no.3 (1988): 589.

131. Wayne Welsh, "Changes in Arrest Policies as a Result of Court Orders Against County Jails," *Justice Quarterly* 10, no. 1 (1993): 113.

132. Terry Baumer and Kenneth Adams, "Controlling a Jail Population by Partially Closing the Front Door: An Evaluation of a 'Summons in Lieu of Arrest' Policy," *The Prison Journal* 86, no3. (2006): 391–92.

133. Ibid., 400.

134. Ibid.

135. Shelden and Brown, "Correlates of Jail Overcrowding," 357.

136. Ibid., 358.

137. Pontell and Welsh, "Incarceration as a Deviant Form," 113.

138. Lloyd Ohlin and Frank Remington *Discretion in Criminal Justice: The Tension Between Individualization and Uniformity,* (New York: State University of New York Press, 1993): 15–16.

139. David Klinger, "Demeanor or Crime? Why Hostile Citizens Are More Likely to be Arrested," *Criminology* 32, (1994): 475.

140. Terry Baumer, "Reducing Lockup Crowding with Expedited Initial Processing of Minor Offenders," *Journal of Criminal Justice* 35, (2007): 273–81.

141. Ibid., 276.

142. Ibid., 281.

143. Ibid.

144. Malcolm Feeley, *The Process is the Punishment* (New York: Russell Sage Foundation, 1979): 241–243.

145. Francis Cullen, John Wright, and Brandon Applegate. "Choosing Correctional Interventions that Work: Defining the Demand and Evaluating the Supply." *Control in the Community: The Limits of Reform?* (Newbury Park, CA: Sage Publications, 1996), pp. 69–116; Belinda Rodgers McCarthy and Bernard McCarthy, *Community–Based Corrections,* (Belmont, CA: Wadsworth Publishing, 1991); John Smylka and William Selke, *Intermediate Sanctions* (Cincinnati, OH: Anderson Publishing, 1995); Michael Tonry and Mary Lynch, "Intermediate Sanctions." in *Crime and Justice,* Michael Tonry ed., Vol. 20. Chicago: University of Chicago Press, 1996: 99–144.

146. Marc Renzama and Evan Mayo–Wilson, "Can Electronic Monitoring Reduce Crime for Moderate to High-Risk Offenders?" *Journal of Experimental Criminology* 1, (2005): 230–31; Lawrence Sherman, et al., *Evidence-Based Crime Prevention: Revised Edition,* (New York: Routledge, 2002): 344.

147. James Austin, Barry Krisberg and Paul Litsky, "Effectiveness of Supervised Pretrial Release," *Crime and Delinquency* 31, no.4 (1985): 531–34.

148. Keith Cooprider and John Kerby, "Practical Application of Electronic Monitoring at the Pretrial Stage," *Federal Probation* 54,(1991): 34.

149. Timothy Cadigan, "Electronic Monitoring in Federal Pre-trial Release," *Federal Probation* 55, (1991): 28–29.

150. Arthur Lurigio, David Olson and Katrina Sifferd, "A Study of the Cook County Day Reporting Center," *Journal of Offender Monitoring* 12, (1999): 11.

151. Christine Martin, David Olson, and Arthur Lurigio. *An Evaluation of the Cook County Sheriff's Day Reporting Center Program: Rearrest and Reincarceration After Discharge.* Chicago, IL: Illinois Criminal Justice Information Authority, (2000): 28–30.

152. Amy Craddock, and Laura Graham. "Recidivism as a Function of Day Reporting Center Participation." *Journal of Offender Rehabilitation, 34,* (2001): 81–100.; Doris MacKenzie, and Claire Souryal. *Multi-Site Evaluation of Shock Incarceration.* National Institute of Justice Research Report (NCJ 150062). (Washington, DC: U.S. Department

of Justice, 1994); Joan Petersilia, and Susan Turner. "Comparing Intensive and Regular Supervision for High Risk Probationers." *Crime and Delinquency* 36, (1990): 87–111.

153. Pontell and Welsh, "Incarceration as a Deviant Form," 18–36.

154. Norval Morris and Michael Tonry. *Between Prison and Probation: Intermediate Punishments in a Rational Sentencing System.* (New York: Oxford University Press, 1990).

155. Michael Tonry, "Stated and Latent Functions of ISP," *Crime and Delinquency* 36, (1990): 174–191.

156. Kathy Padget, William Bales and Thomas Bloomberg, "Under Surveillance: An Empirical Test of the Effectiveness and Consequences of Electronic Monitoring." *Criminology and Public Policy* 5, no.1, (2006): 82.

157. Feeley and Rubin, *Judicial Policymaking*; Welsh, *Counties in Court.*

158. Robert Davis, et al. "Roles and Responsibilities: Analyzing Local Leaders' Views on Jail Crowding From a Systems Perspective," 468–71; Kinkade, Leone and Semond. "Consequences of Jail Crowding," 150–161.

159. Davis, et al., "Roles and Responsibilities," 480.

160. Cunniff, *Jail Crowding.*

161. Welsh, *Counties in Court,* 223–26.

162. Shelden and Brown, "Correlates of Jail Overcrowding," 347–62.

163. Baumer, "Reducing Lockup Crowding," 273–81.

164. Cullen, Wright, and Applegate, "Choosing Correctional Interventions," 163–65; Welsh, et al., "Jail Overcrowding: An Analysis," 361–64.

165. Bleich, "The Politics of Prison," 1127–28.

166. Ibid., 1179.

TWO

Conditions of Confinement

The Social Reality of the Jail Inmate

My first prison experience occurred in 1894 when, as president of the American Railway Union I was locked up in Cook County Jail, Chicago, because of my activities in the great railroad strike that was in full force at the time. I was given a cell occupied by five other men. It was infested with vermin, and sewer rats scurried back and forth over the floors of that human cesspool in such numbers that it was almost impossible for me to place my feet on the stone floor. Those rats were nearly as big as cats, and vicious. [1] —Eugene Debs, *Walls and Bars*, 1927

In addition to a focus on overcrowding and conditions from a criminal justice administration perspective, the social role of the jail has been explored from the individual level of the inmate and from the political role of the jail in the community. Within this literature, the inmate perspective regarding adaptation within the jail environment, the local political rationale for the jail and conditions of the jail has been explored. While the case study literature and the system administration literature provide context to overcrowding and conditions of confinement within prisons and jails from a localized political/governmental perspective, the social role of the jail literature illustrates the context of the incarcerated experience from the perspective of those who are incarcerated.

PRISONIZATION AND INMATE ADAPTATION

The relatively small body of literature regarding the social role of the jail emanates from the larger and more robust literature surrounding prisonization. [2] The preeminent study on prisons which has guided the vast majority of research within incarcerated settings is Gresham Sykes's *The*

Society of Captives: A Study of Maximum Security Prison. Within his analysis of a New Jersey maximum security prison, Sykes explores the social system of the prison setting and its relation to power and authority between guards and inmates, the social system of the inmate world, and inmate collective action. Sykes's perspective argues that inmate culture is developed through the deprivations of imprisonment. Within this culture inmates adapt to functional roles in an effort to negotiate the pains of imprisonment. This research, while a product of the social-structural thinking of its era, provided a launching point for subsequent research associated with adaptation within inmate culture and the incarcerated environment.

Irwin and Cressey argued that inmate culture was imported from the street experiences of the individuals who are incarcerated.[3] This perspective, rooted in subcultural theories of deviance argues that inmate social conditions and adaptation are products of pre-prison identity, race, and ethnicity as opposed to the existing inmate culture that individuals are entering.[4] In addition, Irwin categorizes felons into adaptive roles when serving their sentences.[5] Those inmates "doing time" or "gleaning" are waiting to return to free society with the latter group taking advantage of programming opportunities and the former group merely trying to remain comfortable and avoid problems within the institution. Other adaptive roles posited by Irwin include "jailing," which are those individuals removing themselves from the outside world completely and firmly establishing themselves within the prison world and the "disorganized criminal" who many times becomes the target of victimization.[6] Toch argued that inmates create transactional niches that are congruent with their prioritized needs of stress relief within the incarcerated setting.[7] Toch argues that these niches are homogenous sub-environments related to life experiences prior to incarceration, as well as immediate survival within the prison culture.[8]

More recent perspectives exploring adaptation to the incarcerated setting reify earlier conceptions as posited by Sykes, Irwin and Toch in regard to categorization and rationale of the adaptive role.[9] Schmid and Jones argue that adaptation within the prison setting is correlated with the temporal variable of sentence length.[10] According to these authors, short-time prison inmates marginalize themselves from the prison world and adapt to their environment based on a limited temporal condition. Victor Hassine's *Life without Parole: Living in Prison Today* provides an inmate perspective of adaptation. Hassine categorizes differences among prison adaptation as a dichotomous variable based on generation. The "old heads" or prisoners from previous eras are qualitatively described as "seeking solitude" and "more noble." In opposition, the "young bucks" have infested the inmate general population, importing their violent enterprises into the prison, creating chaos and mayhem.[11] This magnified importation model as it relates to the mass incarceration movement over the past twenty years was recently explored by Melde using face-to-face interviews of Missouri prison inmates. Melde found the basic goal of inmates today remains the same as in the early adaptation literature produced by Sykes, Irwin and Toch.[12] Inmates first and foremost are seeking the maintenance of personal safety and respect of one's fellow inmates.[13] In addition, Melde argues that the concept of an inmate code/convict code as outlined in the early adaptation literature of Sykes and Irwin and reiterated in Irwin continues and is signified by doing one's own time, not interacting with guards and administration and not snitching on other inmates.[14] In regard to the deprivation model of adaptation versus the importation model of adaptation, recent institutional and community culture literature argues that a reciprocal relationship might be occurring. As individuals move back and forth between their communities and prison, importation and exportation are hypothesized to be occurring multidirectionally.[15]

Adaptation and the Jail Environment

John Irwin's *The Jail: Managing the Underclass in American Society* extended the discussion of inmate adaptation to the jail environment. Irwin argued that the nation's jails are merely warehouses for society's rabble class. In addition, Irwin argued that the majority of jail inmates are merely public order violators. These inmates are detached from conventional society and are perceived as offensive and threatening by the public. These attributes, combined with poverty, low educational attainment, unemployment, and minority status, define the rabble class. According to Irwin, the jail is a way to manage the rabble class. Irwin furthered his argument by suggesting that the police and courts use their discretionary powers to arrest rabble-class members and hide them from public view in the nation's jails. In essence, the jail is designed to enforce conformity and adherence to the conventional standards that the rabble class is lacking. Upon entry into jail, those who are not rabble-class members become indoctrinated into the rabble class through a socialization process. Through disintegration, disorientation, degradation, and preparation, inmates are transformed into members of the rabble class.

Backstrand, Gibbons, and Jones argue that Irwin's rabble-class hypothesis of jails is an overstatement.[16] These authors argue that the majority of offenders under jail incarceration are not there for public and petty crimes. Instead, they argue that a large number of booked suspects and convicted time servers in jail have been involved in serious crimes. The authors tested jail population data from two jails across six jail units. Five of the units were tested from Portland, Oregon, and the sixth was from a smaller rural area in Washington. They found that 46.7 percent of the newly booked defendants were charged with felonies. Another 44.3 percent of the newly booked were charged with class A misdemeanors.

The total jail count revealed that 82.5 percent of the inmates were charged with or had been convicted of felony offenses. These authors found there was little evidence to support Irwin's rabble-class proposition.

While the rabble-class hypothesis may be an overstatement in regard to arguing that those incarcerated are petty offenders, the socialization processes experienced by individuals entering jail incarceration as outlined by Irwin provide an indication as to how the jail experience has the capacity to change life trajectories. When community members are arrested, their ties to the conventional world disintegrate.[17] Gibbs describes the processes of disintegration and disorientation of the new jail inmate as a discordant progression where the inmate is between the worlds of the community and the jail.[18] As Klofas argues, the process is less about deprivation and more about the inmate's proximity to the community.[19] Gibbs describes a two-stage process whereby individuals attempting to retain ties to the community experience turmoil and chaos as they enter the jail environment.[20] Turmoil and chaos are soon replaced by boredom in a program-impoverished facility.[21] The perspectives advanced by Irwin and Gibbs, while different in that the former is sociologically based and the latter is social-psychologically based, are similar in that they highlight a qualitative difference in the adaptation to the jail environment as opposed to the adaptation to the prison environment. These differences were further highlighted in an assessment of subcultural values among jail inmates. Garafalo and Clark argue that the subcultural values that were elicited within the prison literature were specific to those jail inmates who had considerable incarceration experience.[22] Rottman and Kimberly describe the jail as an open system whereby the vast majority of individuals are adapting to the environment based on their close proximity to the community and the short duration and repetition in which they move between the jail and community.[23] In addition, these authors argue that the institutional experience of court proceedings also shapes the inmates' adaptation processes.[24] This perspective is similar to what Klofas describes as "retaining a foothold" within the community. In essence, prison adaptation is defined by isolation whereas jail adaptation is defined through pseudo-isolation.

The pseudo-isolation that defines the jail adaptation experience serves to reify and magnify many of the preexisting differentiations between those who become incarcerated within the nation's jails and the rest of the population. While the jail is a holding facility for an amalgamation of offenders and defendants within the criminal justice system including pretrial detainees, convicted misdemeanants, convicted felons awaiting sentencing, probation and parole violators, transfers from state prison, as well as the mentally ill and homeless, there are commonalities among these differing groups. As Michael Welch explains, the profile of jail inmates is that of disproportionately poor, young, black, Hispanic, uneducated, and unemployed persons with drug abuse problems.[25] This population has expanded in volume through criminal justice policies focusing on increased arrest and incarceration, tougher sentencing policies in the 1990s, a war on drugs, increased correctional construction and a general increase in punitiveness.[26]

The social use of the jail and the adaptation process of the incarcerated citizen provide further structural background as to the complexity of overcrowding and conditions of confinement from the many times overlooked perspective of those incarcerated. It is through these areas of literature that the consent decree regarding overcrowding at the Cook County Department of Corrections can be viewed and analyzed. Furthermore, it is through the institutional functionality and disfunctionality of this particular megajail that we can explore the local-level culpability of the flourishing correctional industrial complexes.

Adaptation and the Cook County Department of Corrections (CCDOC)

While much of the emphasis surrounding the consent decree dispute revolves around population and space, aggregate level population numbers, multimillion dollar building projects and demographic changes across the institution, these areas do not entirely capture the overall day-to-day living issues within the CCDOC campus. Within the consent decree dispute, daily conditions regarding environmental health within the facilities, physical health issues of the inmates, and inmate services related to the limited constitutional rights that prisoners are afforded all shape the discourse and themes that are presented by the differing disputants. Within these differing themes specific frames emerged that provided insight into the daily living conditions within CCDOC.

Environmental Health

The frames within the consent decree dispute surrounding the environment within the confines of CCDOC were focused within three predominant areas of argument. Areas of argument included the issues of inmates sleeping on floors; the sanitary and maintenance conditions of CCDOC facilities; and the staffing, security and injury within the CCDOC environment. As these argumentative frames emerged, became dominant and in some cases resided within the consent decree dispute, a clearer picture of CCDOC living conditions was revealed.

The issue of inmates sleeping on floors continued to be the flashpoint for all issues discussed surrounding the consent decree dispute throughout the years 1993 through 2003. As the phenomenon of inmates sleeping on floors continued, emerging frames focusing on changing occupancy levels within cells became a suggested solution. In 1995, the John Howard Association argued that maximum population levels for each division could be achieved if CCDOC administrators were to adopt and adhere to a triple occupancy population ceiling.[27] In 1996 after a renovation project within Division I, CCDOC administrators installed two permanent beds in each cell of the renovated areas. The effect of adding a second bed to each of these cells in Division I was a violation of the consent decree that specified Division I shall house one man per cell.[28] In addition during 1996, CCDOC awarded a contract to procure 1,600 portable beds. CCDOC administrators argued that these beds were to prepare for emergency situations where mass arrests created high occupancy levels. The John Howard Association argued that portable beds, while better than no beds, were an all-too-convenient resource to accommodate more inmates.[29]

By July of 1996, the consent decree had been modified to allow for double-celling in most of Division I, thereby increasing capacity levels within this particular division. By the end of 1996 the number of inmates sleeping on floors exceeded 750 persons on thirteen separate occasions.[30] The end of 1997 marked the ninth consecutive year of inmates sleeping on floors at the jail.[31] In 1999, a review of CCDOC's director's logs revealed that on three different dates it appeared that no inmates had slept on floors. Yet, the John Howard Association pointed out that this could not be confirmed when accounting for classification strategies that exacerbate overflow populations within specific divisions.[32]

Within each year of the data the overflow population was affirmed by all parties, and the framing of the problem was positioned as to the extent of the overflow population and which divisions within CCDOC were experiencing the highest level of overflow population.[33] As the disputants came to realize that overflow populations were a consistent issue without an easily identifiable solution, they began to focus more and more on the living conditions within the divisions at CCDOC.

The rhetoric surrounding the cleanliness and safety of living conditions within CCDOC was a constant point of contention within the consent decree dispute between 1993 and 1995. Through visual inspections performed by John Howard Association staff and the plaintiffs' attorneys, environmental health standards within the institution were consistently coming under scrutiny. For example, in 1994 the John Howard Association described the following conditions:

> In many of the older Divisions of the jail (i.e., I, II, V, and VI) bathroom and shower facilities remain in poor condition. Most of the areas are routinely dirty and foul-smelling and are affected by the same problems described in previous reports. Shower stalls remain dirty, with visible soap scum and flaking paint on walls and floors; in addition one or more stalls in one-third to one-half of the living units have clogged drains and are filled with stagnant water. In Division V and VI, shower stalls are lined with ceramic tiles, many of which are broken and/or missing, resulting in mold and mildew that is difficult to eradicate; in addition, this condition constitutes a safety hazard for inmates who could be cut on the jagged surfaces. Toilets, sinks and urinals are rou-

tinely foul-smelling and dirty, with many urinals still encrusted with mineral deposits.[34]

In addition, inmates were consistently being removed from cold and damp cells and allowed to sleep in dayrooms which were warmer in temperature.[35] There was a consistent short supply of hot water due to water heating equipment that was insufficient for the inmate population and the fact that showers were left running twenty-four hours a day. Insects and rodents were especially problematic within the older divisions.[36] Water seepage and leaking roofs became chronic problems during winter months.[37] Inmates were issued extra blankets to combat the cold and wet conditions.[38]

In the fall of 1994, the John Howard Association was contacted by staff from the Chicago Lawyers' Committee for Civil Rights Under Law, which had been contacted by numerous female inmates at CCDOC. One of the complaints alleged that none of the toilets were working in particular cells in Division IV. This lack of working toilets was corroborated by John Howard Association staff.[39] By November, toilets and floor drains had backed up and were flooding units in Division IV. Staff and inmate workers were issued boots and other protective equipment to minimize risk of contamination from the emanating sewage.[40]

As the frames associated with cleanliness within the institution moved from emergence to dominance in the mid-1990s, many of the sanitation issues called to attention by the John Howard Association were being addressed. Exterminators were providing more frequent spraying for insects and rodents. Extermination contractors were training correctional officers and providing oversight for additional pest control after regular business hours.[41] Construction projects were initiated to address seepage and leaking roofs. Cleaning supplies, power washers, mops and brooms were made more readily available for inmate workers to use for bathroom sanitation. By 1997, while sanitation within specific older divisions continued to remain problematic and challenging, other divisions were reported to be relatively problem free.

> Walls, floors, and ceilings in bathrooms and showers in Division V and VI were frequently dirty, as were sinks, toilets, and urinal in these areas. In Division V and VI, sanitation of bathrooms and showers is seriously compromised due to damaged or missing floor and wall tile, as well as dirty floors, walls and flaking paint. Despite these problems, sanitary conditions in bathrooms and showers in many other divisions have been reasonably good. This description applies to Divisions I, II, III, IV, IX and XI.[42]

The rodent and insect issue moved from a dominant frame in 1993 and 1994 into a residual frame by 1997, with the John Howard Association stating that the vermin control program had met with reasonable success.[43] In regard to some of the more acute sanitation issues in Divisions

V and VI, the John Howard Association concurred with CCDOC administrators that it is difficult to find effective cleaning products that are not
potentially dangerous in the hands of inmate workers.[44] By 1998, the
court monitor stated that mechanical and sanitary maintenance had vastly improved from previous years, yet there remained chronic and unre-
solved problems in particular divisions.

> In Division II, a project to repair and/or replace much of the plumbing
> system in dormitories constructed in the late 1950's had not begun as of
> late January 1998, with no date scheduled for initiation of this project.
> As a result, shower areas on lower floors in several buildings are still
> affected by water leakage from showers on upper floors. In some of
> these areas, plaster has been heavily damaged, and ceilings are covered
> with plastic to prevent plaster and other debris from falling on inmates
> and staff.[45]

While the frames surrounding sanitation and mechanical maintenance
moved from emerging frames to dominant frames in the mid-1990s, the
frames began to move toward the residual as the 1990s progressed. By
1998, the John Howard Association summed up the ongoing sanitation
and mechanical maintenance frames as an issue whereby Cook County
failed to devote sufficient resources to adequately maintain the buildings
of the CCDOC complex.[46]

In 1997, Cook County administrators invited a team of auditors from
the American Correctional Association (ACA) Commission on Standards
and Accreditation to the CCDOC campus for an on-site review of the
correctional facilities. The ACA is an independent association of corrections experts based in Maryland which audits approximately three thousand detention facilities nationwide. CCDOC was graded on over four
hundred standards during this independent audit. CCDOC received a 97
percent compliance rating during the audit process.[47] By 1999, the John
Howard Association stated that routine mechanical maintenance needs
in most divisions, such as inoperative toilets in cells, had been rectified to
a significant degree.[48] In addition installation of air filtration equipment,
further efforts to rectify plumbing problems, vermin control and facility
temperature control had all been improved.[49]

In 1999, the John Howard Association argued that the older facilities
on the CCDOC campus should be replaced due to their need of constant
repair and upkeep.[50] Poor sanitary conditions as well as insect infestation
continued to be reported by plaintiffs' counsel.[51] CCDOC administrators
countered these claims with the following argument:

> The success the Defendants have achieved over the past ten years in
> every aspect of the Consent Decree has largely been ignored by the
> Plaintiffs in their response. Out of 3,000 jails the ACA audits for accred-
> itation purposes, only 97 have received accreditation and the CCDOC
> is the only "mega-jail" to receive such high accreditation scores.[52]

Following ACA accreditation, reports filed by the court monitor and the county between 2001 and 2003 followed a similar cadence. The John Howard Association provided the court a listing of sanitation and mechanical maintenance shortcomings by division. For example:

> Division I: shower areas continue to deteriorate, peeling paint, rust, problematic sanitary conditions; Division II: Seepage to lower floors from shower areas, missing fire exit signs, damaged flooring, missing legs and seats on chairs; Division VIII: Conditions of bathrooms poor, with inadequate lighting and poor plumbing problems. [53]

Following the specific listing of shortcomings the John Howard Association would provide a generalized statement as to the progress achieved by Cook County officials.

> In general, reasonably sanitary conditions have been maintained in all divisions throughout the period covered in this report. This accomplishment is commendable in light of the significant increase in inmate population and crowding that have affected a number of divisions. [54]

Cook County officials responded with the presentation of funding and planning solutions toward the needed renovations and repairs highlighted by the court monitor.

In addition to inmates sleeping on floors and the sanitation and mechanical maintenance of the divisions, another environmental health area not mutually exclusive to the aforementioned areas was that of vandalism, security, and staffing within CCDOC.

The data clearly reflects that sanitation and mechanical maintenance, especially within the older divisions, was related to a lack of upkeep and investment by Cook County officials throughout previous sheriffs' administrations. In addition to neglect on the part of government officials, inmate vandalism played a large part in mechanical and sanitation problems throughout the facility. For example, through 1993 and 1994 the John Howard Association reported mechanical maintenance upgrades of locks on cells doors. While many of these upgrades were due in large part to replacing old locking technology with new locking technology, vandalism was also a contributing factor. In Divisions V and VI locking upgrades were initiated during 1994 based on improved technology. [55] In addition, newer facilities such as Division IX were undergoing renovation to locks and doors caused by inmate vandalism.

> In Division IX, where sanitary conditions are reasonably good, there are growing problems with damage caused by inmate vandalism. JHA staff has seen evidence of damaged cell doors and locks (e.g. hinges broken, steel door handles removed for use as tools and weapons); electrical switches, outlets, and fixtures; and other building system (weather-stripping) around windows removed. [56]

As lock repair renovations continued, living units were emptied and beds became unavailable. The amount of time these beds remained unavailable was not always under CCDOC administrators' control. Cook County sheriff's officials relied on county tradesmen (in this case union locksmiths) who are under the management helm of the Department of Facilities Management (DFM) to upgrade old locks and repair vandalized locks and doors. Inter-conflict based on scheduling and manpower between CCDOC and DFM was being resolved by 1995 as DFM prioritized the issue of lock maintenance by adding an additional six full-time locksmiths to the existing seven who had already been retained at CCDOC.[57] According to the John Howard Association, by 1997 significant improvement in lock maintenance had been achieved, yet there was still concern about the amount of time needed for these repairs.

Vandalism was not merely concentrated within the areas of locks and doors within the CCDOC campus. Many of the other sanitation and maintenance issues were also heightened by inmate vandalism. In the Division II dormitories, vandalism by inmates contributed to the difficulties in regulating temperature. Plastic insulation was removed from windows, and windows were broken when inmates were warm. When seasonal temperatures dropped, inmate complaints of cold and drafts increased.[58] Inmates also covered and clogged air vents to reduce cold drafts in their cells, which in turn created subsequent heating and cooling problems in other common areas. Also in Division II, antiquated metal ceiling tile and the framing supports accompanying these tiles were removed and made into weapons by inmates.[59] Additional vandalism included removal and damage of lightbulbs and electrical switch plates, purposeful clogging of plumbing and toilets, activation of sprinkler systems, fire damage, and destruction of chairs, tables and bedding. As the court monitor stated in 1994, "CCDOC staff and tradesman made reasonable efforts to undo the damage but were frequently unable to keep up with the continued assault."[60]

In addition to a lack of tradesmen to keep up with CCDOC sanitation and maintenance repairs due to years of governmental neglect and continued inmate vandalism, correctional officer staffing also came under scrutiny between 1993 and 2003. In 1993, CCDOC administrators and the Cook County sheriff allocated 50,000 dollars for an in-depth officer staffing analysis to be conducted by an out-of-state consultant.[61] Also, during this time period existing correctional officers who were assigned to departments with minimal inmate contact (i.e., records and supplies) were reassigned to security areas and replaced by civilian employees. In addition by February 1993, 168 new correctional officers were hired at the CCDOC. These management approaches were introduced in an effort to address the burgeoning problem of an increasing inmate population and a decreasing correctional officer staff.

From March 1994 through the end of September 1994, staff shortages were most evident and severe during lunch relief hours in the middle of shifts, and as the John Howard Association noted it was commonplace to find one correctional officer attempting to supervise two or more living units during these times.[62] In consideration of the staffing shortages and based upon the aforementioned staff analysis, CCDOC administrators entered into arbitration hearings with the correctional officer's union in an attempt to reorganize and increase staffing flexibility. By October 1994, CCDOC implemented its new "5/2" work week schedule affording CCDOC with an additional 12,000 workdays per year without increasing correctional staff.[63] In addition to the "5/2" work week a centralized roster management system was initiated to provide consistent analysis and management of changing staffing needs across all divisions.[64] The objective of these two changes was to limit having one correctional officer cross-watching two or more living units. As the John Howard Association specified in its 1996 monitoring report, "for purposes of clarity, it should be noted that, in many of these instances, the location of living units does not allow for direct surveillance of both units simultaneously by one correctional officer."[65] By 1997, CCDOC staffing shortages were an established pattern in all divisions. Observations of these shortages by the John Howard Association staff were confirmed by many divisional superintendents. During correctional officer lunch relief it became common practice to lock inmates in their cells. In 1997, staffing of jail divisions had decreased by 101 correctional officers from the previous year.[66]

Much of the decrease in correctional officer staffing was attributed to an early retirement program offered to Cook County employees. Proposed and passed by county commissioners, the fiscal rationale of the early retirement program was to reduce the salary structure of positions within county government where individuals with long tenure were collecting higher salaries. Following early retirement the CCDOC began graduating training academy classes of new correctional officers that would fill the retired positions at lower yearly salaries. Yet, with increasing inmate populations, additional reduction of correctional officer staff due to termination and medical leave, CCDOC officials were constantly plagued by staff shortages.

> Most divisions routinely operated with six to fifteen fewer CO's than authorized. These shortages were least acute immediately following graduation of classes of cadets, but these gains have invariably been short lived: all divisions then begin to lose staff once again, due to termination of employment and bids for transfer to other divisions and assignments.[67]

While CCDOC administrators were attempting to regain positions lost due to the county-wide early retirement program, they were also being challenged by two other factors which frustrated staffing management.

First, CCDOC divisions carry staff on their rosters that are unavailable for work. These individuals are not working due to injury, leave of absence, training and disciplinary problems. The second factor is that the union bidding system allows correctional officers to transfer to different divisions and shifts thereby creating further staffing problems. As a result, cross watching continued throughout many of the divisions and in an effort to reduce cross watching, inmates were locked in their cells.[68]

Environmental health issues within the institution such as sanitation, maintenance, vandalism and staffing were all contributing factors to injury and violence within CCDOC. Reported injury to inmates and staff at CCDOC was calculated by the John Howard Association per 1,000 inmates. The rate of injury to inmates averaged just over sixteen injuries per 1,000 inmates between 1993 and 2003. The injury rate for CCDOC staff averaged just over nine injuries per 1,000 inmates between 1993 and 2003.[69] These averages only indicate reported instances of injury. In addition, the context of how and where these injuries occur within the institution is not revealed when assessing aggregate injury rates. Yet, within the data there are indications of patterns of violence related to particular divisions within CCDOC. For example, the John Howard Association reported that on March 6, 1994, seventeen inmates were injured in a disturbance involving twenty-nine inmates on wing 3-A in Division IX. This instance was attributed to confrontations between rival gangs.[70] By 2000, the plaintiffs' attorney was requesting a detailed review of these patterns including the nature of injuries reported and when and where these injuries were occurring.[71] In 2001, the John Howard Association argued that the rate of injury varied in direct relation to the size of the inmate population and that inmate rates of injury rose as population increased.[72]

By 2002, the John Howard Association stated, "It is somewhat comforting to note that the rate of injuries to inmates has not increased to even higher levels, given the level of crowding at CCDOC in recent months."[73] In addition, the court monitor outlined specific details of incidents of violence which occurred on March 23 and 24, 2002, which resulted in the murder of one inmate and the serious injury of other inmates in the maximum security Divisions IX and X. As a result of these incidents, CCDOC administrators began staffing these maximum security divisions with members of CCDOC's Special Operations Response Team (SORT). SORT members are trained and equipped to handle disturbances and high-risk individuals and situations. After being assigned to these maximum security divisions, where many of the inmates are IDOC prisoners, CCDOC administrators reported that violent incidents were reduced.[74] In addition, the special incarceration units within the maximum security divisions were modified to enhance security. Modifications included installation of heavy-duty food passes in cell doors, the removal and application of handcuffs only within cells, and eyebolts implanted in visiting booths so inmates could be chained to their seats via leg shackles.[75]

The enhanced security within specific divisions that emerged as a result of injury and violence was revisited again in 2003 when on February 27th the *Chicago Tribune* printed an article concerning a suspected cover-up of an alleged mass jail beating of forty-nine inmates in 1999 by SORT. On Wednesday, March 12, 2003, the Board of Commissioners of Cook County, Law Enforcement and Corrections Committee and the Department of Corrections Subcommittee convened a public meeting to address the aforementioned news story. Participants within the meeting included numerous Cook County board commissioners, representatives from the John Howard Association, a representative from Citizens Alert (a nonprofit public watchdog group dealing in law enforcement issues), and other community activists.

The news article coverage of the alleged mass beating and the subsequent public meeting hosted by the Cook County Board repositioned the issue of violence within CCDOC from an emerging frame to a dominant frame. Upon questioning and presentation, the John Howard Association representatives stated that they were aware of an incident on that particular day in 1999 and had received two complaints from inmates who claimed they had been beaten and did not receive medical attention. Furthermore, the court monitor representatives stated they had notified the sheriff of the incident in writing and that the sheriff had responded that an internal investigation was underway.[76]

The John Howard Association argued that incidents such as the alleged mass beating were an indication of the need for independent external investigations, the establishment of an independent inmate advocate office and in general further resources and staffing across CCDOC which according to the president of the John Howard Association was in "crises mode on a daily basis."[77] John Howard Association representatives further stated that the federal court had not been made aware of the incident within monitoring reports submitted during 1999. Cook County Commissioners questioned why four years after the incident had taken place there were now forty-nine alleged victims as opposed to the original two complainants, why the internal investigation had not been concluded and why the John Howard Association had not followed up on the status of the investigation. Citizens Alert representatives and community activists called for an external investigation by independent prosecutors.[78]

The John Howard Association representatives stated that they had received conflicting narratives from those involved in the melee. On one hand, inmates were claiming they were the victims of abuse of force by members of SORT. On the other hand, CCDOC administrators were claiming that necessary force was used to quell a disturbance. Further testimony revealed that the two individuals who had initially complained on the day of the violent incident had filed a pending lawsuit related to the incident within the Cook County court system. In addition, the sheriff had appointed a three-member panel that included a former President of the Chicago Bar Association, the immediate past public defender of Cook County and the president of the John Howard Association to investigate the incident further. Commissioners questioned the coincidence of a news story of an incident from four years earlier being printed during the same week that the CCDOC Superintendent Ernesto Velasco was being considered by the state legislature as director of the Illinois Department of Corrections.

Referring to presentation material distributed by the John Howard Association, commissioners began an extended discussion on overcrowding at CCDOC and lack of services in general for CCDOC inmates who were disproportionately poor and of minority status. Finally, commissioners discussed the state of Illinois' avoidance of taking financial responsibility for CCDOC inmates and heaping the fiscal responsibility on local taxpayers.[79]

After this discussion, the meeting was opened to questions from the general public and citizen activists. Former death row inmate Aaron Patterson[80] and other citizen activists made impassioned claims of systematic torture within CCDOC, white supremacist rule, and outright murder being conducted by CCDOC employees. As the meeting devolved into unsubstantiated generalizations concerning all CCDOC employees and the Cook County Sheriff's Office the meeting was adjourned.[81]

The conditions related to inmates sleeping on floors, poor sanitary and building maintenance, staffing shortages, security, and injury all shaped the environmental health within CCDOC. As the consent decree disputants shaped the parameters of discourse surrounding these environmental health conditions a background narrative emerged and became dominant that provided a description of what it is to be a citizen within the confines of CCDOC.

Physical Health

In addition to conditions of environmental health within the institution the consent decree dispute also addressed physical health conditions of inmates residing at CCDOC. Frames surrounding food service, health care and personal hygiene dominated the discourse surrounding the theme of physical health.

In 1994, inmates were consistently lodging complaints concerning food service and the cold lunches they were served daily. The John Howard Association confirmed to the federal court that indeed there was legitimacy to these complaints. In addition to the quality of some of the food being provided, the John Howard Association argued that particular sanitation issues related to food service were problematic. Included within this spectrum were food trays encrusted with food from previous meals and food service workers transporting and delivering food to inmates without wearing gloves or washing their hands.[82] By 1995, the sanitation complaints posited by the court monitor to the federal court included dirty and damaged drinking containers and food trays sitting on heavily traveled hallway floors prior to and after serving. Complaints related to the quality of food also continued during this time period with the John Howard Association noting "there is little variation in the selection of lunch meat served, with two selections comprising much of a week's menu—one bologna type product and one chicken loaf product."[83]

By 1997, the emerging frame of food service had been addressed by CCDOC administrators. Cook County issued a four-year, $38.1 million contract to a new food service vendor at CCDOC. The new vendor initiated a menu that included three hot lunches to inmates weekly, a wider variety of lunch meats and enhanced delivery. Under the new contract, the cost per meal was approximately 78 cents per meal, an increase of 4.4 percent over the 74.7 cents per meal cost with the previous vendor.[84] By 1997, inmate complaints concerning food service had waned except for residual complaints concerning cold lunches. The John Howard Association reported that few of the remaining complaints appeared to be substantive.[85] CCDOC officials went so far as to present a review of the comprehensive menu to the federal court. Within this presentation CCDOC officials disclosed that bologna is served only once during a seven-day cycle, and breaded meats (a particular source of inmate complaint) are served eight times during a thirty-five-day cycle.[86] One area of concern related to food service that lasted through 1997 was the issue of inmate labor. Food service at CCDOC was heavily dependent on inmate labor to keep the per meal costs low. The availability of inmate labor was inconsistent due to the fact that inmates were required to be medically screened by health-care personnel prior to food service work. This particular impediment was resolved by eliminating medical screening as unnecessary under City of Chicago and correctional health-care standards.[87]

In 1998 during their on-site observations at CCDOC, the John Howard Association reported that the handling of food and the food itself at CCDOC was generally good. According to the court monitor all lunch meat was being stored in refrigerated storage, under proper temperature and sanitary conditions. In addition John Howard staff sampled lunch meats within the central kitchen and after delivery to the divisions and found the food to be "consistently palatable and quite tasty."[88] While sanitary and maintenance conditions within the central kitchen remained an issue of constant vigilance, the food service frame that emerged in 1994 became a dominant frame between 1995 and 1997 had moved to the residual by 1999.

Frames regarding health care within CCDOC cover a wide array of issues and areas. Included within frames surrounding the quality of health care, issues related to medical, psychiatric and dental needs emerged within the consent decree dispute. In 1994, the court monitor posited the emerging frame of increased complaints and problems associated with health services at CCDOC. While discussion concerning the development of the new Cermak Health Facility had already begun by 1993, the John Howard Associations assessment of health services in 1994 added an increased level of urgency surrounding this emerging issue.

> Since the submission of the JHA report of September 24, 1993, complaints received and verified by JHA staff about problems with health services at CCDOC have risen to alarming levels; in addition, the range of inmate health problems for which treatment has been delayed includes a higher proportion of acute illness and other conditions than at any time since 1989, when the first JHA report to this court was submitted.[89]

By 1995, John Howard Association staff was describing a range of health problems including minor respiratory problems, open wounds, decaying teeth, and significant psychiatric problems.[90] While the court monitor did acknowledge that these acute problems detract from the overall efforts and excellent care that Cermak Health Service staff were providing to thousands of inmates, the emergence and dominance of these frames served to illustrate not only the need for the new health facility but the expedient construction of the new facility.

Prior to the construction and completion of the new facility, CCDOC officials countered the John Howard Association observed reports with indications that they were aware of the health issues and were already addressing problems within the system. Corroborated by the John Howard Association, improvements included the replacement of correctional officers with mental health professionals in the psychiatric screening process and a partnership with the Isaac Ray Center of Rush Presbyterian St. Luke's Medical Center clinicians in stabilizing inmates in psychiatric crises more rapidly.[91] In addition, officials at Cermak Health Services instituted a new procedure to assist inmates in bringing their individual health concerns to the attention of medical staff. Also, health-care officials reorganized and modified the CCDOC pharmacy in an effort to reduce prescription processing time. The latter improvement was based on complaints by inmates of failure to receive medications in a timely manner. As observed by the John Howard Association and confirmed by CCDOC staff, many divisions were forced to house inmates receiving psychotropic medications.[92] The timeliness of receiving medication related to mental health problems is imperative to patient mood stability.

In 1997, plaintiffs' attorneys complained of inadequate dental care within the institution. Plaintiffs received complaints from inmates that they were not receiving prompt dental care and pain relief related to dental problems.[93] By 1998, Cermak Health officials had hired a new chief of dental services, and the Cook County Board of Commissioners approved the hiring of three additional part-time dentists to serve the detainee population.[94]

By 1998, crowding within CCDOC was exacerbating the already over-burdened health-care system within the institution. This was particularly evident in the area of psychiatric treatment of inmates. As crowding within the forty-bed acute psychiatric unit increased, CCDOC officials responded by utilizing specially designated living units within other divisions for this special needs population. Problematic with this solution was that these divisions were not equipped, designed, or staffed for such special populations. During 1998, the John Howard Association received a similar number of complaints about health services as in previous years. Yet, complaints regarding dental care and administration of prescription medicine were diminished.[95] As the new Cermak Health Services opened in 1999, defendants provided the federal court with an overview of the aggregate health-care services provided at CCDOC during the previous year and into the beginning months of 1999.

> In 1998, over one-hundred thousand inmates received diagnostic intake screening. From January 1, 1999 through July 30, 1999, approximately sixty-six thousand inmates were screened at intake. In 1998, over forty thousand inmates visited sick call. From January 1, 1999 through the end of August, 1999 there were over twenty-nine thousand sick call visits.[96]

The opening of the new health-care facility in 1999 increased the bed availability for medical services by sixty-seven beds and psychiatric services by eighty-seven beds.[97]

By 2001, pursuant to the Harrington consent agreement[98] correctional officers and supervisors had made noteworthy strides in receiving training in mental illness identification, and the John Howard Association reported virtually no complaints regarding the administration of psychotropic medication. The latter was attributable to the effectiveness of the medication administration program whereby Cermak Health Service nursing staff delivers medication to detainees within their respective housing units.[99] Yet, while medication delivery and dental health became residual frames within the consent decree dispute, complaints about access to health services for medical issues continued to increase. Complaints ranged from problems being seen in sick call in a timely fashion to significant delays in scheduling surgical procedures.[100]

An additional frame within the consent decree dispute related to physical health and conditions of confinement revolved around exercise and personal hygiene. In regard to exercise, the consent decree requires that detainees incarcerated for less than sixty days are entitled to two hourly exercise periods per week. Detainees held for longer are entitled to three hourly exercise periods per week.[101] Problems meeting this requirement have been attributed to staff shortages and inclement weather during winter months, which has precluded outdoor exercise activity.[102] This emerging frame did not become a dominant frame between 1993 and 2003. In 1998, plaintiffs' attorneys argued that Divisions I, IV and V do not afford even the two hourly exercise periods weekly for short-term detainees, much less anything close to the three hourly exercise period the decree requires for longer-term detainees.[103]

More robust were the plaintiffs' and John Howard Association's framing of personal hygiene problems within CCDOC. Between 1993 and 2003 personal hygiene supplies including soap, toothpaste, toilet paper, towels, clothing and bedding became points of contention between disputants within the consent decree. For example, in 1995 the John Howard Association received hundreds of complaints regarding the size of standard-issue soap bars. While CCDOC administrators were supplying soap and other personal hygiene provisions per the consent decree requirement, the quality and amount of those provisions became a dominant frame within the dispute. The court monitor's report to the federal judiciary in 1995 went so far as to provide the measurements of soap bars issued to inmates. "The bars measure approximately 2.5" x 1.25" x 0.5" and weigh roughly 0.5 ounces, roughly the same size as the small courtesy bars provided in motels."[104] In addition to soap, the John Howard Association also challenged the quality of sanitary napkins being provided to female inmates in Division IV. "The essence of these complaints is that the quality of the items issued is such that individual inmates need more of these napkins than if commercial brands were available."[105]

In addition to questioning the suitability of personal hygiene items, the John Howard Association also called attention to the condition of mattresses, bedding and clothing in many divisions. In 1995, the John Howard Association reported that many mattresses are "stained, dirty, ripped and torn, often with the stuffing removed." CCDOC supervisory staff admitted that mattresses are rarely, if ever, disinfected prior to reissue.[106] In addition, CCDOC confirmed inmate complaints that clean uniforms are frequently not furnished on a weekly basis, and some inmates do not receive clean garments for two weeks or more.[107] In regard to soiled clothing complaints and inconsistent laundry service CCDOC officials relaxed standards and allowed inmates to hand launder their own correctional uniforms within their cells.[108]

By 1996, the John Howard Association continued to report the inconsistent personal hygiene provisions that were being issued to inmates. CCDOC administrators responded with a listing of hygiene and personal items issued to inmates upon arrival to CCDOC. These items included one mattress, one blanket, two sheets, one pillow and pillowcase, one towel, one washcloth, one bar of soap and one tube of toothpaste. In addition, CCDOC administrators began replacing cotton mattresses with vinyl mattresses in an effort to reduce damage and increase cleanliness.[109] By 1998, the John Howard Association was reporting that the great majority of inmates were being provided with the personal hygiene items required by the consent decree. "Throughout the period, soap, toothpaste and toothbrushes, disposable razors, toilet paper, and sanitary napkins have been delivered to all divisions in sufficient quantities on a regular basis to meet inmate need."[110]

In relation to soiled uniforms the John Howard Association suggested decentralizing the laundry facilities at CCDOC and providing washers and dryers at each of the divisions.[111] In 1997, CCDOC officials addressed the soiled uniform problem by arguing that the reason clean uniforms are not available to inmates is a combination of inmates hoarding uniforms, as well as intentional and accidental damage to uniforms caused by inmates. In addressing this problem, CCDOC staff became vigilant in retrieving hoarded uniforms through cell shakedowns that occurred in at least one living unit in every division on a daily basis.[112] The John Howard Association responded to these claims stating that while "very few damaged uniforms have been observed, damage to bed sheets still occurs with some frequency."[113] In addition, the court monitor observed bedding material being used for clotheslines, light switch extension and for a myriad of other purposes.[114]

Physical health frames including food quality and sanitation, physical, mental, and dental health care, and personal hygiene quality and supplies emerged and dominated specific time periods within the data surrounding the consent decree dispute. Coupled with the frames encompassing environmental health a clearer picture developed as to the individual experiential day-to-day subsistence within CCDOC.

Inmate Services

Beyond environmental and physical health frames, another area of conflict within the institution in regard to the consent decree revolved around inmate services. Consistent with prisoner's rights and judicial oversight of correctional facilities, inmates were to receive specific services and avenues for complaint and redress within the institutional environment. Within the Duran consent decree the areas of law library access, inmate grievance processes, and disciplinary procedure became focal points within the consent decree dispute.

Beginning in 1994, sporadic complaints began to surface from inmates who were claiming that they were being given insufficient time within the CCDOC law libraries.[115] By 1995, John Howard Association staff was observing delays in moving inmates to the law libraries. In addition to the delayed visits, which were attributed to staff shortages, the court monitor was also receiving complaints regarding CCDOC's failure to provide updates and other current supplements for many of the critical reporter series that constituted a large part of the library holdings.[116]

The emerging frame of library holdings was addressed in 1996 as library materials were updated with $1 million expenditure by CCDOC administrators. In addition, CCDOC administrators pointed out that each of the nine law libraries on the CCDOC campus were served by a fully license notary public.[117] These financial investments temporarily quelled the court monitor's focus on law library conditions leading to the assessment that during 1996, inmates in all divisions had access to legal materials and were able to receive visits without significant delay.[118]

In 1998, the emerging frame of law library access became a dominant frame as the plaintiffs' attorneys focused on the completion rate of library requests as stipulated within the John Howard Association 1997 court monitoring report.

> Defendants have never been in substantial compliance with this provision, as measured by the "completion rate" the number of law library visits made divided by the number requested and received. Paragraph 6 (A) of the Decree provides, in part, that "all pre-trial detainees shall have access to the law libraries and shall be allowed to use the law libraries during reasonable hours, but each pre-trial detainee shall be allowed at least one library visit per week for at least one hour."[119]

The John Howard Association concurred with the plaintiffs' assessment stating that delays in gaining access to the law libraries continue to affect a significant percentage of inmates in a few divisions. The completion rate within the Division VIII library was just over 36 percent compared to the substantial compliance rate per the consent decree, which was supposed to be in the 85 percent to 90 percent range.[120]

CCDOC attorneys reframed the law library access assessment by questioning the veracity of the completion rate data compiled by the John Howard Association and relied upon by the plaintiffs' attorneys in their argument of library access noncompliance.[121] The inherent inaccuracy as professed by Cook County officials was that the completion rate data did not take into account two important data issues. First, the base number of requests being made did not account for inmates who were making more than one request per week. In essence, CCDOC officials were arguing that as particular inmates made more than one request per week or even daily requests to visit the law library this was leading to an inflation of the input data used in the completion rate calculation. Second, CCDOC officials argued that the completion rate did not take into account canceled library visits due to conflicting court appearances, medical appointments, or just plain refusal by inmates who decided they did not want to visit the library that particular time of day.

By 1999, the frame of law library access was moving toward the residual with the John Howard Association observing that delays in access continued within some divisions but that in general CCDOC law libraries were fairly accessible. In addition, the court monitor noted that procedures for accessing law libraries had become easier for inmates due to the issuance of a new inmate handbook outlining utilization guidelines.[122] The completion rate as measured by the John Howard Association in 1999 had improved to an overall divisional rate of 74 percent.

By 2002, the frame of library access was again emerging as an issue of interest within the consent decree. As the John Howard Association began disaggregating library requests by division they found that over 50 percent of all requests were being made by inmates within Divisions I, IX and XI. The library access completion rate for these divisions was just over 62 percent in 2001. As noted by the court monitor, particularly problematic with this completion rate was that the residents of Divisions IX and XI were often maximum security inmates. As these individuals were facing retrials, resentencing, and appellate court proceedings they were the inmates within CCDOC who were most in need of consistent access to legal research material.[123]

Beginning in 1993, under the guidance of the program services unit of the Cook County Department of Corrections, the inmate grievance process began an overhaul in an attempt to allow for greater inmate access, improved tracking and prompt resolution of inmate complaints.[124] This program overhaul was the result of previous court monitor assessments and what the John Howard Association termed "years of inactivity" in making changes to the process.[125] While CCDOC administrators termed the changes an overhaul, the John Howard Association was less than enthusiastic in referring to these changes as "some progress in developing and implementing a workable inmate grievance procedure."[126]

The court monitor's criticisms of the grievance procedure prior to the 1993 changes and after were based on utilization and response. According to the John Howard Association analysis during 1994, a total of 1,907 grievances were filed by CCDOC inmates. This translated to an average of approximately 159 grievances filed monthly in an institution whose daily population was 8,907 and experienced 83,622 admissions throughout the year.[127] In addition, the response rate to grievances varied from month to month during this time period. In April 1994, there was a 97 percent response rate and in December of 1994 there was a 39 percent response rate.[128] In essence, the court monitor was arguing that considering the size of the population one would assume many more grievances would be filed, and of the grievances filed many did not receive a timely response. In addition, John Howard Association staff argued that the process in place did not differentiate grievances based on seriousness or urgency.[129]

By 1996, the revamped grievance process and criticisms postulated by the court monitor created a dialectic whereby CCDOC administrators reporting to the federal court increased overall responsiveness to grievances. From January to November 1995, over 63 percent of all grievances filed received a response.[130] By 1996, the John Howard Association revealed that eight out of every ten grievances received some type of response.[131] The court monitor reported that the response increase was due in a large part to the modification of routing procedures whereby division superintendents were now being held accountable for response rates.[132] Still problematic from the court monitors perspective was the underutilization of the grievance process by inmates.

In 1997, plaintiffs' attorneys stipulated to the federal court their concern toward the inmate grievance process and the need for further review of these processes. "None of these issues are yet ripe for judicial intervention, but if negotiated resolution proves impossible, counsel for plaintiffs may bring them before the court."[133] The plaintiffs' attorneys then argued before the court that according to the consent decree the John Howard Association was complicit in the problems of utilization and response rate within the grievance process due to its lack of oversight. These statements by the plaintiffs' attorneys thrust the grievance procedure process into a dominant frame during the remaining months of 1997.

By May of 1997, the John Howard Association had produced and submitted to the court a review of the inmate grievance procedure at CCDOC. Within the review, the court monitor described how grievances were collected and logged within the institution, as well as the appropriate time frame for collection and response within the various stages of the grievance process. Grievances were to be collected daily (Monday through Friday) by caseworkers from the human services program. Investigation, fact-finding and written decisions were to be completed within five days of receiving the grievance. Review of the findings and a written recommendation by the director of Human Services to the executive director was to occur within five days of the written decision. Finally, review of the recommendation, issuance of a written decision and initiation of implementation by the executive director was to occur within ten days of the receipt of a recommendation.[134] Basically, the consent decree called for a twenty-day process excluding weekends, which would have the capacity of adding another ten days to the process if a grievance was submitted on a Saturday.

After a full explanation of the process, the John Howard Association reviewed a sample of grievances in an effort to track the actual response time compared to the response time stipulated within the consent decree. Using a sample of thirty-six grievances (n=36), an amount that would be equivalent to less than 2 percent of the total number of grievances filed in 1994, they found that 52 percent of the grievances were collected within two days and 72 percent were collected within three days. Evaluating the twenty-three grievances (n=23) that were dated revealed a nine-day average for written decisions. Many of the responses merely stated "action will be taken" without any further indication as to what action would be taken. All of the grievances analyzed within the sample were resolved at the superintendent level or below, and none of the grievances indicated any recommendations of any kind to the executive director level. While the analysis provided by the John Howard Association was not strong from a social scientific perspective, the limited findings clearly indicated, as the court monitor stipulated, that the grievance procedure remained a matter of high priority.[135]

A review of the aggregate 1997 grievance response data by the John Howard Association led the court monitor to conclude that once again the grievance process was being underutilized by inmates.[136] The plaintiffs' attorneys argued that the delays in processing are especially problematic when the grievances are of an emergency nature in which a detainee claims that there is an immediate threat to their health and safety.[137] The defendants responded with a review of grievance utilization within the first eight months of 1998 which indicated a utilization increase of 77 percent over the 1997 rates. They argued that 16 percent of the increase was due to a change in commissary operation from an in-house service to a contractual service and that the remaining increase was attributable to a revised and distributed inmate handbook which contained a written outline of the grievance procedure for inmate use.[138] Problematic with the increased utilization of the grievance process was that the already challenged response rate was under even more stress than previous years.

While the plaintiffs' attorneys commended the substantial improvement in utilization rates and foresaw that these front-end process improvements would lead to similar improvements in response rates, this was not the case.[139] By 1999 the John Howard Association was bemoaning the grievance response rates and requesting process revisions as promised by CCDOC administrators. According to the court monitor the response rate in 1998 was 56 percent as opposed to the response rate of 81 percent in 1996 and 1997.[140] In 1998, CCDOC administrators issued a new department general order in an effort to increase accountability toward the grievance policy.[141] Through 1999 and 2000, the John Howard Association reported no improvement in the grievance response rate overall, and the most glaring problem was associated with chronic patterns of poor response by the health services staff.[142]

In response to this dominant frame CCDOC officials began a trial program in September 2001 whereby detainee workers were enlisted to collect grievances on a daily basis.[143] The purpose of this trial program was to speed up the collection of grievances, which CCDOC staff and officials had identified as a contributing factor to the low grievance response rate. In addition, and corroborated by the John Howard Association, CCDOC administrators argued that many grievances, such as accusations of excessive use of force, are not susceptible to quick resolution and require thorough and substantial investigation. Within CCDOC's analysis of response rates it became apparent that many delays in response were attributable to staff properly referring grievances for further investigation but failing to inform the detainee of the referral status of the grievance.[144] Finally, Cermak Health Services officials argued that the response rates published by the John Howard Association were not accurate and suggested that court monitor staff work with Cermak Health Services staff to garner the official data directly from them.[145]

By 2002, the John Howard Association was reporting that over 78 percent of the grievances filed were being answered in a timely manner as opposed to the 39 percent response rate reported in 2001. Much of this was attributed to the level of responsiveness initiated by the Executive Office of the Sheriff, who began meeting with CCDOC administrators and staff involved with the grievance procedure.[146] The John Howard Association commended CCDOC on its improvement and stated that these changes may have increased the efficiency of the grievance process and brought it closer to compliance with the consent decree. Yet, within this commendation the John Howard Association again cautioned CCDOC officials on a grievance utilization rate that revealed only one of every fifty inmates at CCDOC had been filing grievances during the period covered within their latest report.[147]

Another dominant frame that persisted throughout the years of this study was related to disciplinary procedures at CCDOC. The disciplinary process within CCDOC consisted of a single disciplinary review board, composed of a security supervisor (i.e., a lieutenant or sergeant), a correctional officer and a caseworker who would hear cases in all divisions in which an inmate was charged with violating CCDOC rules.[148] The continuing frame throughout the data regarding disciplinary hearings was the high percentage of disciplinary cases dismissed due to the inability of CCDOC staff to meet provisions of the consent decree. Data collected on the disciplinary process by the John Howard Association included not only the amount of disciplinary actions filed but also the disposition and the reason for those cases that were initiated and not acted upon. The reason for nonaction in disciplinary processes included reports that were deemed nondisciplinary, the discharge of an inmate prior to conclusion of a disciplinary hearing, failure to provide a hearing within the seventy-two hour time line stipulated within the consent decree and incomplete reporting by CCDOC staff.

Dismissal rate data garnered by the John Howard Association excluded cases not deemed disciplinary, as well as cases whereby the inmate had been discharged. The majority of dismissed disciplinary cases were the result of incomplete reporting by correctional officers. In 1999, approximately 9 percent of the disciplinary cases were dismissed due lack of timeliness and incomplete reporting. By 1997, approximately 20 percent of disciplinary cases were dismissed. Between 1997 and 2002 the dismissal rate hovered at approximately 21 percent.[149] In other words, one out of every five discipline cases was dismissed due to CCDOC failing to meet the provisions of the consent decree.

Disaggregating the 20 percent dismissal rate by timeliness and incomplete reports revealed that just under 5 percent of the dismissals were due to failure of the CCDOC disciplinary board to convene a hearing within seventy-two hours and just over 16 percent were due to CCDOC staff failing to properly file disciplinary reports. According to the John Howard Association, the occurrence of incomplete reports is problematic in that it may be responsible for releasing inmates from segregation who are responsible for significant problems at CCDOC.[150] In addition, intentional failure to properly file disciplinary reports may provide particular CCDOC staff the ability to apply short-term segregation in a capricious manner and in avoidance of disciplinary standards.

In regards to conditions of confinement at CCDOC, oversight of inmate services including disciplinary procedures, grievance processes and law library access remained a focal point of the consent decree between 1993 and 2003. In addition to environmental and physical health concerns the conflict associated with inmate services provides a panorama of the conditions of confinement that inmates and staff at CCDOC grappled with on a daily basis. With respect to addressing these conditions of confinement between 1993 and 2003, federal Judge George Marovich stated as early as 1996:

> The report makes clear that the Department of Corrections continues to improve its facilities and services in a variety of significant respects and to rectify problems identified in previous reports. But in general, it would appear to me that a sincere effort is being made to deal with problems that are not unique to the Cook County Department of Corrections.[151]

While living conditions within CCDOC remained under scrutiny, and the attorneys for the plaintiff consistently reiterated that progress toward compliance with the consent decree is much different than compliance with the consent decree, the federal court clearly acknowledged progress as an accomplishment within itself. As the population of inmates continued to increase the quality of confinement increased also, albeit at an incremental and many times frustrating cadence.

NOTES

1. Eugene Debs, *Walls and Bars* (Montclair, NJ: Patterson Smith Publishing, 1973): 27.

2. Donald Clemmer, *The Prison Community* (New York: Holt, Rinehart and Winston, 1958); John Irwin, *The Felon* (Berkeley: University of California Press, 1970); Jacobs, *Statesville: The Penitentiary*; Gresham Sykes, *The Society of Captives: A Study of Maximum Security Prison* (Princeton, NJ: Princeton University Press, 1958); Hans Toch, *Living in Prison: The Ecology of Survival.* (New York: Free Press, 1977).

3. John Irwin and Donald Cressey, "Thieves, Convicts, and Inmate Culture," *Social Problems* 10, (1962).

4. Irwin and Cressey, "Thieves, Convicts," 152–53; Irwin, *The Felon*.

5. Irwin, *The Felon*, 7–35.

6. Ibid., 61–85.

7. Toch, *Living in Prison*, 181–85, 194–200.

8. Ibid., 204–5.

9. Sykes, *Society of Captives*; Irwin, *The Felon*; Toch, *Living in Prison*.

10. Thomas Schmid and Richard Jones, "Prison Adaptation Strategies of First-time, Short-term Inmates," *Journal of Contemporary Ethnography* 21, (1993): 457–60.

11. Victor Hassine, *Life Without Parole: Living in Prison Today* (New York: Oxford University Press, 2009): 35.

12. Chris Melde, "Penal Reform and the Stability of Prison Adaptive Modes," *Journal of Crime and Justice* 31, (2008): 75–77.

13. Ibid., 76.

14. Ibid.

15. Dina Rose and Todd Clear, "Incarceration, Social Capital, and Crime: Implications for Social Disorganization Theory," *Criminology* 36, (1998): 467–68; Jacob Stowell and James Byrne, "Does What Happens in Prison Stay in Prison? Examining the Reciprocal Relationship Between Community and Prison Culture," in *The Culture of Prison Violence*, eds. James Byrne, Don Hummer, and Faye Taxman (Boston: Pearson Publishing, 2008): 37–38.

16. John Backstrand, Don Gibbons, and Joseph Jones, "Who is in Jail? An Examination of the Rabble Hypothesis," *Crime and Delinquency* 38, no.2 (1992): 227–28.

17. Irwin, *The Jail*, 3 (see intro. n. 1); Ralph Weisheit and John Klofas, "The Impact of Jail: Collateral Cost and Affective Response," *Journal of Offender Counseling, Services and Rehabilitation* 14, (1989): 62–63.

18. John Gibbs, "Disruption and Distress: Going From Street to Jail," in *Coping with Imprisonment*, ed. Nicolette Parisi (Beverly Hills, CA: Sage Publications, 1982): 33–37.

19. John Klofas, "The Jail and the Community," *Justice Quarterly* 7, no.1 (1990b): 74.

20. Gibbs, "Disruption and Distress," 38–39.

21. Ibid., 40.

22. James Garafalo and Richard Clarke, "The Inmate Subculture in Jails." *Criminal Justice and Behavior* 12, 1985: 415–34.

23. David Rottman and John Kimberly, "The Social Context of Jails," in *Correctional Institutions*, eds. Robert Carter, Daniel Glaser, Leslie Wilkins (New York: Harper Row, 1985): 137–38.

24. Ibid., 135–37.

25. Welch, "Jail Overcrowding," 251–76.

26. Alan Elsner, *Gates of Injustice: The Crises in America's Prisons* (Upper Saddle River, NJ: Prentice Hall, 2006); Mauer, *Race to Incarcerate*; Tonry, *Thinking About Crime*.

27. The inevitable emergency situation being referenced by CCDOC administrators was the accommodation of arrestees following street disturbances in the aftermath of the Chicago Bulls winning another National Basketball Association championship.

28. John Howard Association, *Court monitoring report for Duran v. Sheahan et al. 74 C 2949: Crowding and conditions of confinement at the Cook County Department of Corrections and compliance with the consent decree* (Chicago, 1996): 53.

29. Ibid., 87–88.

30. John Howard Association, *Review of the inmate grievance procedure at the Cook County Department of Corrections, Duran v. Sheahan et al. 74 C 2949* (Chicago, 1997): 6.

31. John Howard Association, *Court monitoring report*, 1998, 5 (see intro., n.18).

32. John Howard Association, *Court monitoring report for Duran v. Sheahan et al. 74 C 2949: Crowding and conditions of confinement at the Cook County Department of Corrections and compliance with the consent decree* (Chicago, 1999): 6.

33. John Howard Association, *Court monitoring report for Duran v. Sheahan et al. 74 C 2949: Crowding and conditions of confinement at the Cook County Department of Corrections and compliance with the consent decree* (Chicago, 2000): 5–7; John Howard Association, *Court monitoring report for Duran v. Sheahan et al. 74 C 2949: Crowding and conditions of confinement at the Cook County Department of Corrections and compliance with the consent decree* (Chicago, 2001): 7; John Howard Association, *Court monitoring report for Duran v. Sheahan et al. 74 C 2949: Crowding and conditions of confinement at the Cook County Department of Corrections and compliance with the consent decree* (Chicago, 2002):7.

34. John Howard Association, *Court monitoring report for Duran v. Sheahan et al. 74 C 2949: Crowding and conditions of confinement at the Cook County Department of Corrections and compliance with the consent decree* (Chicago, 1994): 47–48.

35. Ibid., 50.

36. John Howard Association, *Court monitoring report*, 1994, 54; John Howard Association, *Court monitoring report for Duran v. Sheahan et al. 74 C 2949: Crowding and conditions of confinement at the Cook County Department of Corrections and compliance with the consent decree* (Chicago, 1995): 67–68.

37. John Howard Association, *Court monitoring report*, 1994, 51.

38. Ibid., 63.

39. John Howard Association, *Court monitoring report*, 1995, 68–70.

40. Ibid., 70.

41. "Defendants' Status Report," in *the United States District Court for the Northern District of Illinois Eastern Division, Dan Duran et al., Plaintiffs v. Michael F. Sheahan, Sheriff of Cook County et al., Defendants. 74 C 2949, Judge George M. Marovich,* (1994): 36.

42. John Howard Association, *Court monitoring report*, 1997, 61.

43. Ibid., 63–64.

44. John Howard Association, *Court monitoring report*, 1998, 62–63.

45. Ibid., 63–64.

46. John Howard Association, *Court monitoring report*, 1998, 70.

47. "Defendants' Status Report," in *the United States District Court for the Northern District of Illinois Eastern Division, Dan Duran et al., Plaintiffs v. Michael F. Sheahan, Sheriff of Cook County et al., Defendants. 74 C 2949, Judge George M. Marovich,* (1998): 6–7.

48. John Howard Association, *Court monitoring report*, 1999, 76.

49. Ibid., 74–80.

50. Ibid., 85.

51. "Plaintiffs' Response, to Defendant's Status Report and to John Howard Association Monitoring Report," in *the United States District Court for the Northern District of Illinois Eastern Division, Dan Duran et al., Plaintiffs v. Michael F. Sheahan, Sheriff of Cook County et al., Defendants. 74 C 2949, Judge George M. Marovich,* (2000): 4–5.

52. *District of Illinois Eastern Division, Dan Duran et al., Plaintiffs v. Michael F. Sheahan, Sheriff of Cook County et al., Defendants. 74 C 2949, Judge George M. Marovich,* (2000): 8.

53. John Howard Association, *Court monitoring report*, 2001, 58.

54. Ibid., 65.

55. John Howard Association, *Court monitoring report*, 1994, 51.

56. Ibid., 54.

57. John Howard Association, *Court monitoring report*, 1996, 60.

58. John Howard Association, *Court monitoring report*, 1994, 50.

59. John Howard Association, *Court monitoring report*, 1997, 67.

60. John Howard Association, *Court monitoring report*, 1994, 50.

61. "Defendants' Supplemental Status Report," in *the United States District Court for the Northern District of Illinois Eastern Division, Dan Duran et al., Plaintiffs v. Michael F. Sheahan, Sheriff of Cook County et al., Defendants. 74 C 2949, Judge George M. Marovich,* (1993): 9.

62. John Howard Association, *Court monitoring report*, 1995, 85.

63. "Defendants' Status Report," in *the United States District Court for the Northern District of Illinois Eastern Division, Dan Duran et al., Plaintiffs v. Michael F. Sheahan, Sheriff of Cook County et al., Defendants. 74 C 2949, Judge George M. Marovich,* (1995): 28–29.

64. "Defendants' Status Report," in *the United States District Court for the Northern District of Illinois Eastern Division, Dan Duran et al., Plaintiffs v. Michael F. Sheahan, Sheriff of Cook County et al., Defendants. 74 C 2949, Judge George M. Marovich,* (1996): 42–43.

65. John Howard Association, *Court monitoring report,* 1996, 73.

66. John Howard Association, *Court monitoring report,* 1998, 36–37.

67. John Howard Association, *Court monitoring report,* 1999, 130.

68. John Howard Association, *Court monitoring report,* 2001, 73–74; John Howard Association, *Court monitoring report,* 2004, 72–74 (see intro., n. 5).

69. Ibid., 92–94.

70. John Howard Association, *Court monitoring report,* 1994, 114.

71. "Plaintiffs' Response," 2000, 6.

72. John Howard Association, *Court monitoring report,* 2001, 98.

73. John Howard Association, *Court monitoring report,* 2002, 93.

74. Ibid., 94.

75. Ibid., 94–95.

76. *Cook County Board Report of the Committee on Law Enforcement and Corrections,* the Board of Commissioners of Cook County (Chicago, 2003): 3–4.

77. Ibid., 1.

78. Ibid., 4.

79. Ibid., 3.

80. Aaron Patterson was released from IDOC's death row after seventeen years. He was subsequently pardoned by former Illinois Governor George Ryan and the confession that led to his conviction has been alleged to have been produced through the use of police torture. These issues of Chicago Police torture in the 1980's continue to be investigated by the Department of Justice. Subsequently, Mr. Patterson has been incarcerated on federal gun charges.

81. *Cook County Board Report,* 2003, 4–5.

82. John Howard Association, *Court monitoring report,* 1994, 66.

83. John Howard Association, *Court monitoring report,* 1996, 72.

84. John Howard Association, *Court monitoring report,* 1997, 78–81.

85. John Howard Association, *Court monitoring report,* 1998, 75.

86. "Defendants' Status Report," 1998, 39.

87. Ibid., 41.

88. John Howard Association, *Court monitoring report,* 1999, 96.

89. John Howard Association, *Court monitoring report,* 1994, 95.

90. John Howard Association, *Court monitoring report,* 1995, 118.

91. "Defendants' Status Report," 1995, 3, 121.

92. John Howard Association, *Court monitoring report,* 1995, 121.

93. "Plaintiffs' Response to Defendant's Status Report and to John Howard Association Monitoring Report," in *the United States District Court for the Northern District of Illinois Eastern Division, Dan Duran et al., Plaintiffs v. Michael F. Sheahan, Sheriff of Cook County et al., Defendants. 74 C 2949, Judge George M. Marovich,* (1997): 10.

94. "Defendants' Status Report," 1998, 75–76.

95. John Howard Association, *Court monitoring report,* 1999, 125.

96. "Defendants' Status Report," in *the United States District Court for the Northern District of Illinois Eastern Division, Dan Duran et al., Plaintiffs v. Michael F. Sheahan, Sheriff of Cook County et al., Defendants. 74 C 2949, Judge George M. Marovich,* (1999): 36.

97. John Howard Association, *Court monitoring report,* 1999, 123.

98. A coinciding consent decree *Harrington V. Kiley* et al., 74 C 3290, U.S. District Court, Northern District of Illinois, was filed under 42 U.S.C. section 1983 alleging Cook County and the Illinois Department of Mental Health failed to provide necessary mental health care in the CCDOC.

99. John Howard Association, *Court monitoring report,* 2001, 77.

100. Ibid., 76–77.

101. John Howard Association, *Court monitoring report,* 1998, 113.

102. John Howard Association, *Court monitoring report,* 1994, 105.

103. "Plaintiffs' Response, to Defendant's Status Report and to John Howard Association Monitoring Report," in *the United States District Court for the Northern District of Illinois Eastern Division, Dan Duran et al., Plaintiffs v. Michael F. Sheahan, Sheriff of Cook County et al., Defendants. 74 C 2949, Judge George M. Marovich,* (1998): 13–14.

104. "Defendants' Status Report," 1995, 77.

105. Ibid., 80.

106. John Howard Association, *Court monitoring report,* 1994, 62.

107. Ibid., 60.

108. John Howard Association, *Court monitoring report,* 1995, 7–8.

109. "Defendants' Status Report," 1996, 50–51.

110. John Howard Association, *Court monitoring report,* 1999, 88.

111. John Howard Association, *Court monitoring report,* 1997, 76.

112. Ibid., 72.

113. John Howard Association, *Court monitoring report,* 1999, 89.

114. Ibid., 89.

115. John Howard Association, *Court monitoring report,* 1994, 87.

116. "Defendants' Status Report," 1995, 37.

117. "Defendants' Status Report," in *the United States District Court for the Northern District of Illinois Eastern Division, Dan Duran et al., Plaintiffs v. Michael F. Sheahan, Sheriff of Cook County et al., Defendants. 74 C 2949, Judge George M. Marovich,* (1997): 54–55; John Howard Association, *Court monitoring report,* 1998, 96.

118. John Howard Association, *Court monitoring report,* 1996, 89–92.

119. "Plaintiffs' Response," 1998, 12.

120. John Howard Association, *Court monitoring report,* 1998, 97.

121. "Defendants' Status Report," 1998, 47–48.

122. John Howard Association, *Court monitoring report,* 1999, 75, 118.

123. John Howard Association, *Court monitoring report,* 2002, 79–80.

124. "Defendants' Status Report,"1994, 30–31.

125. John Howard Association, *Court monitoring report,* 1994, 106.

126. Ibid.

127. "Defendants' Status Report," 1995, 130.

128. Ibid., 134.

129. John Howard Association, *Court monitoring report,* 1995, 136.

130. "Defendants' Status Report," 1997, 73.

131. John Howard Association, *Court monitoring report,* 1997, 118.

132. Ibid., 121.

133. "Plaintiffs' Response," 1997, 10.

134. John Howard Association, *Review of the inmate grievance procedure at the Cook County Department of Corrections, Duran v. Sheahan et al. 74 C 2949* (Chicago, 1997): 3.

135. Ibid., 9.

136. John Howard Association, *Court monitoring report,* 1998, 117–118.

137. "Plaintiffs' Response," 1998, 16–17.

138. "Defendants' Status Report," 1998, 66–67.

139. "Plaintiffs' Response," 1998, 16–17.

140. John Howard Association, *Court monitoring report,* 1999, 5.

141. "Defendants' Status Report," 1998, 66–67.

142. John Howard Association, *Court monitoring report,* 2000, 87.

143. "Defendants' Status Report," in *the United States District Court for the Northern District of Illinois Eastern Division, Dan Duran et al., Plaintiffs v. Michael F. Sheahan, Sheriff of Cook County et al., Defendants. 74 C 2949, Judge George M. Marovich,* (2001): 22.

144. "Defendants' Status Report," in *the United States District Court for the Northern District of Illinois Eastern Division, Dan Duran et al., Plaintiffs v. Michael F. Sheahan, Sheriff of Cook County et al., Defendants. 74 C 2949, Judge George M. Marovich,* (2000): 22.

145. Ibid., 24.

146. John Howard Association, *Court monitoring report,* 2002, 84.

147. Ibid., 84.

148. John Howard Association, *Court monitoring report*, 2004, 108.

149. John Howard Association, *Court monitoring report*, 2002, 88.

150. Ibid., 87.

151. "Status Report of Proceedings before the Honorable George M. Marovich," *In the United States District Court for the Northern District of Illinois Eastern Division, Dan Duran et al., Plaintiffs v. Michael F. Sheahan, Sheriff of Cook County et al., Defendants. 74 C 2949, Judge George M. Marovich*, (1996): 1.

THREE

The City within the City

Altering Population and Space

As our economies produce abundance, wealth, power, and convenience, the jail endures. —Sean McConville, "Local Justice: The Jail,"
1995[1]

The Cook County Department of Corrections (CCDOC) is the largest
single-site jail facility in the United States. CCDOC is situated on over
ninety-six acres of land located just over three miles southwest of Chicago's downtown business center. The CCDOC campus consists of eleven
different divisions each with its own superintendent and staff. Currently,
there are approximately 10,000 inmates residing at any given time within
this small city situated within Chicago's confines. While the majority of
these inmates are pretrial detainees (approximately 85 percent) the population also includes convicted felons awaiting transport to the Illinois
Department of Corrections (IDOC), IDOC inmates returning to Cook
County for hearings and trials, and convicted misdemeanants. In addition, there are approximately 1,500 correctional officers and additional
service staff that work within this enclosed city daily.

Ten of the eleven divisions are connected by underground tunnels
whereby inmates are received, transferred, released, and transported to
court hearings. Within the receiving area, below Division V, it is not
uncommon to have bullpen cages packed full of newly arrested incoming
inmates in civilian clothes who have been separated by street gang affiliation. At the same time, within other bullpen cages reside individuals in
street clothes waiting processing back into the community. In addition,
some of these large group holding cells are filled with IDOC inmates
arriving and leaving from CCDOC, and CCDOC inmate residents who
have been grouped into bullpen cages for transport to their court hear-

ings for that particular day. As these cages are emptied and filled inmates are led in lines by correctional officers in and out of differing cages as they are processed for entry and release. This is one of the most vibrant areas within the CCDOC campus albeit in a Kafkaesque manner.

The 2004 annual budget for CCDOC was approximately 200 million dollars. In addition to inmate cells, dayrooms, and recreation yards, the CCDOC complex includes a kitchen facility that can produce up to 50,000 meals per day, a hospital, a high school, law libraries, barbershops, commissaries, dental clinics, and laundry facilities. In essence, the CCDOC campus is a city within a city.

CROWDING WITHIN THE WALLS

At the heart of the consent decree dispute is the issue of population management within the CCDOC campus. As the John Howard Association aptly states, "The critical issue of overcrowding has to be addressed and solved to hold any promise of compliance in other areas."[2] Based upon this overarching frame there is a consistent analysis of population change by all parties involved in the dispute between 1993 and 2003. The basis of these population calculations is drawn from observations, analysis and data derived from logs, documents and records provided to the John Howard Association through meetings with Cook County administrators and on-site visits at CCDOC. Initially, the rhetoric of both the court monitor and defendant focused on the front end of the criminal justice process and its impact on the CCDOC population.

> The number of arrests of defendants charged with committing violent crimes continues to rise at an alarming rate. During the first quarter of 1994, 10,125 felony cases were initiated by Cook County. At this rate, more than 40,500 felony cases will be initiated in 1994, an eighteen percent (18 percent) increase over the 34,284 cases in 1993.[3]

While the disputants point toward the increasing arrests and charging of defendants by law enforcement agents within Chicago and the outlying suburbs of Chicago, the John Howard Association positions the starting point of the dispute directly on the population within the institution. While the disputants acknowledge the increasing arrest rates, the agencies responsible for these increases are not directly involved within the overcrowding dispute. Narrowing the focus toward a discussion of who is in the jail as opposed to how many individuals are being transported to the jail as arrestees limits the context of finding solutions concerning the overcrowded population to the administrators of CCDOC.

The John Howard monitoring reports present two differing measures of population to the federal courts. First, overall population numbers are presented which calculate the average number of inmates incarcerated during each year across all eleven divisions at the Cook County Jail Campus. Second, the overflow population is measured and presented. This calculation is presented to the federal court as an indication of how many inmates housed at CCDOC are above the capacity threshold of the institution. In other words, how many of the inmates who are incarcerated are residing in the institution without a bed.[4] These two differing measures are reflected within table 3.1 and serve to provide a cursory overview of the extent of the overcrowding crisis at CCDOC.[5]

These calculations illustrate the basis of a consistently dominant frame of the consent decree dispute and drive many, if not all,of the other frames which are posited by the differing disputants within the time period being studied. Prior to exploring the numerous frames that are derived from the initial discussion surrounding the population calculations it is important to recognize that even at this initial stage of the dispute the interpretations of these objective frequencies are framed differently by the claims-makers within the dispute.

Through the use of aggregating and disaggregating the population frequencies, as well as selectively choosing beginning and ending points to frame the extent and direction of the overcrowding problem, the stakeholders describe the population frame using the metaphors of a glass half empty versus a glass half full.

Table 3.1. Cook County Department of Corrections Institutional Growth between 1993 and 2003

	Average Daily Population	Year to Year Change	Available Beds	Year to Year Change	Occupancy Level	Average Overflow Population	Year to Year Change
1993	8,881	+1.0%	7,953	+20.1%	111.7%	1,543.4	-36.8%
1994	8,907	+0.3%	7,927	-0.3%	112.4%	1,455.7	-5.7%
1995	8,751	-1.8%	7,683	-3.1%	113.9%	1,360.4	-6.5%
1996	9,035	+3.2%	8,857	+15.3%	102.0%	624.7	-54.1%
1997	9,153	+1.3%	9,262	+4.6%	98.8%	414.1	-33.7%
1998	9,475	+3.5%	9,360	+1.1%	101.2%	531.9	+28.4%
1999	9,492	+0.2%	9,639	+3.0%	98.5%	304.3	-42.8%
2000	9,953	+4.9%	9,721	+0.9%	102.4%	535.4	+75.9%
2001	10,642	+6.9%	9,720	0.0%	109.5%	1,147.1	+114.3%
2002	11,082	+4.1%	9,827	+1.1%	112.8%	1,419.6	+23.8%
2003	10,664	-3.8%	10,100	+2.2%	105.6%	990.3	-30.2%

(John Howard Association, 2004:4)

An example of this approach is reflected within the data: "the over-flow population in the CCDOC has fallen from 1,667 in October of 1993, to 1,419 as of April 15, 1994. This represents a fourteen percent decrease in overcrowding over a six month period. The only Divisions affected by overcrowding continue to be I, V, and VI."[6] Through the practice of dis-aggregating the population frequencies by month and choosing a begin-ning month with a high frequency and an ending month with a low frequency the overcrowding decrease percentage is inflated. The argu-ment is being framed by Cook County officials as moving in a positive direction toward resolution of the overcrowding problem at a pace that is not necessarily shared by the other disputants.

While CCDOC official argue that the glass is half full in regard to the overcrowded population, the attorneys representing the plaintiffs frame the population argument as the glass being half empty. In regard to the presentation of the population data during 1999, the plaintiffs responded less than enthusiastically concerning progress.

> The monitoring report documents the lowest level of average over-crowding in many years. Nonetheless, because the decree standard is that no one should be sleeping on floors, ever, defendants remain out of compliance with the decree in this crucial area: overcrowding has been reduced but there is still overcrowding. Progress towards full compliance is very different from achieving full compliance and then maintaining it.[7]

This approach whereby the defendant frames the overcrowding problem as a public policy issue moving toward resolution and the plaintiff frames the overcrowding problem as a consistent failure to achieve com-pliance is manifest throughout the data between 1993 and 2003. These polemic arguments are continually tempered by the John Howard Asso-ciation's conciliatory perspective in the analysis of population, overflow population and progress toward compliance with the consent decree.

The John Howard Association's summation of the progress toward resolution is less optimistic than the defendants' and less pessimistic than the plaintiffs'.

> The data presented in the John Howard report, which was taken from CCDOC records, indicates the 1994 average daily overflow population of 1,455 is at its lowest point since 1991. Specifically, this figure is below 1991's average daily level of 1,499 and represents a 5.67 percent de-crease from the 1993 overflow population of 1,543.[8]

While pointing out indeed Cook County is moving in a positive direc-tion, there is more than an eight percentage point difference between the defendant's summation of the overflow population and the court moni-tor's conclusion. In essence, the differing stakeholders aggregate and dis-aggregate the population and overflow data in an effort to frame their argument toward differing perceptions of the overcrowding problem.

The reliance upon these subjective presentations of data emanating from the same official source is an ongoing approach that is used by all of the disputants in an effort to define the seriousness of the overcrowding problem and its relation toward compliance with the consent decree. Problematic with this approach is the official data that serves to define these differing argumentative frames does not actually represent the extent of the overcrowding problem. In fact, the actual number of inmates who are sleeping on floors at CCDOC remains unknown, yet is perceived to be much higher than the official source data reveals regardless of how it is presented by the differing stakeholders.

The inability to provide an actual count of the inmates who are sleeping on floors is a product of using an inmate classification system within the institution. As pointed out by the John Howard Association Report of 1996, "adherence to classification categories causes uneven distribution of the inmate population within CCDOC as a whole and within individual divisions."[9] While all the parties within the dispute recognize the benefits of safety, security and services that a classification system provides within a correctional institution, the by-product of classification exacerbates the overflow population problem. Within the differing divisions at CCDOC inmates are housed according to classification categories. These categories are based on variables such as age, disciplinary status, offense, psychiatric/medical needs, and educational participation. The result of classification is that individual inmates are assigned to housing units regardless of bed availability. In addition, specialized units such as segregation and protective custody are reserved only for those individuals who qualify within that particular classification. The outcome is that while some living units have overflow populations, other living units have vacant beds. Therefore, the use of CCDOC official source data on population that compares the number of beds to the number of inmates is a simplistic representation of the actual overcrowding problem.

The actual overflow population within living units across the entirety of CCDOC is difficult to assess. What can be assessed is which of the eleven jail divisions do not have overflow problems. By 2000, Divisions I, II, and XI were exempted from overcrowding due to facility design or inmate classification.[10] Yet, overcrowding within particular living units in the other divisions remained quite severe between 1993 and 2003. A descriptive example of this overcrowding when viewed at the living unit level reveals the following:

> On December 22, 1997, Division VI had 948 beds available and held 1,057 inmates with an apparent overflow population of 109 inmates; however, 217 inmates were actually sleeping on floors on that date, almost double the number apparent. In this instance, four of the 23 living units were completely triple-celled, holding 60 inmates in space designed for 40, and seven additional living units were operating at 125

percent to 150 percent of their design capacity, with the majority of cells holding three inmates each.[11]

The unintended consequence of inmate classification is an enhanced overflow population within particular subsets of the inmate population. While the John Howard Association was commending CCDOC officials on improved classification policies and procedures, these improvements were creating further challenges in the management of overflow populations.[12]

An emerging frame in relation to addressing the aforementioned classification improvement versus the hidden overflow problem was presented by the John Howard Association in its 1997 status report to the federal court:

> The implications of this situation are clear: to accomplish this goal without inmates sleeping on floors, CCDOC administrators need to establish adjusted capacity ceilings for each division and commit to operating within these limits.[13]

This emerging frame was endorsed wholeheartedly by the plaintiffs' attorneys in 1998 when they argued to the federal court that the 9,299-bed facility should create a maximum population ceiling of 7,900–8,375 inmates.[14] Yet even in 1997, the John Howard Association was backing away from its posited emerging frame as being detrimental to the safety, security, and services that an improved classification system had provided.

> Based on visits to all divisions during the past year, JHA staff found that the vast majority of inmates at CCDOC are housed in appropriate divisions and living units according to their respective needs. Although some inmates may be forced to sleep on floors as a result of the working classification system, the benefits of assignment to appropriate living units and services available in these units normally outweigh the problems associated with crowding.[15]

By 1998, Cook County officials had reframed the argument as an unavoidable trade-off between overcrowding and proper classification. Further, they argued that "short of building the jail so that all units always have some excess capacity, there is no way to avoid this marginal overcrowding problem—and of course building a jail intentionally too large would be socially, politically and fiscally irresponsible."[16] By the end of 1998, the implementation of a capacity ceiling as an emerging frame had been reduced to a residual frame.

ALTERING POPULATION CAPACITY

Disputants monitoring population growth at CCDOC proffer agreement that the overcrowding issue will not be solved through a predominant focus on building new jail cells. This agreed upon mantra by all disputants is stipulated time and time again within the pages of each report that is presented to the federal court.

> Defendants continue to recognize that population management issues should not be addressed solely through bricks and mortar.[17]

> The persistence of such substantial overflow population constitutes persuasive evidence for the now-familiar maxim that we cannot build our way out of the problem of crowding in correctional institutions.[18]

> Moreover as the court has emphasized, it is unlikely that defendants can build their way into full compliance.[19]

Coupled with these general statements regarding the agreed upon false promise of building one's way out of the overcrowding problem, plaintiffs, defendants and the federal court monitor alike embarked on an expansion of space that had never been seen before within Cook County. In addition to new building projects, renovation and repair to existing structures and property on the CCDOC campus reached new heights between 1993 and 2003. So while each of the disputants verbally acknowledged the inability of building their way to compliance, their actions between 1993 and 2003 presented a different reality.

Between 1993 and 2003 four new building projects and dozens of renovation projects were completed on the CCDOC campus. New building projects included the Division XI facility at a local taxpayer cost of 120 million dollars, a new central kitchen at a local taxpayer cost of 28 million dollars and the new health facility at a local taxpayer cost of 42.8 million dollars. In addition, new building included the construction of a boot camp facility that was funded through federal and state tax dollars. Renovation projects included division and living unit repairs and campus wide renovations. Included in these projects was a 1.2 million dollar security lighting upgrade, the 4.6 million dollar LIFE Safety project, which upgraded fire alarm systems throughout differing divisions and the 3.5 million dollar renovation to correct ground settlement problems in and around Division IV.

The new and improved infrastructure during this time period led to an overall expansion in bed space throughout the CCDOC campus. Including the construction of Divisions IX and X, which occurred just prior to the time period being examined within this study, the CCDOC increased capacity in an enormous fashion.

According to the John Howard Association, since 1988 the defendant's facility expansion and rehabilitation efforts have realized an approximately 70 percent increase in the overall capacity of CCDOC.[20] The building expansion within this growth period was at the very least tacitly approved by all of the disputants involved within the consent decree.

Figure 3.1.   Division X, Maximum Security

Cook County officials were explicitly direct in this approach, stating that expansion of facilities is mandated.[21] By 1996, the John Howard Association was cautioning the federal court, as well as Cook County officials, as to this mandated expansion.

> Cook County officials would be well advised to carefully evaluate the total costs of construction, debt service, and operation of these facilities; moreover, they should also assess how much time elapsed before these earlier generations of beds, numbering in the thousands, were filled, and inmates were once again sleeping on floors.[22]

Yet, the promise of more beds through building and renovation was seductive enough that Cook County officials were given a measured concurrence that this was indeed a prudent approach. Even in instances when living units were emptied for renovation needs and inmates were forced into further overcrowded living conditions, there was an agreement on the necessity of these policy decisions. As federal court Judge George Marovich stated:

> You have been going through a great deal of renovation, and that has caused some problems over at Division I, but I see that, while it may be a technical violation of the consent decree, it is something that maybe is necessitated and will be alleviated in a reasonably short period of time.[23]

Figure 3.2.   Division X, Security Tower

Specific and most important to adding bed space within the walls of CCDOC was the construction of Division XI.

Division XI of the CCDOC campus was promised to be a key element toward compliance with the consent decree and the ending of over-crowded conditions at the jail facility. The construction of this 120 million dollar 1,600-bed maximum security facility had already broken ground and was proceeding as scheduled in 1993. By 1995, inmates were being transferred from other jail divisions to the new complex located across California Boulevard from the remaining CCDOC campus.

A description of this new facility that was provided to the federal court by county officials provides the underlying promise of improved conditions and enhanced security and order.

> This ultra-modern facility incorporates the latest designs to maximize security and safety to both the inmate population and CCDOC staff. Inmate services and programs will also be augmented by the design of this maximum security facility. Division XI is located just east of Cali-fornia Boulevard and north of Thirty-First Street. The eighteen acre site provides inmates and staff with six hundred forty-nine thousand square feet of space. The immense structure encompasses a one hun-dred forty-nine thousand square foot central core with four adjacent one hundred seventeen thousand square foot pods. Each pod contains one hundred and ninety-two cells with three-hundred and eighty four beds and six-thousand square feet of outdoor recreation area. The pods

Figure 3.3.   Division XI

are divided into individual triangular blocks, each containing twenty-four cells capable of holding forty-eight inmates. Each block opens into a dayroom area where inmates eat meals and participate in programming offered by CCDOC. The design of this facility reflects the contemporary philosophy of correctional officials to offer agreeable surroundings for the inmate population. For example, instead of painting the interior of the facility battleship grey, each pod is decorated in a unique color, such as orange, yellow, blue and green—colors which are designed to yield a tranquil atmosphere. In an effort to reduce noise levels, a special insulating material called "pyrok" was utilized which was a critical element in providing a more pleasant environment for inmates and staff.[24]

By 1997, plaintiffs' attorneys were already questioning the assurances given by county officials that the construction and opening of Division XI would alleviate crowding. "Counsel for defendant's anticipated that once Division XI was brought to its population capacity, defendants might shortly come into substantial compliance with the decree."[25]

In addition to the Division XI building project, county official embarked on the construction of a 28 million dollar central kitchen and a 42.8 million dollar health facility. The 65,000-square-foot kitchen facility began construction in April 1994. The new kitchen opened at the beginning of 1996 with the capability of serving fifty thousand meals per day.[26] The old central kitchen, which had been opened in 1975, was then tar-

Figure 3.4.   Division XI, Security Tower

geted for renovation into a 300-bed dormitory-style living unit for minimum security inmates. Coinciding with the opening of the new central kitchen in 1996, Cook County officials broke ground for the new Cermak Health Facility to be completed by the end of 1998.

In addition to the renovation of the old central kitchen, numerous other renovation projects were in constant progress between 1993 and 2003. The purpose of these constant renovations was twofold. First, renovations such as the old kitchen facility were being completed to increase the number of beds available within the CCDOC campus. Second, much of the renovation work was being done to correct dilapidated building conditions that had been ignored under the helm of previous Cook County administrators. The result of all these renovations became a process of musical chairs, or in this case musical beds. For example, in reference to particular renovations taking place in 1993, the defendant's counsel explained to the federal court:

> Because evacuation is necessary during the renovation/rehabilitation period only one wing can be worked at a time. It is projected that work in each of the eight wings will take approximately four to five months to complete, with the first wing completed by April/May 1994, and the remaining wings completed in four to five month increments thereafter.[27]

This process of inmate relocation and building renovation resulted in many living units being uninhabitable for months on end. The result of this process was the loss of beds within living units, which in turn escalated overflow populations within the jail. Within Division I, between 1994 and 1996 it was estimated that 300–325 beds at any given time were unavailable due to construction closures.[28] Considering this ongoing issue the John Howard Association posited the argument that because of the consistent maintenance and renovation projects throughout CCDOC, administrators would be well advised to close one living unit in every jail division at any time for repairs and preventative maintenance.[29] While this approach provided order to the issue of renovation it did not necessarily take into consideration the problem of an increasing population entering into the CCDOC complex. As Cook County administrators pointed out as retort to the John Howard Association argument:

> Although the Association report recommends the closure of one living unit in every jail division at any time for repairs and preventative maintenance the report recognizes that population surges may require utilization of every living unit on the complex. In light of that reality, the CCDOC and Department of Facilities Management have continued to conduct preventative maintenance by removing inmates for eight hour time periods.[30]

Rather than closing living units for extended periods, as was the initial renovation approach, or providing a closed living unit in each division per John Howard's suggestion, CCDOC officials opted to remove inmates in eight-hour increments to allow construction crews to work. The success of this approach, as well as the other two approaches, was tethered to the day-to-day inmate population numbers and the previously mentioned classification system that dictated overflow population within the differing divisions. For example, in 2001 several renovation projects were discontinued due to inmate population surges.[31] In essence, the cadence of renovation projects was controlled by the cadence of inmates who were entering CCDOC on a daily basis. Between 1993 and 2003, 2,147 beds were added across CCDOC. Of these 2,147 beds, 1,600 beds were the result of the construction of Division XI, and 547 new beds were created through renovation. The overflow population when comparing inmates to beds dropped from 1,543.4 in 1993 to 990.3 in 2003; in other words, a reduction of 553 inmates sleeping on floors. Of course, these calculations do not reflect the actual overflow population, which is controlled by the inmate classification system. As the plaintiffs' attorneys' state, "The actual number of inmates sleeping on floors is ordinarily somewhat higher than the average overflow population, and may be significantly higher."[32]

CHANGING POPULATIONS

Between 1993 and 2003 specific categories of inmates placed particular strain on the already overcrowded institution. While the majority of inmates residing at CCDOC were male arrestees in a pretrial status, female pretrial inmates and Illinois Department of Corrections (IDOC) inmates placed new strains on the already overburdened overflow population. In addition, new categories of inmates with classification status revolving around mental health, physical health and drug addiction emerged as areas of concern when addressing overflow populations.

During 1993 until the end of 1994, references to female inmates within the consent decree dispute were relegated to discussion by the John Howard Association that these inmates should have access to health-care and addiction services at the same rate as their male counterparts. Yet in 1995, review of CCDOC daily director's logs by JHA staff revealed that the size of the female population began to increase beginning in October 1994. In addition to the male overflow populations in Divisions I, V and VI, crowding of female inmates in Division IV had become a daily phenomenon.[33] JHA related that this new overflow population was the cause of great concern due to the following four reasons:

1. a substantially increasing daily population;
2. peak populations for females that have exceeded 775 inmates during November and December 1994;
3. a significantly larger overflow population than is readily apparent;
4. the expected duration of repair work (projected for 12–24 months) during which living units must remain vacant.[34]

This emerging frame within the consent decree dispute was thrust into dominance by 1996. Between 1995 and 1996 occupancy levels for female inmates at CCDOC were in the range of 140 percent to 150 percent.[35] CCDOC officials reacted to this dominant frame in an attempt to ameliorate the female overcrowding problem. Plans were forwarded for the modification of Division V in an effort to add an additional 186 beds. This short-term approach was coupled with the development of a third female division that would increase the CCDOC female capacity to 1,225 female pretrial detainees. The reaction by CCDOC officials and the subsequent expansion of bed space for the increasing female population was applauded by the federal court. As Judge George Marovich stated in March of 1996:

> What Plaintiffs have presented to this Court over the last two status hearings was overcrowding of the women's division and that there was no plan. And I want to commend publicly, and JHA's report pointed out, that the defendants have now embarked on a plan that we feel has a really good opportunity to alleviate the overcrowding in that division.[36]

By the end of 1996, CCDOC's female population, which had been housed exclusively in Division IV, was divided and transferred to the former drug unit in Division III. After these transfers no female inmates were forced to sleep on floors or other areas not designed as sleeping quarters. CCDOC's female housing capacity had been increased by over 50 percent in just over a year.[37]

In addition to the burgeoning female pretrial detainees, the CCDOC also houses convicted offenders awaiting transport to the Illinois Department of Corrections (IDOC). These inmates are a mixture of individuals who have either recently been convicted within Cook County and are awaiting transport to IDOC, as well as those individuals who are residing at CCDOC having been implicated on new charges or as a witness in an ongoing trial. The former convicted individuals have actually been transferred back from IDOC facilities to CCDOC for the geographic proximity of CCDOC to the Cook County criminal courts. IDOC inmates residing at CCDOC can be a problematic population for a number of reasons, yet the most basic problem, in regard to the consent decree, is that these individuals are using bed space that is intended for pretrial detainees. In regard to this particular subgroup of inmates residing at CCDOC, Cook County officials began a new program implemented by agreement with IDOC to increase the number of inmate transfers to IDOC. By increasing the IDOC transfer schedule from one group transfer per week to three group transfers per week, CCDOC was attempting to free up bed space for pretrial detainees.[38] Yet by 2000, a dramatic turn of events changed a manageable IDOC relationship into an emerging overflow population problem.

Beginning in May of 2000, the state of Illinois implemented a new parole enforcement initiative. This aggressive parole enforcement policy, known as "Operation Windy City," mandated that state inmates arrested on a violation of parole be held in the county jail, without bond or the option to participate in alternative release programs offered through the Sheriff's Office and the Cook County judiciary. State inmates were to be held within the CCDOC while they await parole hearings and/or the adjudication of newly acquired charges. So while the number of admissions to CCDOC was not changing significantly, the legal status of many of the inmates was limiting the discretion of the sheriff and the local judiciary in regard to bond and release.

The state parole initiative created 160 new parole agents who were equipped with enhanced communication technology and drug testing equipment. According to representatives from the Illinois Department of Corrections (IDOC), during fiscal year 2001 there were 29,000 IDOC inmates on parole and 368 parole agents, of which 240 were working in Cook County.[39]

While jail inmates classified as "parole holds" are not a new issue in and of itself, the state-initiated parole policy change rooted in a "tough on crime" accountability perspective created quantitative and qualitative changes in the Cook County Jail population. CCDOC officials began compiling data on parole hold inmates being held at the jail in July of 2000. In July 2000, 482 inmates, representing 5 percent of the total inmate population, were classified as "parole holds." By May of 2001, there were 1,386 or 12.8 percent of the inmate population classified as parole holds.[40] According to the Cook County Judicial Advisory Council, the new parole violator initiative would cost Cook County taxpayers an additional 18 million dollars per year.[41] In addition to the quantitative increase in parole holds, a qualitative change in population also occurred as a larger number of inmates housed at CCDOC were former residents of the Illinois Department of Corrections. While many pretrial detainees are experiencing temporary incarceration at CCDOC, many IDOC inmates residing at CCDOC are in the midst of long-term prison sentences.

By May of 2001, the plaintiffs' attorneys were requesting intervention from the federal court in regard to the parole hold population crisis.

> Surely, this court should not tolerate the continued use of the jail as a base for incarceration of persons whose custodial care is properly the responsibility of IDOC when the effect of this use of the jail is a gross transgression of that provision of the decree guaranteeing that each class member will be afforded a bed.[42]

While the attorneys for the plaintiff acknowledged that this particular issue was not under the direct control of Cook County officials, they argued that until county officials could address the parole issue with the state of Illinois, pretrial detainees (i.e., class members of the Duran decree) should be afforded beds prior to parole violators.[43] During this time, Cook County officials, specifically the sheriff's department, began meeting with the principals involved with the problem population. Upon meeting with the IDOC, the Illinois Prisoner Review Board, the Cook County state's attorney, local judiciary and the John Howard Association, the Sheriff's Office provided the following three-pronged solution: 1) Establish a special court to handle the parole population with simultaneous hearings on the parole hold issue as well as the pending criminal charge; 2) the state should open a temporary facility in the Chicago area for holding and processing parole violators; and 3) the state should fund a local expansion of electronic monitoring for the parole population.[44] While these meetings were successful in bringing the differing parties together, a determination was made by the agencies involved that the creation of a special court was not feasible due to implementation difficulties.[45] In addition the other two suggestions were postponed for further review and consideration. In frustration, on April 9, 2002, the Cook County Board of Commissioners passed a resolution requesting that the governor of the state of Illinois provide funding to develop and implement a plan in conjunction with Cook County to resolve the local problems created by the new parole initiatives implemented by thestate of

Illinois.[46] According to Charles Fasano of the John Howard Association, by the end of 2002 and through 2003, the Illinois Department of Corrections had been participating within the Duran consent decree status hearings and concerns revolving around parole populations at CCDOC. While individuals with parole holds who had acquired a new charge remained a complicated subpopulation to process, the number incarcerated at CCDOC had been reduced from 1,500 individuals to approximately 600 individuals by March 2003.[47]

While the emergent frames surrounding female inmates and IDOC inmates moved from dominant to residual between 1995 and 2003, numerous other emergent frames continued to surface intermittently throughout the period of study. As each of the disputants became more enveloped in analyzing the CCDOC population data, frames surrounding the expanding population in need of physical and mental health services became apparent. Specifically, drug treatment services were already being offered to a limited number of pretrial detainees who had been released from CCDOC. By February 1993, five different agencies including Gateway Foundation and Catholic Charities were providing over 200 community treatment beds to house inmates awaiting mandatory drug treatment ordered by the court. In addition Cook County officials had budgeted an additional 7.5 million dollars to purchase future community treatment beds through other nonprofit organizations.[48] In 2000, plaintiffs' attorneys argued that the subpopulation residing at CCDOC in need of drug treatment services should be offered treatment within CCDOC if requested.

> Substance abuse treatment programs should be broadly available to the inmates who wish to participate in such programs. Plaintiffs request defendants to prepare proposals to provide such treatment by the time of the next report. While substance abuse treatment may not be considered part of the consent decree, to the extent that such treatment could reduce length of stay in the jail or prevent repeated incarceration, plaintiffs suggest that provisions of such treatment would contribute to reductions in the overcrowding of the jail and improve conditions of confinement overall.[49]

Defendants argued that drug-dependent inmates should be selectively chosen to participate in any CCDOC treatment programs. Defendants argued that the average length of stay of a CCDOC inmate is approximately forty-nine days and that treatment programs are only beneficial when an individual is exposed to treatment for a minimum amount of time.[50] In essence, CCDOC officials were arguing that it would be fiscally irresponsible to offer treatment to pretrial detainees who would either be released or convicted and transferred to IDOC prior to finishing a treatment program.

In addition to crowding associated with pretrial inmates suffering from drug dependency problems, another emerging public health frame began to amplify in resonance. As the general population of female inmate overcrowding began to subside it became apparent that bed space for women with acute psychiatric and medical needs was inadequate. According to the John Howard Association, crowding affecting all inmates with major psychiatric problems housed in the Cermak Health Services facility occurred with increasing frequency during the second half of 1997. During August 1998, crowding in these units was a daily phenomenon, with an average of ten inmates and a maximum of twenty-five inmates sleeping on floors in the acute psychiatric intensive care unit.[51] The overcrowding of this special-needs population of inmates continued through 1999 before and after the opening of the new Cermak Health Services facility.[52]

In regard to population and space, the consent decree dispute surrounding overcrowding at CCDOC revolved around the three main concepts of defining crowded populations, altering the confines of CCDOC and addressing demographic changes within those crowded populations. During the time frame of 1993 through 2003 the average daily population of CCDOC increased by 1,783 inmates. According to the average overflow population derived from CCDOC logs, there was a reduction of inmates sleeping on floors of 553.1 inmates. Yet, the emerging frame presented by the John Howard Association that factors in classification strategies revealed that this average overflow population was not only higher than presented in official data; it was changing on a daily basis. Between 1993 and 2003, hundreds of millions of taxpayer dollars were spent on new construction, alteration and repair in an effort to increase bed space within the CCDOC facilities. In addition to growing population and expanded building projects, the population was changing demographically. Women inmates were increasingly entering CCDOC at a higher rate, and female capacity was subsequently increased by 50 percent between 1993 and 2003. Parole policy changes within the state of Illinois were increasing the convicted inmate population and challenging bed space reserved for pretrial detainees. Finally, the emergence of burgeoning populations of mentally ill, drug dependent and physically ill detainees were being recognized as an imminent policy problem. Within all of these dominant, emerging and residual frames surrounding the themes of population and space, one particular detail remained constant. Between 1993 and 2003, on all but a few days, pretrial detainees were sleeping on floors in violation of the consent decree.

NOTES

1. Sean McConnville, "Local Justice: The Jail" in *The Oxford History of the Prison: The Practice of Punishment in Western Society*, eds. Norval Morris and David Rothman (New York: Oxford University Press, 1995): 292.

2. "Plaintiffs' Response," 1997, 3 (see chap. 2, n. 93).

3. "Defendants' Status Report," 1994, 9 (see chap. 2, n. 41).

4. The overarching emphasis of the consent decree is that each resident shall have a permanent bed in a cell during their residence at CCDOC.

5. John Howard Association, *Court Monitoring Report*, 2004, 4 (see intro., n.5).

6. "Defendants' Status Report," 1994, 9.

7. "Plaintiffs' Response to Defendant's Status Report and to John Howard Association Monitoring Report," in *the United States District Court for the Northern District of Illinois Eastern Division, Dan Duran et al., Plaintiffs v. Michael F. Sheahan, Sheriff of Cook County et al., Defendants. 74 C 2949, Judge George M. Marovich,* (1999): 5.

8. John Howard Association, *Court monitoring report*, 1995, 7–8 (see chap. 2, n. 36).

9. John Howard Association, *Court monitoring report*, 1996, 86 (see chap. 2, n. 28).

10. John Howard Association, *Court monitoring report*, 2000, 5 (see chap. 2, n. 33).

11. John Howard Association, *Court monitoring report*, 1998, 94 (see intro., n. 18).

12. "Defendants' Status Report," 1995, 39, (see chap. 2, n. 36).

13. John Howard Association, 1997, 71 (see chap. 2, n.30).

14. "Plaintiffs' Response," 1998, 4 (see chap. 2, n. 103).

15. John Howard Association, *Court monitoring report,* 1997, 136–37.

16. "Defendants' Status Report," 1998, 4 (see chap. 2, n. 47).

17. "Defendants' Supplemental Status Report," 1993, 1 (see chap. 2, n. 61).

18. John Howard Association, *Court monitoring report,* 1995, 28.

19. "Plaintiffs' Response," 1999, 2.

20. John Howard Association, *Court monitoring report,* 1998, 1–2.

21. "Defendants' Status Report," in *the United States District Court for the Northern District of Illinois Eastern Division, Dan Duran et al., Plaintiffs v. Michael F. Sheahan, Sheriff of Cook County et al., Defendants. 74 C 2949, Judge George M. Marovich,* (1992): 2.

22. John Howard Association, *Court monitoring report,* 1996, 21–22.

23. "Status Report of Proceedings before the Honorable George M. Marovich," *In the United States District Court for the Northern District of Illinois Eastern Division, Dan Duran et al., Plaintiffs v. Michael F. Sheahan, Sheriff of Cook County et al., Defendants. 74 C 2949, Judge George M. Marovich,* (1996): 3.

24. "Defendants' Status Report," 1996, 13–14 (see chap. 2, n.64).

25. "Plaintiffs' Response," 1997, 1.

26. "Defendants' Status Report," 1996, 7.

27. "Defendants' Status Report," in *the United States District Court for the Northern District of Illinois Eastern Division, Dan Duran et al., Plaintiffs v. Michael F. Sheahan, Sheriff of Cook County et al., Defendants. 74 C 2949, Judge George M. Marovich,* (1993): 3.

28. "Defendants' Status Report," 1997, 10 (see chap. 2, n. 117).

29. John Howard Association, *Court monitoring report,* 1998, 69.

30. "Defendants' Status Report," 1997, 6.

31. John Howard Association, *Court monitoring report,* 2001, 55 (see chap. 2, n. 33).

32. "Plaintiffs' Response," 1997, 3.

33. John Howard Association, *Court monitoring report,* 1995, 4.

34. Ibid., 100.

35. John Howard Association, *Court monitoring report,* 1996, 83.

36. "Defendants' Status Report," 1996, 5.

37. John Howard Association, *Court monitoring report,* 1997, 7.

38. "Defendants' Status Report," 1997, 12–13.

39. Cook County Board Report of the Committee on Law Enforcement and Corrections, 2001.

40. John Howard Association, *Court monitoring report,* 2001, 26.

41. Cook County Judiciary Advisory Council, *Analysis of Cook County jail crowding and costs caused by new state parole enforcement procedures* (Chicago, 2001).

42. "Plaintiffs' Response to Defendant's Status Report and to John Howard Association Monitoring Report," in *the United States District Court for the Northern District of Illinois Eastern Division, Dan Duran et al., Plaintiffs v. Michael F. Sheahan, Sheriff of Cook County et al., Defendants. 74 C 2949, Judge George M. Marovich,* (2001): 2.

43. "Plaintiffs' Response," 2001, 3.

44. Cook County Board, Committee, 2001.

45. "Defendants' Status Report," 2001, 4 (see chap. 2, n.143).

46. Resolution Cook County Board of Commissioners, *Resolution Sponsored by the Honorable John H. Stroger, Jr. President of the Cook County Board of Commissioners,* April 9, 2002 meeting, (Chicago, 2002): 2.

47. Cook County Board, Committee on Law Enforcement and Corrections, 2003.

48. "Defendants' Supplemental Status Report," 1993, 11–12.

49. "Plaintiffs' Response," 2000, 8 (see chap. 2, n. 51).

50. "Defendants' Status Report," 2000, 5 (see chap. 2, n. 144).

51. John Howard Association, *Court monitoring report,* 1998, 87.

52. John Howard Association, *Court monitoring report,* 1999, 65.

FOUR

Expanding the Jail into the Community

Growth, Development and Mutual Interest

> Reform of our jails requires either that we drastically reduce the size of the rabble class, a highly remote possibility, or that we abandon our self-serving fictions about crime and deviance. I believe that instead of arguing over which particular reform proposal might work, we should concentrate our efforts on the second task, that is, on developing and disseminating a more honest perspective on the nature and causes of crime and deviance and on the limits and consequences of various control policies.[1] —John Irwin, *The Jail*, 1985

As the consent decree dispute continued to focus on aggregate population numbers, building expansion and the day-to-day conditions that existed within the walls of CCDOC, disputants began addressing the increasing interior population of CCDOC through the expansion of programming outside of the jail confines. Between 1993 and 2003, disputants within the consent decree began not only to address how many defendants were in the differing CCDOC divisions, but also how long they had been there and how they should be removed from CCDOC and placed within the community while awaiting court processing. The emergence and dominance of pretrial release mechanisms within Cook County were directly shaped by the consent decree dispute between 1993 and 2003. In addition, development and changes within release mechanisms increased the number of pretrial defendants under the control and surveillance of the Cook County Sheriff's Office.

LENGTH OF STAY WITHIN THE JAIL

In addition to the increasing number of inmates who were arriving at the CCDOC campus between 1993 and 2003, another focal point of the consent decree was the amount of time that individual inmates were spending within the confines of the jail complex. The length of stay (LOS) of inmates was an issue frame that fueled discussion of release mechanisms throughout the consent decree dispute. In 1996, CCDOC provided data to the federal court reflecting that 33 percent of the inmates entering the correctional facility were released within seventy-two hours.[2] Furthermore, upon review by the Cook County state's attorney and the John Howard Association, the remaining 67 percent of the inmates were not individuals with low bond amounts who merely lacked the small amount required to post bond. Individuals with low bond amounts incarcerated for petty crimes were generally released through a variety of pretrial release programs. Individuals who were not released from CCDOC were either individuals facing serious charges or, commonly, individuals with a current lower level charge who possessed an outstanding arrest warrant or a previous serious charge that precluded pretrial release mechanisms and low bond structures. In other words, individuals relegated to CCDOC were generally being held on serious charges or were in a high monetary bond or no monetary bond status. In essence, and stipulated by all of the disputants, LOS was less influenced by inmates unable to meet low bond requirements and more often related to slow court processing.[3]

When examining the LOS data within the Cook County Department of Corrections it is important to keep in mind the magnitude of daily admission and release of individuals from the confines of the jail. Between 1993 and 2003, 1,032,590 citizens were booked into CCDOC custody. On average there were 257 individuals per day entering the facility over an eleven-year period.

When combining these data with the aforementioned 1996 LOS status report figures presented by the Cook County State's Attorney's Office we can ascertain the dimensions of the populations that are being referred to as simple percentages within the dispute. For example, as stated in the previous paragraph, in 1996 33 percent of the inmates were released within seventy-two hours while 67 percent of the inmates were incarcerated longer than seventy-two hours. In other words, 28,418 citizens spent up to three days within the jail while 57,697 spent more than three days within the jail. It is also important to note that these two groups are not necessarily mutually exclusive in that multiple stays at the jail within the one-year time period for single individuals is not uncommon.

While acknowledging the greatest source of increasing LOS at CCDOC, disputants avoided a direct confrontation with the local court system that had been acknowledged by all disputants as an indirect cause of the overcrowding problem. As the John Howard Association acknowl-

Table 4.1.   Cook County Department of Corrections Annual Admissions/ Bookings between 1993 and 2003

	Year	Month	Day
1993	79,174	6957.8	216.9
1994	83,564	6963.7	229.2
1995	87,420	7285.0	239.5
1996	86,115	7176.3	235.9
1997	96,130	8010.8	263.4
1998	100,780	8398.3	275.4
1999	99,609	8300.8	272.9
2000	99,438	8286.5	271.7
2001	100,115	8342.9	274.3
2002	103,200	8600.0	282.7
2003	97,045	8087.1	265.9

(John Howard Association, 2010:13)

edged in 1996, there had been a study by the National Center for State Courts which articulated the need for court expansion, and the local judiciary had been lobbying the County Board for expansion, but no plans had been forwarded to address the need.[4] Disputants within the consent decree believed that local court expansion was beyond the locus of control of the consent decree. As federal Judge George Marovich stated:

> I understand that, and I really don't want to be quoted as sticking my nose into something that isn't part of my assigned chore, namely, the monitoring of the conditions of the jail. That's what the consent decree is, not to reorganize the court system. And I don't want anything that I say to be construed as me having an opinion or advice along those lines. But I offer no guidance, no advice. It is an observation. The faster they go through the court system, the less pressure there is on the housing problem; right?[5]

The emerging frame of LOS and its relation to overcrowding was relegated to observation only in regard to the consent decree disputants engaging action within the Cook County court system. This was in opposition to the action orientation that was being applied to local executive branch decision making within the CCDOC. Basically, if LOS was going to be addressed within the consent decree dispute it was going to be addressed through expansion and reorganization of CCDOC's prerelease mechanisms not through changes in the court processing system.

The emerging issue of LOS and its relation to court processing revealed itself again in 2002 when the John Howard Association highlighted further increases in the LOS for inmates at CCDOC. Using 2001 data, the John Howard Association revealed that the average LOS for all inmates within CCDOC had risen to 187 days, or slightly more than six months. In addition, it was revealed that defendants held within the maximum-security divisions LOS was almost ten months. Approximately 33 percent of the CCDOC population is housed within maximum-security divisions.[6] By 2003, over 1,900 inmates had been held at CCDOC for more than a year; over 700 had been held more than two years; and over 100 had been held beyond four years.[7] As Cook County Commissioner Peter Silvestri questioned and commented in 2003, "This is a disgrace on the system. How do we get the system changed without trampling or violating the constitutional rights of these individuals to receive a fair trial?"[8] When examining increasing LOS data it is important to recognize that the average of 187 days stipulated by the John Howard Association in its 2002 report does not represent all admissions to CCDOC but instead accurately represents the LOS for inmates who were not released within one to two weeks of admission.[9] This central tendency measure is also shaped by the approximately 33 percent of inmates housed in the maximum-security divisions whose average length of stay was 297 days or just under ten months. The relevance of this particular length of stay frame is that it draws the dispute toward an acknowledgment of slow felony court processing within the Cook County Circuit Court and the loosely coupled relationship between overcrowding, conditions of confinement and judicial management.

UNSUPERVISED PRETRIAL RELEASE THROUGH CCDOC

By 2003, the Cook County Board was beginning to seriously discuss court processing and its relation to LOS within the CCDOC. Yet, prior to the wider acknowledgment of the connection between court processing and LOS, the consent decree disputants addressed LOS and overcrowding in general through executive branch programming by CCDOC officials. During the earliest years of the consent decree the main form of pre-release enacted by CCDOC officials was the Administrative Mandatory Furlough Program (AMF). AMF was a recognizance bond program offered by the CCDOC to selected inmates who were not given recognizance bonds by the judiciary or individuals who could not afford to pay their monetary bond amount set by the judiciary. AMFs, also known in Cook County as jail I-bonds, were issued predominantly to inmates charged with nonviolent low-level offenses. These individuals would sign their way out of CCDOC with the promise they would return for their court hearing. In 1989, over 35,000 AMFs were issued by CCDOC administrators. In 1992, the Illinois Criminal Justice Information Authority (ICJIA) published an evaluation of Cook County pretrial release mechanisms that focused on the AMF program. The study revealed that the AMF program resulted in high rates of failure to appear, delays in case processing, higher instances of arrest for new crimes and frequent reincarceration.[10] In addition, local level judiciary was voicing displeasure with the AMF program as an executive branch usurpation of judicial authority. Some local judges were actually raising bail amounts, marking arrest reports with "no I-bond" and threatening to hold CCDOC officials in contempt for violating a court order.[11] In spite of the AMF program, jail overcrowding continued to intensify during the late 1980s and early 1990s.

As overcrowding as well as the overcrowding dispute continued to worsen, federal Judge Milton Shadur directed the John Howard Association to compile a comprehensive report on jail overcrowding and conditions with short-term and long-term recommendations. The John Howard Association report to Judge Shadur recommended eleven major changes including an expanded range of mechanisms for supervised release.[12] In addition and concurrently, the jail population was also being investigated by the Bureau of Justice Assistance through the Adjudication Technical Assistance Project (ATAP). ATAP analyzed felony court processing within Cook County and its relation to jail overcrowding.[13] The recommendations of the John Howard Association report, the ATAP analysis, the Cook County Long-Range Master Plan, the ICJIA pretrial release study, and the ever-present high occupancy rates at CCDOC provided strong support for expansion of supervised release programs in Cook County.

SUPERVISED PRETRIAL RELEASE THROUGH CCDOC

In 1993, Sheriff Michael F. Sheahan (1990–2007) created the Cook County Department of Community Supervision and Intervention (CCDCSI). CCDCSI was developed as a separately budgeted, managed, and staffed entity within the Cook County Sheriff's Office. This branch of the Sheriff's Office operated an electronic monitoring program (CCEMU) initially instituted within CCDOC, a day reporting program (CCDRC) and a residential drug treatment program known as the Pre-Release Center (PRC). These programs served as supervised release avenues for felony pretrial male defendants who could not make bail, or did not qualify for the unsupervised release process of AMF. These three supervised release programs within the newly developed CCDCSI served as a prerelease mechanism for male inmates at CCDOC who would otherwise continue to be housed within CCDOC awaiting trial. By 2003, the average daily population of these voluntary programs was over 2,200 individuals with over 95 percent of the participants being in a pretrial status.

With the inception of CCDCSI, by the end of 1993, the electronic monitoring unit (EMU) had increased its active caseload by 41 percent from its original caseload in 1989 when it was managed within CCDOC. While the EMU supervised over 1,100 individuals at the end of 1993, the newly formed day reporting center (DRC) population had reached 162 participants by the end of 1993. The Pre-Release Center (PRC) had reached an average daily population of 133 inmates by the end of 1993. These 1,395 inmates who would have been housed within the CCDOC divisions were now being supervised within an intermediate sanction framework that afforded a sliding scale of restrictive surveillance outside of the CCDOC walls.

Within the EMU, CCDOC inmates were screened for eligibility based upon their current charge, bond amount and criminal history.[14] Eligible individuals who volunteered for the program were issued an electronic surveillance bracelet and restrictions as to their physical movement. The majority of EMU participants were restricted to their homes, and some EMU participants were also allowed to travel outside of their home for education and employment.[15]

DRC participants, of whom the majorities were low-level drug offenders, were assigned to differing "tracks" based upon the type of drug possession charge, their criminal history, and their education or work status. For example, individuals charged with heroin possession, cocaine possession, and marijuana possession were assigned to differing tracks. Within those tracks, individuals who were deemed to have more serious addiction problems were further grouped based on level of seriousness. DRC participants who were employed or in school were assigned to less restrictive tracks than those participants who were unemployed or not in school. In essence, individuals were assigned to an array of supervision whereby they were required to report to the DRC Monday through Friday for a period ranging between three and twelve hours. During this time frame they were drug tested and required to participate in drug counseling classes, life skill courses and educational programming.[16]

The PRC program was an on-site incarceration program for drug addicted inmates. Individuals volunteering and assigned to the PRC lived in a dormitory style setting and participated in an immersed twelve-step program environment twenty-four hours a day, seven days a week. The programming consisted of individual and group counseling, self-help programming, Alcoholics Anonymous and Narcotics Anonymous meetings.[17] In addition, PRC inmates worked in a community garden providing fresh produce to local homeless shelters.[18]

It was not uncommon for individuals who were successful in the more restrictive PRC program to be afforded the opportunity to enter the DRC program. Furthermore, an individual who was failing to meet expectations within the DRC could be reassigned to the more restrictive PRC. Overall, individuals participating in all of the CCDCSI programs were threatened with return to CCDOC should they fail to meet the program requirements of EMU, DRC or the PRC. Length of stay within these programs was contingent upon the culmination of each inmate's court case. After a pretrial felony defendant was processed through the Cook County court system, they were released from CCDCSI programming.

The development and expansion of CCDCSI programs between 1993 and 2003 were predominantly driven through the consent decree dispute process. Beginning in 1993 and coinciding with the opening of CCDCSI, Cook County officials began a consistent campaign of framing CCDCSI as the panacea to the overcrowding problem at CCDOC. Promises of ending overcrowded conditions within CCDOC were abundant.

> The overcrowding in Division I is expected to decline steadily with the implementation of services provided by the Department of Community Supervision and Intervention.[19]

> Once the building is ready for occupancy, it is projected that inmates will be diverted into the day reporting program at a rate of fifty to seventy-five per month until the program reaches capacity. The facility will be designed to accommodate up to 800 pretrial detainees on a daily basis.[20]

By 1994, the John Howard Association was arguing for further expansion of the electronic monitoring program within CCDCSI. "In so far as EMP growth is dependent on the amount of equipment available for use, CCDCSI administrators and Cook County officials should consider providing additional funding for the purchase of equipment to expand this successful program."[21] In addition to expanding the electronic monitoring program through the purchase of more surveillance bracelets, the court monitor and plaintiffs alike argued for loosening the selection criteria for entrance into the pretrial release programs.[22] The John Howard Association remarked in 1995, "The limited growth of CCDCSI release programs is distressing, especially because of the expansion of services offered by these programs to those inmates fortunate enough to qualify."[23] The court monitor stated unequivocally that all release mechanisms must expand their capacities substantially to reduce jail overcrowding.[24]

Cook County officials were in agreement with the John Howard Association concerning the expansion of CCDCSI facilities and services. In 1995, the defendants produced a two-phase construction plan to expand the capabilities of the county supervised pretrial release mechanism. This projected 19.7 million dollar project, known as the South Campus redevelopment plan, was promised to expand the capacity and capabilities of CCDCSI.[25] Between 1996 and 1998 the call for expansion of CCDCSI was a dominant frame throughout much of the dialogue presented by each of the disputants within the decree. As the proposed South Campus

re-development funding was postponed with construction anticipated in
1999, the John Howard Association and the plaintiffs' attorneys argued
that Cook County officials were "penny wise and pound foolish," and the
development of architectural plans would require only a "modest expenditure."[26] Between 1996 and 1998, Cook County officials argued that expansion of services was indeed taking place specifically within the
CCDRC and the PRC. A review of average daily population within
CCDCSI revealed that indeed the average CCDRC population in 1993
expanded from 162 inmates to 434 inmates and the PRC population expanded from 150 inmates to 296 inmates. Yet, the EMU population in
1993 experienced a reduction from an average daily population of 1,166
inmates to 1,014 inmates. Overall, CCDCSI expanded its average daily
population by 266 inmates over a five-year period.[27] Yet, as the Day
Reporting Center and the Pre-Release Center were expanding daily populations they were tapping into the clientele that were also eligible to
receive electronic monitoring services through the EMU program.

Plaintiffs' attorneys argued that the slow pace of CCDCSI expansion
was a contributing source of the continued overcrowding problem at
CCDOC. Plaintiffs' attorneys further argued that this problem could be
resolved by speeding up building expansion plans, purchasing more
electronic monitoring bracelets, lowering the eligibility requirements for
EMU participation, and developing partnerships with nonprofit groups
that could supply off-site shelter to homeless inmates not eligible for
EMU.[28] County officials began reframing the call for expansion of
CCDCSI by focusing on the prerelease mechanisms as successful programs that would be jeopardized by unfettered expansion. Touting visits
by then director of the White House Office of National Drug Policy, General Barry McCaffrey (Ret.), as well as officials from Milwaukee County,
Wisconsin, county officials posited that CCDCSI was a model program
throughout the country.[29] Furthermore, CCDCSI officials provided data
indicating that since the inception of EMU in 1989, nearly 72,000 detainees had been released through the program.[30]

In addition, county officials argued that the success rates of EMU and
DRC, which were measured by reincarceration to CCDOC for violation
of program rules including any subsequent arrest while released, would
be endangered by expansion.[31] The reincarceration rate for program reg-
ulation for DRC participants in 1999 was 14.6 percent of all participants
discharged.[32] In 1999, the supervision success rate for EMU was 75 percent, which CCDCSI officials attributed to more effective and efficient
screening of candidates.[33] Finally, county officials argued that CCDCSI
staff was constantly screening and rescreening inmates within CCDOC as
candidates for any possible openings in their programs. The John Howard Association stated that the PRC had been at constant capacity for
the past five years and that expansion of the PRC and DRC was limited

by space requirements.[34] County officials argued that expansion of EMU must be balanced with security and issues of public safety.[35]

By 1998, the Cook County Board of Commissioners had begun approving budgets and construction plans for the expansion of CCDCSI through the South Campus re-development project. In addition to the space build-out, which county officials were now referring to as a "fast-track" project based on its importance, the county also entered into a new contract for electronic monitoring equipment.[36] The expansion of EMU included more electronic monitoring bracelets, as well as enhanced technology for tracking and archiving EMU participant movements. As Cook County officials stated, "This next generation equipment offers several distinct advantages over the current system, including an increased level of safety and security."[37] As the South Campus re-development plan proceeded and the electronic monitoring equipment and surveillance technology were upgraded, the expansion of EMU and DRC proceeded as originally suggested by the plaintiffs' attorneys and the John Howard Association. During the calendar year 2000, a total of 13,833 CCDOC inmates were placed on electronic monitoring. The average length of participation in EMP was approximately forty-five days, and more than 3,200 electronic monitoring participants who remained compliant with the conditions of supervision were transferred into the DRC program during 2000.[38] In 1993, the average daily population of inmates within EMU, DRC, and the PRC was 1,478 individuals. In 2002, the average daily population of inmates within EMU, DRC, and the PRC was 2,105 individuals, a daily average increase of 627 participants compared to the 1993 population.[39]

Based upon 2002 budget expenditures for CCDOC and CCDCSI divided by their respective daily average populations the savings per defendant were approximately 20 percent less for a defendant being supervised through CCDCSI. The average daily cost for a defendant being incarcerated within CCDOC during 2002 was $43.03 per day. The average cost for a defendant being placed within CCDCSI programming was $34.50 per day.[40] As federal Judge George Marovich stated as early as 1996,

> It is giving you a bigger bang for the buck to have people on electronic monitoring than to have them incarcerated, or to have them on day release rather than being incarcerated, assuming that they are suitable people who do not pose a flight risk and threat to the populace that also concerns us. Right?[41]

The total financial appropriation for CCDCSI during the 2003 fiscal year was 30.7 million dollars. The total appropriation for CCDOC during the same time period was 186.5 million dollars.[42] Together these two entities supervised over 12,000 defendants.

Pretrial Release through the Circuit Court of Cook County

Coinciding with the development, growth and expansion of CCDCSI, and following suggestions posited within the Adjudication Technical Assistance Project (1989), the Cook County judiciary integrated and expanded its Pretrial Services Division (PSD) with the Cook County Adult Probation Department.[43] PSD provided assistance to the Circuit Court of Cook County with the process of setting and enforcing appropriate conditions of bond in criminal cases. PSD provided the court with individualized evaluations of defendants that included the collection and verification of information concerning social and criminal history, potential risk to public safety, and probability of an individual absconding if released from CCDOC. In addition to bond recommendation, the PSD provided general supervision, as well as curfew supervision for those individuals released on monetary bonds and judicial recognizance bonds. While the development and expansion of PSD was outside the authority of the consent decree dispute, the program increased participation and expanded court supervision and services to those individuals released under judicial control. As the defendants and the John Howard Association pointed out, the increase in judicial I-bonds and increased control of release decision making by the judiciary created less of a need for the AMF release program instituted by CCDOC.[44]

The Decline of Unsupervised Pretrial Release in Cook County

As the newly established risk assessment model was applied through PSD, more defendants being released from custody found themselves under the surveillance and control of the Circuit Court of Cook County while waiting court processing. In February of 1994 alone there were 11,771 criminal defendants being supervised through PSD. In addition, CCDCSI was consistently culling the CCDOC divisions for inmates eligible for EMU, DRC and PRC. The result of this two-pronged approach was an increase in the surveillance and control of defendants who were released while awaiting court processing and the decrease of the sheriff's AMF release mechanism. In 1989, there were 35,327 inmates released through the AMF program or an average of over ninety-six individuals each day. By 1995, AMF releases had declined to 10,045 or just over twenty-seven each day. In 1999, the total plummeted to 1,487 AMF releases, almost a 96 percent reduction from the 1989 total. At the same time the recorded CCDOC overflow population within CCDOC went from just over 1,500 in 1993 to a low of just over 300 inmates in 1999.[45] Yet as the year 2000 approached and CCDOC bookings increased, the PSD program through the Circuit Court and CCDCSI programs had reached supervision capacity. In response to population growth, CCDOC administrators again resorted to an increase in the use of the AMF program as a response to the overflow population. In 2000 as well as in 2001, over 6,000 inmates were released on AMF. Cook County sheriff's officials applied a five-day waiting period and strict classification guidelines to those inmates released on AMF. John Howard Association representatives argued that it would be preferable to seek further expansion of EMU rather than increase the number of inmates on AMF.[46]

Supervised Pretrial Release for Female Detainees

In addition to the expansion and increased surveillance of pretrial release mechanisms for male detainees at CCDOC, Cook County officials also developed pretrial release mechanisms for female detainees. While the number of female pretrial detainees in CCDOC's population was much less than male pretrial detainees, female detainees were increasing in number at a greater rate than their male counterparts between 1993 and 2003. Within CCDOC, County officials addressed the increasing female population by modifying existing divisions and developing a new female division. These changes increased the number of beds available for female inmates. Concurrently, the Cook County Department of Women's Justice Services (CCDWJS) began operation in 1993 in an effort to address the growing population of female pretrial detainees unable to make bail. In 2003, the average daily population of CCDWJS programs was just over one hundred individuals. CCDWJS consisted of the Cook County Detention Alternative for Women, which combined the properties of electronic monitoring and day reporting, as well as the Maternity Objectives Management (MOMs) program, which provided residential treatment, life skill counseling and physical health treatment for pregnant and recent mothers with drug addiction problems.

In 1993, the CCDAW active caseload was twenty-eight defendants; by 1995 the active caseload had more than doubled to fifty-nine female defendants. The growth of CCDAW was spurred by the support of the John Howard Association, which argued in 1994 that the lack of comparable female prerelease alternatives was "another example of the unequal treatment afforded women incarcerated in Cook County."[47] In 1995, the John Howard Association argued for an immediate and substantial expansion of release programs based on the increasing number of female detainees within CCDOC.[48] According to the John Howard Association further expansion of CCDAW was limited by a lack of electronic monitoring equipment.[49] In 1998, CCDAW nearly doubled its correctional officer staff and began increasing its caseload with electronic monitoring equipment on loan from CCDCSI. In addition, CCDAW expanded space for drug treatment for female detainees awaiting placement in community-based treatment programs. At the end of 1998, the MOMs program opened, diverting pregnant females from pretrial detention to a therapeutic environment. The MOMs program was designed to foster proper prenatal, postpartum and infant care in a culturally sensitive manner. Supportive medical services including OB/GYN and pediatric care were provided to a daily average of sixteen pretrial defendants between 1993 and 2003.[50] The John Howard Association stated that although the MOMs program was small, it was a critical component of the matrix of release programs available to CCDOC inmates and a particularly important component of gender-specific programming.[51] According to the DWJS between 2001 and 2003 approximately 35 percent to 40 percent of female pretrial detainees who were eligible for CCDAW programs were being served by these prerelease mechanisms.[52] The 2003 appropriated budget for CCDWJS was $4.2 million.

DIVERTING POSTTRIAL CONVICTED OFFENDERS

While CCDCSI and CCDWJS were serving both male and female pretrial defendants who would have been incarcerated in CCDOC or released on the unsupervised AMF program, two other programs were initiated between 1993 and 2003 that served to free bed space for pretrial inmates sleeping on floors. In addition to the EMU, DRC, and PRC, CCDCSI also operated the Sheriff's Work Alternative Program (SWAP). SWAP served misdemeanant and low-level felony offenders who had been convicted and sentenced by the judiciary. Individuals sentenced to this program provided municipal work crews throughout Cook County under the supervision of Cook County sheriff's deputies. In 2003, the average daily population of this post-conviction program was approximately 3,000 individuals.[53] According to Cook County officials it was estimated that approximately 50 percent of SWAP participants otherwise could have been ordered to serve jail sentences, adding to the overall population of CCDOC.[54] Finally, the Cook County Boot Camp (CCBC), funded by a state of Illinois grant, began operation in 1997. The Boot Camp provided an eighteen-week residential program with up to one year of after-care services that included, electronic monitoring, day reporting, education and addiction programming for convicted misdemeanant and low-level felony offenders. In 2003, the average daily population of the CCBC was 220 residential inmates.[55] Because of their legal status as convicted offenders, individuals sentenced to SWAP and CCBC were not members of the Duran class of pretrial detainees. Yet, insofar as these inmates were residing at CCDOC prior to their entry into these two programs, they were part of the overcrowded inmate population at CCDOC. The John Howard Association attributed these two programs in addition to the other CCDCSI and CCDAW pretrial release programs as imperative to managing overflow populations at CCDOC.[56]

As length of stay for defendants confined within CCDOC became an emerging frame, the disputants within the consent decree began to search for alternative approaches to supervision and surveillance of pretrial detainees. Consensus between all disputants focused upon pretrial release programs that removed defendants from incarceration within CCDOC. Adopting an intermediate sanction framework, Cook County officials developed CCDCSI and CCDWJS programming as supervised alternatives to the AMF release program that dominated the early years of the consent decree dispute between 1993 and 2003. The shift from the unsupervised release program of AMF to the supervised release programming of CCDCSI and CCDWJS developed release policies focusing on risk aversion for county officials and increased surveillance for pretrial defendants released into the community. Through PSD and external to the consent decree dispute, reorganization and increased risk assessment within bail decision-making processes at the judicial level served to realign the onus of responsibility for pretrial release with the judicial branch of government within Cook County. Persuaded by the federal court, the John Howard Association and the plaintiffs' attorneys, Cook County officials expanded and developed their pretrial release mechanisms into two new separate departments under the control of the Sheriff's Office. These departments with a combined budget of approximately 35 million dollars supervised over 2,200 pretrial detainees outside the CCDOC confines during 2003.

While the emergence of the LOS frame created the impetus for expansion beyond the walls of CCDOC, the newly developed CCDCSI became a dominant frame within the consent decree dispute between 1993 and 2003. As CCDCSI became more robust in action and words among all of the disputants within the consent decree, the issue frame of AMF moved toward a residual frame.

As the number of AMF releases began to rise again in 2000 and 2001, with an increasing CCDOC population, other emerging frames were posited by disputants. Plaintiffs' attorneys suggested the development of partnership-based community-release shelters for homeless and mentally ill defendants.[57] These partnerships would link the Cook County sheriff with private service agencies such as the Salvation Army and the Safer Foundation. In essence, pretrial defendants would be placed in supervised social/health service settings through the authority of the sheriff of Cook County. Cook County commissioners touted public health initiatives such as the Thresholds Cook County Jail Project, which provided community-based rehabilitation for homeless and mentally ill individuals who seemed to be constantly involved in the revolving door of homelessness and jail incarceration.[58] This particular initiative had been serving approximately one hundred post-release individuals each year. The emergence of a frame rooted in public health and rehabilitation requiring public/private partnerships was countered in 2002 by the emergence of a much more punitive-based frame.

In 2002, with the CCDOC population increasing, the Cook County Sheriff's Office posited the development of a tent city for CCDOC inmates.[59] Based upon increased LOS, drug arrests, and state of Illinois parole holds, the average daily population at CCDOC in April 2002 was above 11,000 inmates for the first time in its history. In response to the increased population at CCDOC, Sheriff Sheahan toured the tent city at the Maricopa County Jail in Phoenix, Arizona. As Sheriff Sheahan stated, "Housing inmates in tents would be a dramatic step, but we are running out of options here at Cook County Jail."[60]

The emergence of the tent city frame failed to gain any traction within the consent decree dispute. In addition, the frames positing community-based public/private health partnership initiatives also failed to reach dominance between 1993 and 2003. The polemic frames of expanding community-based public health programs for pretrial defendants, as well as punitive-based tent city incarceration for pretrial defendants were stifled in favor of a continued focus on the supervised release programs of CCDCSI and CCDWJS. The emergence and dominance of these supervised release programs provided a mean between extremes for all of the disputants involved within the consent decree. On a daily basis in 1993, close to 9,000 individuals were under the control and surveillance of the Cook County Sheriff's Office through the CCDOC. By 2003, with the expansion of prerelease and postconviction mechanisms, on a daily basis over 13,400 individuals were under the control and surveillance of the Cook County Sheriff's Office.[61] This expansion constitutes more than a 32 percent increase in the number of individuals under the control of the Cook County Sheriff's Office over a ten-year period.

NOTES

1. Irwin, *The Jail,* 115 (see intro., n.1).

2. "Status Report of Proceedings before the Honorable George M. Marovich," *In the United States District Court for the Northern District of Illinois Eastern Division, Dan Duran et al., Plaintiffs v. Michael F. Sheahan, Sheriff of Cook County et al., Defendants. 74 C 2949, Judge George M. Marovich,* (1996): 14.

3. Ibid., 8–10.

4. Ibid., 8.

5. Ibid., 9.

6. John Howard Association, *Court monitoring report,* 2002, 5 (see chap. 2, n. 33).

7. John Howard Association, *Court monitoring report,* 2004, 11–16 (see intro. n. 5).

8. *Cook County Board Report,* 2003, 4, (see chap. 3, n. 50).

9. John Howard Association, *Court Monitoring Report for Duran v. Brown et al. 74 C 2949 Crowding and Conditions of Confinement at the Cook County Department of Corrections and Compliance with the Consent Decree* Chicago IL, 2010.

10. Christine Martin, *Cook County pretrial release study.* (Chicago, IL: Illinois Criminal Justice Information Authority, 1992).

11. Fasano and MacKinnon, "Impact of Litigation," 10 (see intro. n. 2); P. M. Manikas, *Criminal Justice Policymaking: Boundaries and Borderlands, Final Report of the Criminal*

Justice Project, (Evanston, IL: Northwestern University, Center for Urban Affairs and Policy Research, 1990).

12. John Howard Association, *Court Monitoring Report for Duran v. Sheahan et al. 74 C 2949 Crowding and Conditions of Confinement at the Cook County Department of Corrections and Compliance with the Consent Decree,* (Chicago, IL: 1989).

13. Charles Edelstein et al., *An Assessment of the Felony Case Process in Cook County, Illinois and Its Impact on Jail Crowding,* (Washington, DC: The American University, School of Public Affairs, 1989).

14. John Howard Association, *Court monitoring report,* 1998, 32 (see intro., n. 18).

15. John Howard Association, *Court monitoring report,* 1995, 39 (see chap. 2, n. 36).

16. John Howard Association, *Court monitoring report,* 1994, 36 (see chap. 2, n. 34); John Howard Association, *Court monitoring report,* 1995, 48; John Howard Association, *Court monitoring report,* 1996, 40 (see chap. 2, n. 28).

17. John Howard Association, *Court monitoring report,* 1994, 42.

18. John Howard Association, *Review of the inmate grievance procedure,* 1997, 50–51 (see chap. 2, n. 134).

19. "Defendants' Supplemental Status Report," in *the United States District Court for the Northern District of Illinois Eastern Division, Dan Duran et al., Plaintiffs v. Michael F. Sheahan, Sheriff of Cook County et al., Defendants. 74 C 2949, Judge George M. Marovich,* (1993): 3.

20. Ibid., 2.

21. John Howard Association, *Court monitoring report,* 1994, 35.

22. John Howard Association, *Court monitoring report,* 1995, 34; John Howard Association, *Court monitoring report,* 1996, 28; "Plaintiffs' Response," 1997, 29 (see chap. 2, n. 93).

23. John Howard Association, *Court monitoring report,* 1995, 57.

24. Ibid.

25. "Defendants' Status Report," 1995, 13–14 (see chap. 2, n. 63).

26. "Plaintiffs' Response," 1997, 6.

27. John Howard Association, *Court monitoring report,* 2002, 37, 45 (see chap. 2, n. 33).

28. "Plaintiffs' Response," 1997, 9.

29. "Defendants' Status Report," 1997, 32 (see chap. 2, n. 117).

30. "Defendants' Status Report," 1998, 18 (see chap. 2, n. 47).

31. "Defendants' Status Report,"1999, 11–14 (see chap. 2, n. 96).

32. Ibid., 14.

33. Ibid., 11.

34. John Howard Association, *Court monitoring report,* 1999, 52 (see chap. 2, n. 32).

35. "Defendants' Status Report," 1998, 20.

36. Ibid., 21.

37. Ibid., 20.

38. John Howard Association, *Court monitoring report,* 2000, 37–47 (see chap. 2, n. 33).

39. Ibid.

40. Cook County Sheriff's Office, "Cook County Sheriff's Office 2004 Annual Budget," (Chicago, 2004).

41. "Defendants' Status Report," 1996, 8 (see chap. 2, n. 64).

42. Cook County Sheriff's Office, 2004 Annual Budget.

43. John Howard Association, *Court monitoring report,* 1997, 24.

44. "Defendants' Status Report," 1994, 11 (see chap. 2, n. 41); "Defendants' Status Report," 1995, 25.

45. John Howard Association, *Court monitoring report,* 2002, 10, 16.

46. John Howard Association, *Court monitoring report,* 2000, 28.

47. John Howard Association, *Court monitoring report,* 1994, 42.

48. John Howard Association, *Court monitoring report,* 1995, 38.

49. John Howard Association, *Court monitoring report,* 1996, 33.

50. "Defendants' Status Report 1999, 17; "Defendants' Status Report," in *the United States District Court for the Northern District of Illinois Eastern Division, Dan Duran et al., Plaintiffs v. Michael F. Sheahan, Sheriff of Cook County et al., Defendants. 74 C 2949, Judge George M. Marovich,* (2003): 8.

51. John Howard Association, *Court monitoring report,* 2002, 34.

52. Cook County Sheriff's Office, 2004 Annual Budget.

53. John Howard Association, *Court monitoring report,* 2004, 19.

54. "Defendants' Status Report," 1997, 25.

55. John Howard Association, *Court monitoring report,* 2004, 40.

56. John Howard Association, *Court monitoring report,* 1999, 62.

57. "Plaintiffs' Response," 2001, 5–6 (see chap. 3, n.42).

58. Resolution Cook County Board of Commissioners, 2002, 2 (see chap. 3, n. 46).

59. A tent city is a population management approach whereby inmates who do not have bed space or cell space are removed from jail divisions and provided with a tent as their outdoor residence. This policy approach has been enacted at the Maricopa County Jail in Arizona.

60. Cook County Sheriff's Office, "Press Release: Overcrowding May Force Jail Inmates into 'Tent City,'" (Chicago, May 9, 2002).

61. Cook County Sheriff's Office, 2004 Annual Budget.

FIVE

Constructing the Jail within Local Media

Presenting Expansion to the Public

As the book page yields the inside story of the author's mental adventures, so the press page yields the inside story of the community in action and interaction. It is for this reason that the press seems to be performing its function most when revealing the seamy side. Real news is bad news—bad news *about* somebody, or bad news *for* somebody.[1] [2]
—Marshall McLuhan, *Understanding Media*, 1964

In addition to the primary source documents used to analyze the emergent, dominant and residual frames of the consent decree dispute between 1993 and 2003, the media portrayal of CCDOC was also analyzed within the *Chicago Tribune* and the *Chicago Sun-Times*. Using interpretive packages, claims-makers within the consent decree dispute presented specific frames of CCDOC through the media fostering specific interpretations of jail incarceration within Cook County. Each of the newspaper articles was coded for prominence of particular issue frames that were developed based on sociological constructs of punishment. In addition, new frames posited were also identified within the media text population.

Two levels of analysis ensued after data collection. First, the media articles served as the unit of analysis to measure the extent of the frames presented from the a priori developed sociological constructs of punishment and the posterior frames which emerged after coding news articles. After which, the frames were then disaggregated by year and each of the frames was analyzed further. Second, the attribution of frames was linked to the two differing groups of disputants within the decree and then specifically to claims-makers within those groups. The second level of analysis, whereby the claims-makers were the unit of analysis, offered the opportunity to examine how stakeholders within the consent decree dispute presented local incarceration to the public through the newspaper media.

The textual media article population generated through a search of the Lexis-Nexis and Newsbank database systems resulted in 308 articles between the years of 1993 and 2003. Figure 5.1 reveals the number of articles related to the research topic based on the search terms specified within the methodology. The largest amount of print media articles within the *Chicago Tribune* and *Chicago Sun-Times* were published in 1993 and 2003.

Local print media coverage of the Cook County Jail declined throughout the 1990s, reaching a low of ten articles in the year 2000. After which, a steady increase in media articles ensued with a high point of forty-six articles published in 2003.

Applying the signature matrix of jail overcrowding issue packages (refer to appendix) each of the 308 newsprint articles was coded for the dominant frames used to describe the Cook County Department of Corrections. In addition to the original four objective frames within the signature matrix, the coding scheme also revealed two new frames not in-

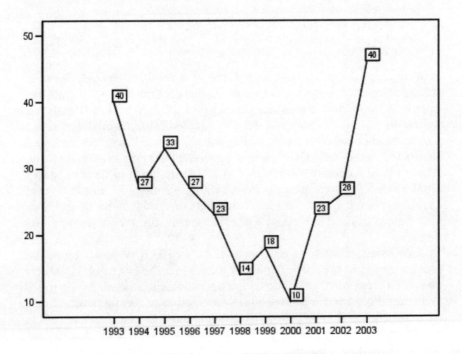

Figure 5.1.   Number of CCDOC News Articles, 1993–2003

cluded within the signature matrix of issue packages. Examples of the a priori frames of order and control, rights of the accused, root causes of arrest and incarceration, and community pursuit of justice, as well as the a posteriori frames of poor conditions and politics in Cook County are exhibited in table 5.1.

The phrasing used within these narratives served to bolster particular interpretations of the reality of the Cook County Department of Corrections for the media audience. Table 5.2 provides the percentage frequency of the differing frames as presented within the print media.

The a priori issue packages accounted for 76.9 percent of the frames exhibited within the print media, while the posteriori issue packages represented the remaining 23.1 percent of the frames presented to the media audience.

ORDER AND CONTROL

The largest percentage of frames presented was within the issue package of order and control with almost one-third of the media narratives focusing upon the dangerousness of the institution and the occupants who reside within the institution. As illustrated in table 5.3, the majority of these narratives were promulgated between 1993 and 1995, as well as in 2003. These four years accounted for over 64 percent of the narratives framed within the order and control issue package.

The media stories presented with a dominant frame of order and control were generally focused within three particular areas. Narratives focusing on dangerousness based on insufficient staffing, dangerousness for the individual employees and dangerousness for the individual inmate. For example, as reflected in a *Chicago Tribune* article:

> Cook County Jail continues to be plagued by staff shortages that create security and safety risks for both guards and inmates, a prison watchdog group said Monday, but the solution may hinge on the resolution of a labor dispute with the union representing the guards.[3]

This particular example fits squarely within dangerousness based on insufficient staffing with a solution rooted in increasing order and control through more staff or a better managed staff. This type of order and control frame is different from the narratives focusing explicitly on the environmental safety of correctional officers within the institution. For example:

> The men-accused murderers, rapists and drug dealers are behind thick steel bars reaching from floor to ceiling. The women guarding the "cage" are accustomed to the insults hurled at them by the inmates; they say it's an occupational hazard. "Some of them call us bitches or make sexually explicit remarks," said Hargraves, 38, a correctional offi-

Table 5.1.   The Frames Used to Describe CCDOC in the Newsprint Media

Frames	Samples of Phrases Classified
1. Order and Control	The staffing levels pose a potentially grave threat in maintaining a minimally safe institution. Something is going to explode out there and everybody is going to point fingers. It's better than handing them a slip of paper and hoping they show up for court.
2. Rights of the Accused	Most of the people there are cloaked with a presumption of innocence. Appalling mass strip-searching policy. Investigation into the allegation of Civil Rights Violations.
3. Community Pursuit of Justice	The Sheriff's Work Alternative Program (SWAP) which permits nonviolent offenders to pay for their crimes outside of Cook County Jail instead of behind its walls. Non-violent inmates awaiting trial are released but must make daily contact with jail officials. Three-hundred inmates will stay home with electronic monitoring.
4. Root Causes of Arrest and Incarceration	Drug-addicted prisoners meet with counselors who guide them through the first stages of recovery. Cook County jail has become the largest mental institution in Illinois.
5. Politics in Cook County	The Republican state's attorney is trying to stop the Democratic Sheriff's pet project of a boot camp. Cook County Sheriff Michael Sheahan faces a tough challenger in Republican rival Leroy Martin.
6. Poor Conditions	But the group was more critical of general maintenance problems ranging from clogged toilets to inmates sleeping on floors. Inmates still complain about stench from backed-up toilets, foreign objects in food and poor ventilation. After renovation it will be divided into six units with 50 beds each.

Table 5.2.   Representation of Frames in all Newspaper Articles between 1993 and 2003

Frame	Percentage
1. Order and Control	31.2
2. Rights of the Accused	18.8
3. Community Pursuit of Justice	15.9
4. Root Causes of Arrest and Incarceration	11.0
5. Politics in Cook County	14.0
6. Poor Conditions	9.1

cer who has worked at the jail for 15 years. "Some of them just need an attitude adjustment."[4]

In addition to order and control frames regarding insufficient staffing and the dangerousness associated with being a correctional officer, further order and control frames provide the media reader with a view of danger from the inmate perspective.

> Convicted robber Anton Mims was stabbed to death in a gang fight Saturday in Division Nine—a section for convicts returned from prison for pending court matter. On Sunday two pretrial inmates were stabbed with homemade knives and two others suffered head injuries in beatings with a 16-inch towel bar yanked from a cell in Division Ten, another maximum security wing.[5]

While narratives describing the dangerous environment for inmates tend to be based on violent victimization and offending, all of these narratives draw the reader toward a similar constructed conclusion of the Cook County Department of Corrections.

The order and control frames paint the CCDOC environment as disorganized, understaffed, violent and dangerous. The recourse to these frames from a news reader perspective is to increase safety through increased authority. For the reader, policies based on the hiring of more correctional officers, further control and expanded surveillance of inmates and staff logically follows. Considering that 31.2 percent of the frames promulgated within local media articles focus upon order and control, one would postulate that the general public absorbing these narratives would be more than likely to view CCDOC as an institution in need of addressing these concerns through expanded punitive frameworks, expanded surveillance and increased accountability.

Table 5.3.   Issue Frames Presented in Local Newspapers by Year and Type between 1993 and 2003

	Order and Control	Rights of Accused	Comm. Pursuit	Root Causes	Cook County Politics	Poor Condition	Total
1993	18	4	13	9	0	11	55
1994	14	3	2	7	2	0	28
1995	20	2	2	2	5	3	34
1996	4	2	8	4	7	2	27
1997	3	6	6	1	4	5	25
1998	4	4	2	1	3	0	14
1999	3	5	1	4	3	2	18
2000	3	1	1	1	4	0	10
2001	6	9	4	2	2	1	24
2002	8	0	8	2	7	2	27
2003	13	22	2	1	6	2	46
Total	96	58	49	34	43	25	308
Percent Total	31.2%	18.8%	15.9%	11.0%	14.0%	9.2%	100%

RIGHTS OF THE ACCUSED

The second largest frame consisting of 18.8 percent of the total population of stories presented by the media concerning the CCDOC between 1993 and 2003 was the issue frame of rights of the accused. The issue within this frame is how due process and civil rights are secured for pretrial inmates within the overt control of the institution. Between 1993 and 2002 there were on average three articles exhibiting this frame per year between both newspapers analyzed. Yet, as reflected in table 5.3 an increase in news articles exhibiting this issue occurred in 2003 with twenty-two narratives presenting the rights of the accused frame. Forty-eight of the fifty-eight total news stories within this category were focused on two particular incidents related to inmate civil rights. The first incident, and the subject of twenty narratives, was based on strip searches of female inmates conducted between 1994 and 1996. These narratives were published between 1996 and 2001, accounting for twenty of the twenty-seven narratives of this time period. The second incident was the alleged physical abuse of inmates by members of the Special Operations Response Team of the CCDOC. All of these articles were printed during 2003 and accounted for eighteen of the twenty-two narratives during that year.

Reflected within the news media presentation of both of these incidents were stories reflecting violations of civil rights, degradation, and violence on the part of Cook County correctional officers against inmates sequestered in the jail. A firsthand witness presentation of the strip search narrative was provided in a 2001 editorial published in the *Chicago Tribune*:

> Along with 15 to 40 other women at a time, she would be told to spread her legs, squat three times and cough, in order to free any hidden contraband. If someone didn't do it just so, everybody had to do it again. And again. She would be instructed to spread her buttocks. To lift her breasts. To lift her stomach, if she had flab. Menstruating women had to remove their sanitary napkins, often causing blood to drip to the floor. Townsend, last in jail in February on drug possession charges, remembers the guards joking and calling the women "whores" and "bitches."[6]

The physical abuse incident also provided the media reader with a narrative description of civil rights abuse and violence within CCDOC as described by a former correctional officer,

> Breaking what he said was a code of silence and testifying under oath as part of a lawsuit brought by the five inmates, former guard Roger Fairly, 37, said the shackled inmates were dragged and shoved into a windowless room where they were beaten after a disturbance in which several guards were injured. "I saw them hitting them with elbows, stomping on their faces and heads, kicking them in the face," Fairly testified. "I yelled at them to stop because what I saw was too violent. But they didn't."[7]

The underlying premise behind these frames is that executive branch line-level workers and their supervisors must be investigated and provided with oversight to ensure the civil rights of the accused. Subsequently both of these civil rights issues were subjected to local and federal investigations, as well as lawsuits.

COMMUNITY PURSUIT OF JUSTICE AND BALANCED NEEDS

The community pursuit of justice and balanced needs frame accounted for 15.9 percent of the overall frames presented within the local newspapers analyzed between 1993 and 2003. The majority of these narratives highlight the purported emancipative nature of newly developed and expanded Cook County sheriff programs that removed individuals from CCDOC and placed them under surveillance within a community setting. Included in these programs were an electronic monitoring program, a day reporting program, and a boot camp for male detainees as well as similar furlough programs for female detainees. The issue frames within these narratives are focused on the individual inmate's connections with their community and how those connections can be re-established and strengthened.

> The program began in October 1998 as a way to help mothers like Jones keep their children as they try to kick drug habits and to improve parenting skills, said Cook County Sheriff Michael F. Sheahan.[8]

> For just as many years, prison reform groups such as the John Howard Association kept beating the drum that there was a better way-one that not only would improve conditions at the jail, but also would reduce the likelihood that the same people would keep trooping into the lock-up, and would increase the likelihood of turning them toward more useful lives and in the long run and save the county money.[9]

The issue frames within this category continually posit two arguments to the reader: first, as illustrated above, the redemptive nature of those eligible individuals who are incarcerated at CCDOC, and second, the fiscal responsibility of government officials in opting for these alternatives in lieu of full-time incarceration within CCDOC for detainees. In addition, both of these arguments are premised with descriptions of classification and eligibility which express the importance of public safety through differing levels of surveillance depending upon the particular inmate and program.

ROOT CAUSES OF ARREST AND INCARCERATION

The root causes of arrest and incarceration frame accounted for 11 percent of the issue frames presented. Just over half of these narratives reported growing trends in the number of individuals incarcerated at CCDOC suffering from tuberculosis, HIV, homelessness and mental illness issues. In addition, these narratives, as well as others within this category, attributed incarceration and the aforementioned maladies to poverty, lack of education and addiction. As Reverend Jesse Jackson was quoted in his 1994 annual Christmas address to the inmates of CCDOC:

> Today our civil wrongs constitute the No. 1 threat to our progress. The surrender to drugs, dropouts and violence, the abandoned families and alienated children are not only eroding our base, they are also fueling the politics of fear, anger and repression.[10]

While the root causes of crime and incarceration frame was limited in number compared to some of the other issue frames, there was at least one media article positing this issue frame for every year analyzed. A higher number of frames within this category were initiated in 1993 and 1994 when problems of defendant drug dependency were coupled with the expansion of the aforementioned community-based programs outlined within the previous issue frame of community pursuit of justice and balanced needs.

COOK COUNTY POLITICS

An issue frame that emerged as the data was being coded for the previously discussed frames was that of Cook County politics. Within these narratives CCDOC became an election issue, as opponents were attempting to unseat Cook County officials, and an issue of public argument between elected official awarding business contracts at CCDOC. These narratives accounted for 14 percent of the issue frames presented between 1993 and 2003. Included within this group of narratives were editorial political endorsements by the local media sources being analyzed. During election years, candidates running against incumbents for Cook County Board president and Cook County sheriff proposed approaches to alleviate overcrowding such as placing inmates in floating barges on the Chicago River and mandating that inmates sleep in shifts so they could share a bed.[11] In addition, many of these narratives captured political arguments between Cook County officeholders as to bidding processes for CCDOC contracts, as well as legal representation associated with CCDOC lawsuits.[12]

AMELIORATING POOR CONDITIONS

The final issue frame presented within the newspapers analyzed related directly to ameliorating poor building and living conditions within the CCDOC facilities. Just over 9 percent of the narratives coded were framed around the issue of building and living conditions that inmates and correctional officers resided in at CCDOC. Twenty-four out of twenty-eight of these narratives were critical of the quality of building conditions that existed within CCDOC. The majority of these frames were posited in 1993 when eleven narratives were framed in this manner. Within these narratives, claims of grossly inadequate health facilities, lack of air conditioning, poor food quality, rodents and dirty conditions were presented in media coverage.[13] While criticism of conditions continued within the issue frames presented in later years, the number of narratives devoted to this frame lessened in number; and the narratives focused specifically on renovation and construction, as well as the financial investment involved with these changes.[14]

CLAIMS-MAKERS

The issue frames presented provide an indication as to what the news-paper media consumer is privy to in regard to CCDOC and the ongoing federal consent decree. The issue frames and the extent to which they are presented have the capacity to shape the public's view of CCDOC, its inmates, and its employees. The second level of analysis provides an indication as to who is making claims within the media, to what extent, and within which issue frames. The claims-makers are categorized into the two groups of primary claims-makers and secondary claims-makers.

Primary claims-makers included the federal judiciary, the plaintiffs' attorneys, the John Howard Association and community activists. Secondary claims-makers included the Cook County Sheriff's Office, the Cook County State's Attorney's Office, the Cook County Board of Commissioners and the Cook County judiciary. As illustrated in table 5.4 just over 26 percent of the issue frames were attributed to primary claims-makers as the primary source. Almost two-thirds of the frames posited within the media narratives were informed by the secondary claims-makers. The remaining 10.4 percent of the 308 issue frames were attributed to other claims-makers not directly involved with the consent decree dispute process. These claims-makers included correctional researchers, outside local and state law enforcement agencies, public health officials and newspaper editorial boards.

The representations of frames by the particular claimants within the primary and secondary categories were then disaggregated by issue frames within table 5.5. Almost half of the narratives posited by sources from the Cook County Sheriff's Office and the John Howard Association can be attributed to the order and control issue frame.

Table 5.4.   Frames Produced by Claims-Makers between 1993 and 2003

	Number of Frames	Percentage of Frames
Primary Claims-makers	81	26.3%
Secondary Claims-makers	195	63.3
Other Claims-makers	32	10.4
Total	308	100

Table 5.5. The Representation of Frames by Claims-Makers

Frame	Federal Judiciary	Plaintiffs' Attorneys	John Howard Association	Community Activists	Cook County Sheriff's Office	Cook County States Attorney's Office	Cook County Board of Commissioners	Cook County Judiciary	Other
Order and Control	5.9%	14.3%	47.6%	—	49.3%	28.6%	21.4%	14.3%	18.2%
Rights of the Accused	82.3	50.0	9.5	36.7%	5.0	21.5	17.9	42.9	15.2
Community Pursuit of Justice	—	—	14.3	13.4	21.1	7.1	10.7	14.3	27.3
Root Causes of Arrest and Incarceration	5.9	—	—	40.0	6.3	7.1	3.5	14.3	30.3
Politics in Cook County	—	—	—	6.6	10.6	35.7	39.3	7.1	9.0
Poor Conditions	5.9	35.7	28.6	3.3	7.7	—	7.2	7.1	—

These two claims-makers are the primary sources representing both groups involved within the dispute. The context of the order and control issue frames presented by these claims-makers focused upon violence within the institution as a result of overcrowding, gang affiliation, and lack of supervision for inmates. The issue frame that is being presented to the largest degree by both the primary and secondary claims-makers who are closest to the day-to-day operations within the institution is that of a correctional facility in need of order, safety, and control. In addition, the Cook County State's Attorney's Office, the chief prosecutor within the county, relied upon this issue frame over 28 percent of the times they were referenced as a primary source and the Cook County Board of Commissioners over 21 percent of the time. The only claims-makers who were not a source within the order and control frame were community activists.

The Cook County Sheriff's Office was limited in the extent that it framed CCDOC issues within the realm of the rights of the accused. While all claims-makers referenced the rights of the accused when used as primary sources within the media, the Sheriff's Office was least likely among claims-makers to reference this frame. When used as a primary source, the federal judiciary framed CCDOC issues within the rights of the accused category over 80 percent of the time. In addition, the plaintiffs' attorneys, community activists and the Cook County judiciary relied heavily on this issue frame.

The community pursuit of justice frame was invoked by the Sheriff's Office within 21.1 percent of the narratives where they were cited as the primary source. In addition the John Howard Association and the Cook County judiciary promulgated this frame in just over 14 percent of the narratives that they were cited as primary sources. Community activists invoked the community pursuit of justice frame just over 13 percent of the time they were cited as primary sources.

While claims-makers outside of the consent decree dispute who were categorized as "other" only accounted for 10.4 percent of the primary sources within the media narrative population, over 57 percent of the frames posited by these individuals was either within the realm of community pursuit of justice or root causes of incarceration. Community activists also framed CCDOC issues within the frame of root causes of incarceration more often than any other issue frame.

The issue frame of poor conditions in relation to CCDOC was posited by the plaintiffs' attorneys in over 35 percent of the narratives where they were referenced as the primary source. In addition, the John Howard Association posited this frame in 28.6 percent of the narratives in which they were attributed as the primary source. The Cook County Board of Commissioners framed CCDOC within the issue of poor conditions 17.9 percent of the time they were referenced as the media source. The remaining secondary claims-makers referenced this frame much more sparingly.

Overall, the media analysis revealed a decrease in news stories related to CCDOC as the 1990s progressed and then an increase in stories beginning in 2001 through 2003. Over 31 percent of the interpretive packages presented within the media were within the order and control frame. In addition, incendiary incidents were responsible for increased framing within specific issue packages. This finding was particularly relevant within the rights of the accused frame. Secondary claims-makers were the primary media source within almost two-thirds of the media frames produced between 1993 and 2003. Within the interpretive packages, the Cook County Sheriff's Office and the John Howard Association were most likely to frame news stories under the order and control frame. In opposition, when the federal judiciary, local judiciary, and the plaintiffs' attorneys were used as the primary source within media articles they were most likely to position CCDOC issues within the rights of the accused frame. Finally, the root causes of arrest and incarceration frame was the dominant perspective fostered by community activists and those individuals not directly involved with the consent decree dispute.

NOTES

1. Marshall McLuhan, *Understanding Media: The Extension of Man*, (Corte Madera, CA: Gingko Press, 2003): 276.

2. Italics in original.

3. Andrew Fegelman, "150-Patient Jail Hospital to Be Built," *Chicago Tribune*, July 8, 1993, sec. B2.

4. Susan Kuczka, "Female Jail Officers Fight Back Against Harassment," *Chicago Tribune*, October 15, 1993, sec. B1.

5. Frank Main and Carlos Sadovi, "County Jail to Return Convicts to Prison," *Chicago Sun-Times*, March 26, 2002, pg.7.

6. "Strip-Searching Women in Jail," *Chicago Tribune*, April 8, 2001, sec A18.

7. Maurice Possley & Steve Mills, "Former Guard Allege 2nd Mass Beating," *Chicago Tribune*, February 28, 2003, sec. A1.

8. Carlos Sadovi, "Jail Program Helps Moms Learn Skill of Parenting," *Chicago Sun Times*, January 1, 2001, p. 12.

9. "A Sign of Hope at Cook County Jail," *Chicago Tribune*, September 27, 1993, sec. A14.

10. William Raspberry, "Inmates Have the Power to Change Their Destinies," *Chicago Tribune*, December 30, 1994, p. 19.

11. Bill Zwecker, "Morris Barges in with Jail Plan," *Chicago Sun-Times*, August 9, 1994, p.18; Abdon Pallasch, "Longtime Cop Vies for Sherriff's Badge," *Chicago Tribune*, October 7, 1998, p. 10.

12. Andrew Fegelman, "Lack of Manpower Creates Safety Risks, Jail Watchdog Group Says," *Chicago Tribune*, November 9, 1994, sec. B2; Robert Becker, "County's Politicians Make Bickering Their Way of Life," *Chicago Tribune*, November 2, 1999, sec. B1.

13. Fegelman, "150-Patient Jail," sec. B2; Terry Wilson, "Jail Menu Has Strike Against It," *Chicago Tribune*, April 14, 1993, sec. B8.

14. Lorraine Forte, "New Hospital to Save Jail Cash," *Chicago Sun–Times*, July 18, 1997, p. 57.

SIX

The Politics of Local-Level Punishment

Presiding over the Culture of Control

Class actions brought for or against representatives of a group were developed by courts of equity as an answer to the practical problems of multi-party litigation. They are made to order for litigation by transient jail inmates aimed at general jail conditions. Where jail inmates are uneducated, unaware of their rights or of the means for implementing them, or unrepresented by council, a class suit can provide the only practical means for presenting their grievances to the court. Class suits frequently are more efficient and economical than individual action and save time for the courts, defending prison officials, and attorneys.[1]
—Ronald Goldfarb, *Jails: The Ultimate Ghetto of the Criminal Justice System*, 1975

The identification of promoted meanings in regard to local-level incarceration by the differing stakeholders within the Cook County criminal justice system, the federal judiciary, the John Howard Association, plaintiffs, and community activists revealed a dynamic disputing process. The advancement of particular promoted meanings by the differing stakeholders within the dispute reveals the concept of framing. In essence, framing exposes dynamic promoted meanings presented within the dispute as pre-organized efforts whereby structures of everyday thinking contribute to a structure of dominance.[2] The subsequent cultural interplay is a continuous generation of meaning within a dialectic of moral entrepreneurship, moral innovation and transgression.[3]

Within these processes three specific areas of discussion can be added to the larger criminal justice literature regarding jail incarceration: first, an examination of the implicit role all disputants played in expanding the social control apparatus of the Cook County criminal justice system; second, an examination of the role of a loosely coupled criminal justice system failing to fully address local-level incarceration problems; finally and most importantly, the chronicling of contextual changes in the social reality of local-level incarceration within a large urban criminal justice system spurred by a conglomeration of stakeholder decision making. The importance of examining these three areas provides a link between cognitive policymaking and its connection to cultural and policy analysis. The end result of dynamic frame building and frame setting by claims-makers over a ten-year period (see figure intro.1) are quantitative and qualitative changes to local-level incarceration reflecting an expanded culture of control.

EXPANDING THE CULTURE OF CONTROL

Addressing overcrowding and conditions of confinement problems within CCDOC resulted in net-widening within the Cook County criminal justice system. Through the consent decree dispute and as a consequence of a loosely coupled criminal justice system, wider, stronger and different control mechanisms served to expand the Cook County sheriff's locus of control over citizens entering into criminal justice processes.[4] The federal judiciary and all of the disputants involved within the consent decree were actively involved with the resulting criminal justice expansion.

A wider net of control was produced as all of the disputants agreed to or at the very least acquiesced to increasing the number of jail cells through new building projects. Between 1993 and 2003, 2,147 beds were added across CCDOC. The vast majority of these jail beds were the result of new jail construction. This expansion occurred despite recognition by all of the disputants that brick and mortar solutions would have little positive impact on overcrowding. In addition, previous research revealed that building expansion within other jurisdictions has been found to have very little if any impact on overcrowding.[5] Further widening of social control occurred with the development of the Cook County Department of Community Supervision and Intervention. CCDCSI, a separately managed and budgeted entity within the Cook County Sheriff's Office, introduced an array of intermediate sanction-style controls for pretrial felony defendants outside the walls of CCDOC. By 2003, the average daily population of these programs was over 2,200 individuals. Throughout this period of expansion, all of the disputants referenced CCDCSI as a panacea to jail overcrowding that required further expansion. Finally, a wider net was also cast upon post-convicted misdemeanants and low-level felons who were enlisted in the Sheriff's Work Alternative Program and Sheriff's Boot Camp. By 2003, the combined population of these programs was over 3,200 individuals. In essence, a combined increase of over 7,500 individuals under the control of the Cook County Sheriff's Office ensued based upon the three aforementioned reforms emanating out of the consent decree. In 1993 prior to these expansions, the average daily population at CCDOC was 8,881 inmates. By 2003, there were over 16,381 individuals within the sheriff's net of social control.

In addition to wider nets of social control, stronger nets of social control were also produced as a result of a loosely coupled criminal justice system within Cook County. Through an increasingly punitive criminal justice system arrests flooded CCDOC. Courtroom processing of defendants was slowed as a result of more arrests. This stronger net of social control increased length of stay within the CCDOC facility. In 1996, 33 percent of the inmates entering the correctional facility were release within seventy-two hours. By 2002, the average length of stay for CCDOC inmates was over six months. In addition, the unsupervised release program known as Administrative Mandatory Furlough (AMF) was effectively replaced by the surveillance and control of the Pretrial Services Division within the county probation department and CCDCSI. In 1989, over 35,000 inmates were released through the recognizance-based AMF program. By 2001, just over 6,000 inmates were released through this unsupervised release program. Within a twelve-year period executive branch release on recognizance was diminished by over 82 percent. This reduction was heralded as a policy success by not only the Cook County Sheriff's Office but also the federal judiciary and the John Howard Association.

As the AMF program was offered to fewer inmates and the length of stay within the institution continued to increase, finding volunteers for the newer CCDCSI intermediate sanction-style programming was not problematic. Yet, while volunteers for the programs were easily recruited, stipulations regarding criminal history, current charges and community-based housing stability resulted in many volunteers being judged unqualified for DCSI opportunities. For example, releasing a pretrial low-level drug possession defendant to the electronic monitoring or the day reporting program was hampered by a previous charge or conviction for domestic battery or by an individual who was homeless. A domestic violence background was judged by CCDCSI internal policy to be a non-starter in regard to program eligibility. Confining a suspected or convicted domestic violence perpetrator to their home on the sheriff's orders appeared risky and illogical from a public safety perspective. In addition, electronic monitoring equipment required that the user of the equipment inhabit a residence with a landline telephone. Individuals who were homeless or could not offer proof of active landline service were not eligible for the electronic monitoring program. In essence, individuals whose current charges were within the catchment area for CCDCSI programming were sequestered to confinement based on variables not necessarily connected to their current legal predicament.

As wider and stronger nets of social control were implemented within Cook County, different nets of social control were utilized as CCDCSI programming included intermediate sanctions based upon specific types of drug use, employment and educational history, family ties, and prior criminal histories. The Cook County Day Reporting Center (CCDRC) grew to ten differing tracks based on the aforementioned variables and daily drug testing results.[6] For example, an individual with a marijuana possession charge would initially be placed in one of the CCDRC marijuana tracks requiring daily urinalysis testing and on-site supervision for ten to twelve hours a day. If the individual remained drug and arrest free they would be moved to a less controlling track where they may only spend six to eight hours under direct supervision. In addition if they provided proof of employment or school enrollment they would be placed in a track which allowed them to continue their employment and/ or education. Pretrial detainees of the CCDRC would successfully and unsuccessfully move back and forth within these different tracks until their court case was processed.

Female inmates as an increasingly growing demographic were also included in the expansion of wider, stronger and differing nets of social control including some individuals diagnosed and entering treatment for post-traumatic stress disorder. The increase in female detainees mirrored national level increases in female detainees in prisons and jails.[7] The expansion of differing social controls for pretrial defendants, female and male, diagnosed with mental illness problems included specific classification categories and the utilization of psychotropic medications for mood alteration. Consent decree disputants, including the plaintiffs, argued for even further net-widening through executive branch ordered pretrial defendant placement in community-based mental health and drug dependency centers. Expansion rooted in an ideology of benevolence, initiated through the consent decree dispute, pushed the Cook County criminal justice system firmly into the area of public health. CCDOC became one of the largest mental health centers in the United States.[8]

Media stories were also instrumental in reinforcing net-widening. Order and control frames posited by Cook County criminal justice actors and the John Howard Association focused heavily on institutional violence and violent offenders. Over 31 percent of the frames presented in the media revolved around issues of the need for or the increasing of order and control in regard to institutional violence and violent offenders. Interestingly, according to the primary source documents, the rate of injury to inmates averaged just over 16 injuries per 1,000 inmates between 1993 and 2003. Within the media analysis, over 47 percent of the frames posited by the John Howard Association and over 49 percent of the frames posited by the Cook County Sheriff's Office were related to order and control. While the frames presented by claims-makers were indeed based in fact, they were in actuality selected observations of extremes within the institutional setting. For example, a frame presented concerning the need for increased order and control that cites the stabbing of an inmate or a gang altercation becomes naturalized for the reading public, which then perceives this violence to be more widespread than the objective data indicates. Simplistic presentations of complex social problems have been posited to shape public perceptions of crime in the news media.[9] In reality, stabbings and gang altercations within CCDOC are most likely to occur within the maximum security divisions where IDOC inmates are housed and within the intake and processing areas where inmate transiency is heightened. Yet, these frames reinforce agenda setting toward increasing stronger nets of social control within the facility as a whole and across all defendants within the facility. According to Chermak, stakeholders within criminal justice institutions have a financial and ideological stake in how social problems are presented to the public.[10] As the reading public generalizes that it is likely inmates and correctional officers will be victimized by violence in the jail setting, they are more likely to acquiesce toward an agenda of expanded order and control. One may argue that media outlets are enlisted to present dominant frames or particularly emphasized narratives to the general public and that these narratives are promulgated by claims-makers advancing an ideological agenda.

In addition, agenda setting culminating in wider and different nets of social control was also reinforced within media claims. Over 21 percent of the claims posited by the Cook County Sheriff's Office focused upon the frame of community pursuit of justice. In addition, the Cook County state's attorney, Cook County Board of Commissioners, Cook County judiciary, John Howard Association, and community activists also promulgated this frame within the media. Frames positing the redemptive and fiscally prudent nature of expanding community corrections programming for pretrial defendants provide what appear to be plain descriptions of benevolent services that save the taxpayer the cost of incarcerating low-level felons and misdemeanants within the county jail. Conjoined to benevolence and taxpayer savings, the Cook County Sheriff's Office was expanding the number of citizens under its control and the budgetary allocation of its office.

The expansion of the Cook County Sheriff's Office into the realm of community-based correctional supervision programs was acceded to by all of the disputants involved within the consent decree. Also, the primary stakeholders within the dispute, including the federal judiciary, argued that through further expansion of these programs the overcrowding problem within CCDOC would soon be solved. As the Cook County Department of Community Supervision and Intervention continued to expand, it soon became clear that the community-based programming of electronic monitoring and day reporting were replacing the recognizance bond program of Administrative Mandatory Furlough. Individuals who would have been free pending trial were now under the supervision of the Cook County criminal justice system. Individuals who were sequestered within the CCDOC were increasingly spending more time within the facility and more time within their cells.

THE LOOSELY COUPLED NONSYSTEM

Loose coupling within the Cook County criminal justice system and federal judiciary failure to fully address a loosely coupled criminal justice system resulted in a piecemeal approach to overcoming overcrowding and conditions of confinement problems within the Cook County Department of Corrections. Proactive solutions to addressing conditions of confinement and overcrowding were hampered by horizontal as well as vertical loose coupling. Among Cook County and city of Chicago criminal justice officials, horizontal loose coupling between the Chicago Police Department, Cook County judiciary, and Cook County correctional officials narrowed accountability and responsibility associated with increasing jail populations. Vertical loose coupling between state of Illinois, Cook County and city of Chicago officials further narrowed accountability and responsibility. Finally, among the consent decree disputants themselves, loose coupling was enhanced through a lack of agreed upon baseline measurements when assessing overcrowding and conditions of confinement.

Within the length of stay theme, a frame emerged which posited an expansion within the Cook County Court system in an effort to alleviate overcrowding by speeding up inmate processing. In essence, it was argued that more courtrooms and more judges would speed the flow of criminal justice processing. Within other jurisdictions proactive uniformity in addressing court backlog problems has been introduced with differing degrees of success contingent upon individual-level discretionary decisions of line-level criminal justice agents.[11] Expedited processing through judicial expansion emerged, yet failed to gain any traction within the consent decree dispute. The Cook County judiciary and the Cook County Board of Commissioners selectively ignored this emerging frame and the tight coupling between local courts and corrections that would be required for implementation. Similar to other jurisdictions, there is an acknowledgment within judicial communities of the social problem of overcrowding, yet a discord as to responsibility in regard to this problem.[12] In addition, ignoring an approach of proactive uniformity across the courts and corrections reified the overcrowding problem as a CCDOC dilemma as opposed to a Cook County criminal justice predicament. Remaining a loosely coupled nonsystem reinforces the blame avoidance perspective of correctional overcrowding for local judiciary and the courts.[13]

Vertical loose coupling was evident between the state of Illinois and Cook County specific to the increase in Illinois Department of Corrections parole holds within CCDOC that emerged in 2000. Rooted in state-level policy changes related to politically motivated crime control measures, IDOC parole hold inmates began to swell within CCDOC confines, and the emergent frame became dominant in 2001. Attempts at addressing a loosely coupled criminal justice system, in this case engaging the IDOC, toward proactive problem solving proved difficult. Suggestions by the Cook County Sheriff's Office for the state of Illinois to establish a specialized court, a temporary holding facility for parole holds and increased electronic monitoring funding were postponed and dismissed. In other words, promoting a tightly coupled system to address the crisis situation was ignored by a local judiciary not beholden to the federal court. Yet, while formal changes in processing were not implemented, the political pressure applied by the Cook County Board and the Sheriff's Office did lead to a decrease in parole holds by almost two-thirds by 2003. By 2003, the parole hold population had become a residual frame within the consent decree.

In addition to the vertical loose coupling that was evident between the state and the county an additional vertical/horizontal loosely coupled relationship was in existence between the city of Chicago and Cook County. The primary source data emanating from the federal court dispute made little if any reference to the city of Chicago's accountability toward local correctional overcrowding. Considering that the vast majority of citizens who are incarcerated within the CCDOC are city residents who are arrested by the Chicago Police Department, the negation of the city of Chicago in proactive problem solving associated with jail overcrowding appears quite baffling. Yet, a bifurcation in local government whereby the city of Chicago is largely responsible for enforcement through the police department and Cook County is responsible for incarceration creates a horizontal dichotomy in responsibility between local police and local corrections. In addition, from a vertical and financial standpoint, the city of Chicago mayoral office controls the enforcement budget through the Chicago Police Department, and the Cook County Board of Commissioners controls the incarceration budget through CCDOC. In essence, vertical loose coupling is occurring as city government fiscally expanded enforcement operations in the 1990s while county government remained fiscally responsible for the aftermath of increased enforcement. Previous quantitative structural analysis of the relationship among participants within Cook County/city of Chicago criminal justice agencies found similar loose coupling.[14]

Finally, loose coupling was enhanced within the consent decree dispute itself. Through an adversarial approach, plaintiffs and defendants alike engaged in a competitive presentation of data that fit their particular perspective of the reality of overcrowding and conditions of confine-

ment. The failure of the federal judiciary to establish agreed upon baseline measurements associated with overcrowding and inmate services
created an environment mired in adversarial disagreement over the extent of the problems within CCDOC as opposed to firmly addressing the
problems through consensus based proactive problem solving rooted in
social scientific data collection. The federal judiciary overseeing the *Duran* consent decree ignored fully implementing the coordinated system
perspective of jail data collection and analysis promulgated by the United
States Department of Justice.[15] Specific portions of these coordinated data
collection objectives require tight coupling of local-level government entities at the county and city level. While all of the disputants within the
consent decree were in agreement that inmates within CCDOC were
sleeping on floors, failing to receive library visits, and failing to have their
grievances heard, the extent of these problem was never agreed upon by
the disputants. The results were piecemeal solutions to poorly defined
problems.

Outside of the immediate claims-makers there are also areas within
the Cook County criminal justice system and the wider governmental
structure that continue to hamper proactive change. First, the political
lack of responsiveness among Cook County officials not directly involved with the overcrowding consent decree was not fully addressed. A
specific area that needed to be addressed was the lack of responsiveness
by the chief judge of Cook County in creating a sustained avenue of
accountability toward overcrowding and conditions within the jail. Previous research analyzing the internal social processes of the Cook County
judiciary revealed that innovations are circumscribed by the tension between loose and tight coupling.[16] In addition, the Cook County judiciary
has historically been more aligned and networked with the partisan politics of the Cook County Board and the Cook County State's Attorney's
Office rather than aligned with the leading consent decree disputants of
the Sheriff's Office and the John Howard Association.[17] Yet, within the
larger criminal justice literature there are examples of tight coupling during short term crises across policing, the courts and corrections.[18] Specifically, tight coupling has occurred across the police, courts and corrections
during short-term crisis situations within the Cook County criminal justice system.[19]

The office of the chief judge of Cook County must apply assertive
leadership approaches in the long term, introducing a transparent management plan that further implements structured avenues of speedier
arraignment and community release at the judicial level.[20] Yet, Jacob
argued that the conciliar/loose coupling style leadership of the chief
judge in Cook County was related to political sponsorship and the partisan political makeup within judicial elections.[21] Cook County and state of
Illinois judicial election structure is mired in city of Chicago/Cook
County ward-level politics. Without a judicial merit selection process

within Illinois it is unlikely that even the most charismatic leader within the Chief Judge's Office would be able to sustain the assertive leadership needed for long-term tight coupling. In essence, responsive action associated with long-term justice policy issues by county judiciary will more than likely continue to take a backseat to the furtive politics of the region. Currently, the Cook County Department of Community Service and Intervention is providing intermediate-style sanctioning to approximately 2,200 pretrial detainees at any given time. In essence, these release decisions are being made by the executive branch of Cook County government as a reactive outcome of the consent decree. Logically, these release decisions should be made by the judicial branch of Cook County government.

Furthermore, on a wider governmental level, there is a continued lack of vested interest in this social problem by the City of Chicago. The separation of city and county government in regard to enforcement, judgment, and detention at the local level exacerbates the overcrowding problem within Cook County. Despite the fact that the vast majority of individuals incarcerated within the Cook County Department of Corrections are residents of the city of Chicago there continues to be a lack of responsiveness toward overcrowding and conditions of confinement by city officials. The development of correctional oversight by city officials has been implemented within other jurisdictions. Within New York City, the deputy mayor of health and human services provides oversight for local detention centers. While New York City is not without its own local detention problems, at the very least there is a structured avenue of accountability within the city government. In addition, a lack of vested interest by state of Illinois legislators representing districts within Cook County and the city of Chicago is also apparent. One would assume the partisan politics of the region are similarly disenfranchising the power of state legislators to effect change for their constituents associated with CCDOC.

An argument toward a tightly coupled criminal justice system whereby police, courts, and corrections work in unison from a horizontal perspective and state, county and city officials work in unison from a vertical perspective is not without its detractors. As Wright argued, the dynamic quality of a fragmented system promotes a balance of power.[22] Yet, within Cook County there is an excessive level of loose coupling in regard to the overcrowding and conditions of confinement problem. Rather than a balance of power the overt loose coupling in Cook County creates an omission of public service. Cook County, city of Chicago, and state of Illinois officials who are not named defendants within the consent decree have displayed a poverty of ambition toward addressing this public policy problem. The failure of the Cook County judiciary, the city of Chicago and the state of Illinois to enter into formal ameliorative action in regard to the consent decree dispute process can be considered a calculated form of blame avoidance. If different agencies and levels of government actively address this social problem in a positive manner within the confines of the federal consent decree, they may create the possibility of being added as defendants within the decree. Once added as defendants, the federal judiciary has the capacity to demand fiscal appropriations and policy changes from those agencies and levels of government. Avoiding legal culpability within an ongoing federal consent decree would be considered politically astute from the perspective of even the most novice of politicians.

CONTEXTUAL CHANGES FOR THE INCARCERATED

Conditions of confinement within CCDOC were incrementally changed for the better between 1993 and 2003. Yet regardless of these incremental changes, the social reality of jail inmate existence within Cook County was tantamount to subsistence living. The parameter of conditions within CCDOC produced the three themes of environmental health, physical health and inmate services. It is the frames emanating from these three themes which provide an indication as to the daily conditions that shaped the lives of inmates between the years of 1993 and 2003. John Irwin's rabble-class hypothesis arguing that jails serve the purpose of warehousing the poor, the ill and the petty offenders of society connotes the enforcement policies which have led to the quantitative increase in jail inmates evident within the population and space parameter.[23] Social theorists analyzing crime control and prisonization from a wider perspective argue that higher incarceration rates are a product of a new form of governing social marginality.[24] Yet, it is within the parameter of conditions within CCDOC that the qualitative existence within the institution is displayed most vividly.

The perspective of connections to the conventional world outside the jail walls disintegrating for the jail inmate and the process of this devolution for individual inmates is exposed through the emerging, dominant and residual frames of the consent decree dispute. Gibbs argued that a two stage process existed where turmoil and chaos are replaced by boredom in an impoverished facility.[25] While Irwin and Gibbs's early jail research posits the adaptation process for inmates, recent correctional literature reifies these adaptation premises within the prison setting.[26] The results emanating from the conditions within the CCDOC parameter suggest that turmoil and chaos coexist with boredom within the impoverished jail facility. In addition, these results describe and analyze the actuality of changing conditions for the adapting inmate as reform decisions were implemented through the consent decree.

As inmates were double and triple celled within particular divisions, appropriating beds for each individual inmate gave way to a general malaise among disputants in solving the problem of inmates sleeping on floors. Instead, a tacit consensus toward managing a facility with inmates sleeping on floors emerged. Descriptions of sanitary conditions including exposure to rodents, bugs, raw sewage, cold, heat, dampness, foul smells, and broken furniture provides a portrayal of chaos and turmoil as lived experience. Many of these particular frames emerged, became dominant, and moved toward the residual as the disputants addressed them within the decree. Yet, the old frames were replaced by new frames as a result of building deterioration and vandalism from inmates. In addition to the dirty and dilapidated conditions, staff shortages increased the correctional officer/inmate ratio leading toward cross-watching between living units and low levels of supervision in general. Realignment of correctional officer work schedules and new correctional hiring did not keep pace with the increasing inmate population. Even though the reported injury rates were relatively low for inmates and correctional officers, unreported injuries, fear of injury, and alleged mass beatings were adding to an environment of at the very least perceived chaos and turmoil.

In addition to the disorientation and degradation of the jail experience that was magnified by the aforementioned environmental health themes of the institution, individual-level physical health themes produced frames surrounding food service, health care and personal hygiene. These emanating frames magnified the institutional disorder which has been alluded to in the wider incarceration research.[27] Food service frames included poor quality of food, serving trays encrusted with old food, trays of food stacked on rodent-infested floors and exposure to communicable diseases carried by the inmate labor serving meals. In addition, health-care frames emerged regarding poor access to diagnosis and treatment for physical, mental, and dental needs. Opportunities for inmate physical exercise were limited due to staff shortages, inmate uniforms were dirty and torn, inmates lucky enough to have a bed slept on dirty and torn mattresses, and personal hygiene items such as soap, razors, towels, and sanitary napkins were of subpar quality when they were available.

Improvements were specifically noted within the areas of food service and personal hygiene. The frames of health care and its emanating subframes remained dominant throughout the period of the study. The vast health-care needs of inmate populations appear to be outside the realm of expertise of criminal justice officials and the consent decree disputants. In addition, inmate health care is not mutually exclusive of the institutional problems related to sanitary conditions, food quality, personal hygiene items and lack of exercise. Also, as exercise became limited based on staff shortages and increased populations, inmates were more likely to spend significant amounts of time locked in their cells thereby magnifying the effects of boredom.

In essence, the theme of environmental health within the conditions parameter provides an institutional perspective of the disorienting and disintegrating process of jail incarceration. The physical health theme and subsequent frames extend the process to the individual level incorporating the perspective of boredom and helplessness inside the impoverished facility. The institutional and individual context of jail incarceration establishes, propels and/or reifies the incarcerated toward second-class citizenship.

Additionally, the media analysis captured the social reality of the jail from two predominantly contested interpretations which served to reify the context of the incarcerated experience. The secondary claims-makers who produced over 63 percent of the frames presented within the media articles focused to a great degree on presenting order and control frames within the media. A reality of jail existence that is violent, unsafe, and potentially always dangerous was presented. These frames present a reality that is in need of expanded authoritative control over impending chaos. On the other hand, the primary claims-makers who produced just over 26 percent of the media frames also tended to focus on a jail reality though many times revolving around the rights of accused defendants and the poor conditions within the facility.

In essence, while many of the media narratives were referring to a similar incident, the framing of the incident varied by claims-maker. As Mather and Yngvesson argue, transformation of disputes occurs through the narrowing and expansion of discourse surrounding a dispute.[28] For example, there is the reality that some inmates conceal contraband within the orifices of their body when entering the Cook County Department of Corrections. This narrative is framed by the Cook County Sheriff's Office as a safety and security hazard creating a potentially unsafe environment. As a reaction to this frame, a wider range of strip searches of male and female detainees was instituted within the correctional facility. At the same time, the federal judiciary and the plaintiff's attorneys were framing the concealed contraband issue and subsequent searches as a violation of pretrial defendant rights based on the contextual environment in which the searches were being conducted. Both of these representations have validity. Both of these representations explain the social reality of the jail. It is within these areas of competing interpretation that the media frame analysis provides the most graphic portrayal of jail existence.

Competing interpretations in relation to increased control versus individual rights revolved around searches, altercations between gang members and correctional officers, use of confinement, access to inmate and health services, as well as facility conditions. Conditions of confinement within CCDOC were incrementally changed for the better between 1993 and 2003. Yet, qualitatively and quantitatively pretrial defendants within the Cook County Department of Corrections were living in an overcrowded and impoverished facility and many continued to sleep on floors. Within this daily existence the jail inmates' lived experience was one of chaos, turmoil and boredom.

The Context of Incarceration, Constructed Meaning and the Community

Alternative approaches to controlling crime and social order at the local level require that policy makers within city, county, and state offices look outside of the criminal justice system toward the communities which the local jail is serving. Focusing upon the social role of the jail in the community provides not only a critical assessment of the current conditions of loose coupling and net-widening but also provides opportunities for policy makers to address the culture of control within Cook County. Focusing upon who is served within the Cook County criminal justice system reveals that the majority of individuals passing through the Cook County Department of Corrections are drawn from specific geographical areas of Chicago. In addition, examining the socio-structural underpinnings of those particular neighborhoods and the reciprocal relationship they have with local-level incarceration provides the opportunity to map changes across the community and jail environments.

In an analysis of prisoner reentry within Illinois, Lavigne et al. found that 51 percent of released prisoners from the Illinois Department of Corrections returned to Chicago. Of the approximately 15,000 individuals returning to Chicago in 2001, 33 percent of them returned to six specific communities within the overall 77 Chicago neighborhoods.[29] These particular neighborhoods, Austin, Humboldt Park, North Lawndale, Englewood, West Englewood, and East Garfield are characterized by high levels of poverty, crime, and social disadvantage. Similar findings have been examined by Sampson and Loeffler, who conclude that specific Chicago communities are involved in a negative-feedback loop with mass incarceration.[30] Individuals convicted by the state of Illinois in Chicago and sentenced to IDOC travel through CCDOC. In addition, individuals returning from IDOC to Chicago and who violate parole pass through CCDOC. Focusing upon the reciprocal relationship between the Cook County Department of Corrections and the specific neighborhoods which are served to the greatest degree by the local jail provides a targeted approach to developing a further policy agenda related to the Cook County Department of Corrections.

In addition to the aforementioned incarceration post-release studies, in an analysis of racial disparity in metropolitan Chicago, the Human Relations Foundation/Jane Addams Policy Initiative and the Center for Urban Research and Learning at Loyola University Chicago concluded that segregation, isolation and inequity were most pronounced within African-American and Latino communities on the south and near west sides of Chicago.[31] These are the same neighborhoods most identifiable by prisoner reentry within the Urban Institute post-release study.[32] In addition to disparity among African-American and Latino young men within the Cook County criminal justice system, disparity was also found within the areas of income, employment, education, housing, transportation, health, and child welfare within these neighborhoods.[33] Sampson argues that spatial logic and specifically racial geography explain a reinforcing pattern connecting race, inequality and incarceration within Chicago.[34] These findings become part of a larger discussion as to how penal and welfare institutions have combined to govern socially marginal neighborhoods and their community members.[35] As Wacquant observes, a major contributor to the growth of the carceral system in America is the enlarged role of the jail in confronting city disorder.[36]

Developing a further understanding of the reciprocal relationship that exists between specific communities on the south and near west sides of Chicago and the Cook County Department of Corrections requires an approach emanating from the residential differentiation research literature. Examining the relationship of incarceration to specific neighborhoods across spatial, cultural, economic and political dynamics using a multilevel model has the capacity to identify areas of proactive change at the community level which in turn may limit the number of inmates entering the Cook County Department of Corrections. Identifying dimensions of residential differentiation at the census block level through spatial analysis, identifying differential social organizations that contribute to the solidarity of nonviolence, strengthening the economic stature of targeted neighborhoods and empowering community organizations toward political strength all serve to identify and implement a community justice model. Research that identifies and rigorously evaluates promising programs and policy in these areas is essential. A community justice model that is rooted in a public health framework as opposed to a criminal justice framework is necessary in breaking apart the relationship between local-level incarceration and the specific neighborhoods within Chicago that contribute most toward the jail population.

The premise behind community-based justice initiatives is that beyond the offense against an individual victim, violations against norms are an act against the entire community. In essence, the abstract entity of the community is the victim. Expanding the definition of the victim allows the community and its members the opportunity to address what have been historically referred to as victimless crimes. In substance, a community-based focus addressing the misdemeanor and low-level drug felonies that fuel the reciprocal relationship between the jail and the targeted communities of the south and near west sides of Chicago has the potential to break the fetters between the jail and these specific neighborhoods. A community justice model rooted in a public health perspective is a mixture of functional-based Chicago school ecology, the philosophical premises of communitarianism and the action orientation of epidemiology. Through decentralized community-based programming that promotes positive social capital the negative-feedback loop/reciprocal relationship between the community and the jail can be minimized.

Program development that increases investment at the public level in decentralized mental and physical health facilities within targeted neighborhoods, government and corporate investment in workforce educational programs, and local infrastructure and public transportation development all serve to address problems of isolation and segregation within these particular neighborhoods. Parochial-level investment that increases broad-based neighborhood relations between community members and churches, schools and social clubs and further private-level investment among family, neighbors and friends serves to strengthen the informal and formal social controls necessary for individuals to avoid entering the Cook County Department of Corrections.[37] A challenge with this approach from an implementation standpoint is that these three levels of social capital building must work in unison. For example, it is not enough to increase parochial-level investment and ignore the public and private levels of investment. In addition, rigorous process and outcome evaluations of programs must be implemented in an effort to identify what works, what doesn't work and which programs are promising.[38] Finally, investment in social capital development is subject to an ever-changing political economy. Sustained investment is integral to long-term success.

Movement toward a community justice model which has the capacity to marginalize the use of local-level detention facilities such as the Cook County Department of Corrections requires a change in the current philosophical premises of criminal justice administrators and the public at large. Much of the media data emanating from this research represents a view of the Cook County correctional detainee as an individual who is dangerous and in need of criminal justice control mechanisms. Granted, there are particular individuals who are incarcerated who are dangerous and in need of criminal justice control mechanisms. Yet, is this the vast majority of individuals incarcerated at CCDOC? Following Peter Manning's dramaturgy of police work perspective, criminal justice administrators and consent decree participants must break from the symbolic perspective of "us against them" in regard to community members detained at CCDOC.[39] Through this perspective, punitive conditions of confinement and overcrowding become justified for the criminal justice administrator and a valid approach to the moral service of criminal justice administration. Through media and political representation, the general public buys into this moral service perspective of "us against them" and turns a blind eye toward punitive conditions of confinement and overcrowding.

Active citizen participation or, as Cornel West argues, the critical cultivation of an active citizenry toward democracy is necessary.[40] Through an active citizenry the passivity or unresponsiveness that many of us continue to perpetuate in regard to local-level incarceration of our fellow citizens may be addressed. Addressing unresponsiveness through a targeted community-level approach provides the promise of a distilled policy avenue focusing on the specific source of the increasing jail population. Lowering the quantitative number of jail admissions by addressing co-morbid neighborhood-level public health issues such as alcoholism, drug abuse and mental illness, as well as the public disorder outcomes associated with these health issues in inner-city neighborhoods, is essential for addressing the problem.

CONCLUSION

Federal judicial involvement in local-level jail overcrowding within Cook County began thirty-five years ago with a class action lawsuit. The emanating consent decree which began in 1982 led to a disputing process of contested and promoted meaning regarding conditions of confinement within CCDOC. Through processes of formal adjudication, informal agreements, and media presentations, incrementally better conditions in a continually overcrowded and expanded facility were created. In addition, wider, stronger and different nets of social control were implemented and acquiesced to by all disputants involved in the consent decree. These nets enveloped more and more citizens within the Cook County criminal justice system. In retrospect, much of the acquiescence toward expansion was the result of consent decree disputants working within the confines of a loosely coupled criminal justice system.

Continued federal judicial oversight will have a limited return on investment as it is currently structured. From a federal judicial perspective, there has been a reluctance to expand the dispute beyond the current defendants and parties involved. Expansion of consent decree defendants to include the wider Cook County governmental system, the city of Chicago and the state of Illinois creates the capacity for the federal judiciary to enter a slippery slope of federal oversight in regard to local public health, local law enforcement and the organization of the Cook County Circuit Court system. Yet, each of these particular public service areas is directly and indirectly responsible for the overcrowded conditions within the Cook County Department of Corrections. From the perspective of the local and state agencies and officials who are not named defendants within the consent decree, remaining a safe distance from inclusion within the decree prevents their full commitment toward problem solving. It is apparent that the federal courts are an inappropriate and ill-suited setting to fully or further address the complexity of the social problems culminating in local-level jail overcrowding in Cook County beyond their current capacity as a monitor of previously instituted policy.

The current expanded Cook County criminal justice system was ten years in the making and had been expanding prior to the time period being analyzed in this research. Diminishing a criminal justice system that is many times posing as a public health outlet for the mentally ill and indigent would require replacement with an actual public health response. This seems implausible without the mandated inclusion of a wider group of public service agencies at the local, state and federal level. Until that time arrives, pragmatic solutions which ease the pain of incarceration to areas of home confinement, electronic monitoring, day reporting, and the like as purported by all of the stakeholders within this research seems to be the alternative trajectory within the new localized penal-welfare state. With that being said it is likely we will continue to see further net-widening within the Cook County criminal justice system and more than likely more inmates sleeping on floors.

NOTES

1. Ronald Goldfarb, *Jails: The Ultimate Ghetto of the Criminal Justice System*, (Garden City, NY: Anchor Press, 1975): 403.

2. William Gamson, "Goffman's Legacy to Political Sociology," *Theory and Society* 14, (1985):614–15.

3. Keith Hayward and Jock Young, "Cultural Criminology: Some Notes on the Script," *International Journal on Theoretical Criminology* 8, no. 3 (2004): 259.

4. James Austin and Barry Krisberg, "NCCD Research Review: Wider, Stronger and Different Nets: the Dialectics of Criminal Justice Reform," *Journal of Research in Crime and Delinquency* 18, (1981): 169.

5. D'Alessio and Stolzenberg, "Effect of Available Capacity," 285 (see chap. 1, n. 114); Shelden and Brown, "Correlates of Jail Overcrowding," 360 (see chap. 1, n. 105); Pontell and Welsh, "Incarceration as Deviant Form," 31 (see chap. 1, n. 114); Welsh et al., "Jail Overcrowding," 360–61 (see chap. 1, n. 107).

6. Martin, Olson and Lurigio, *Evaluation of Cook County Sheriff's Day Reporting*, 35 (see chap. 1, n. 151).

7. Harrison and Beck, *Inmates at Midyear 2005* (see chap. 1, n. 99).

8. Elsner, *Gates of Injustice*, 93–94 (see chap. 2, n. 26).

9. Beckett, *Making Crime Pay*, 78 (see intro., n. 43).

10. Chermak, "Presentation of Drugs," 687 (see intro., n. 24).

11. Baumer, "Reducing Lockup Crowding," 279–80 (see chap. 1, n. 140); Baumer and Adams, "Controlling a Jail Population," 399 (see chap. 1, n. 132); James Eisenstein, Roy Fleming and Peter Nardulli, *The Contours of Justice: Communities and their Courts* (Lanham, MD: University Press of America, 1999): 243–48; Shelden and Brown, "Correlates of Jail Overcrowding," 359; Welsh, "Changes in Arrest Policies," 112–13 (see chap. 1, n. 131).

12. Davis, et. al., "Roles and Responsibilities," 469–71 (see chap. 1, n. 158); Kinkade, Leone and Semond, "The Consequences of Jail Crowding," 157–60 (see chap. 1, n. 88).

13. Bleich, "Politics of Prison Crowding," 1125–28 (see chap. 1 n. 86); Shelden and Brown, "Correlates of Jail Overcrowding," 359; Welsh et. al., "Jail Overcrowding," 358.

14. John Heinz and Peter Manikas, "Networks among Elites in a Local Criminal Justice System," *Law and Society Review* 26, no. 4, (1992): 841–49.

15. Cuniff, *Jail Crowding*, (see chap. 1, n. 124); Cushman, *Preventing Jail Crowding*, (see chap. 1, n. 124; Pretrial Services Resource Center, *A Second Look at Alleviating*, (see chap. 1, n. 124).

16. James Eisenstein and Herbert Jacob, *Felony Justice: An Organizational Analysis of Criminal Courts*, (Boston, MA: Little Brown, 1977): 109–24; Herbert Jacob, "The Governance of Trial Judges," *Law and Society Review* 31, no. 1 (1997): 24–25.

17. Eisenstein and Jacob, *Felony Justice*, 121; Heinz and Manikas, "Networks among Elites," 842.

18. Eisenstein, Flemming and Nardulli, *Contours of Justice,* 135–37.

19. Hagan, "So Little Criminal Justice," 120–22 (see intro., n. 71).

20. Center on Sentencing and Corrections, *Los Angeles County Jail: Overcrowding Reduction Project,* (Final Report: Revised). (New York, NY: Vera Institute of Justice, September 2011).

21. Jacob, "Governance of Trial Judges," 14–15.

22. Kevin Wright, "The Desirability of Goal Conflict within Criminal Justice Systems," *Journal of Criminal Justice* 9, (1980): 143.

23. Irwin, *The Jail,* 2 (see intro., n. 1).

24. Katherine Beckett and Bruce Western, "Governing Social Marginality: Welfare, Incarceration, and the Transformation of State Policy," *Punishment and Society,* 3, (2001): 55; David Garland, *The Culture of Control: Crime and Social Order in Contemporary Society,* (Chicago, IL: University of Chicago Press, 2001): 195.

25. Gibbs, "Disruption and Distress," 33–37 (see chap. 2, n.18).

26. Hassine, *Life Without Parole,* 10–11 (see chap. 2, n. 10); Melde, "Penal Reform," 75–77 (see chap. 2, n.12).

27. Elsner, *Gates of Injustice,* 103–30; John Irwin, *The Warehouse Prison: Disposal of the New Dangerous Class* (Los Angeles, CA: Roxbury Publishing, 2005): 150–57; Welch, "Jail Overcrowding," 269–72 (see intro., n. 2).

28. Mather and Yngvesson, "Language, Audience, Transformation," 776–80 (see intro., n. 37).

29. Nancy Lavigne et al., "A Portrait of Prisoner Reentry in Illinois," (Washington, DC: The Urban Institute Justice Policy Center, 2003): 50–51.

30. Robert Sampson and Charles Loeffler, "Punishment's Place: The Local Concentration of Mass Incarceration," *Daedalus,* 139, no. 3, (2010): 29.

31. Center for Urban Research and Learning and the Human Relations Foundation/ Jane Addams Policy Initiative, "Minding the Gap: An Assessment of Racial Disparity in Metropolitan Chicago," (Chicago, IL: Center for Urban Research and Learning, 2003): 4.

32. Lavigne et al., "Portrait of Prisoner Reentry," 50.

33. Center for Urban Research and Learning and the Human Relations Foundation/ Jane Addams Policy Initiative, "Minding the Gap"; Sampson and Loeffler, "Punishment's Place," 24.

34. Robert Sampson, *Great American City: Chicago and the Enduring Neighborhood Effect,* (Chicago, IL: University of Chicago Press, 2011): 97–120.

35. Beckett and Western, "Governing Social Marginality," 53–55.

36. Loïc Wacquant, "Class, Race and Hyperincarceration in Revanchist America," *Daedalus,* 139, no. 3, (2010): 75.

37. Robert Bursik and Harold Grasmick, *Neighborhoods and Crime: The Dimensions of Effective Community Control,* (San Francisco: Jossey-Bass, 1993): 16–18; Albert Hunter, "Private, Parochial and Public School Orders: The Problem of Crime and Incivility in Urban Communities," in *The Challenge of Social Control: Citizenship and Institution building in Modern Society,* ed. Gerald Suttles and Mayer Zald, (Norwood NJ: Ablex Publishing, 1985): 233.

38. Lawrence Sherman et al., *Evidence-Based Crime Prevention, Revised Edition,* (New York, NY: Routledge, 2002): 8–10.

39. Peter Manning, *Police Work: The Social Organization of Policing,* (Prospect Heights IL: Waveland Press, 1997): 27–30.

40. Cornel West, *Democracy Matters: Winning the Fight against Imperialism,* (New York, NY: Penguin Press, 2004): 41.

Conclusion

An analysis of claims-making between 1993 and 2003 associated with the *Duran v. Sheahan* jail overcrowding lawsuit and subsequent federal consent decree revealed numerous changes in the emergent, dominant, and residual frames posited by stakeholders within the formal court proceedings and newspaper media accounts. The use of frame analysis provided a grounded and systematic avenue to explore ten years of qualitative public records and media accounts which captured the changing culture of control within the Cook County Department of Corrections.

I began this volume with a quote from Sheriff Michael Sheahan who stated, "If I knew of all the problems embedded within the jail I may have never run for this position." It is within this public servant's casual presentation of self-reflexivity in which I began delving into the study of jail conditions, expansion, oversight and disputing within CCDOC. As the research moved further and further into a thick description and analysis of local-level incarceration within Chicago, I came to share a similar exasperation that Sheriff Sheahan revealed in our initial meeting. As this volume concludes, I will offer some modest suggestions for change and discuss how those modest suggestions are challenged by the current structure of the local criminal justice environment. In addition, I will address the methodological limitations of the research approach, as well as its overall value in expanding our understanding of the culture of control at the local level. Finally, I will provide an overview on some of the major changes within CCDOC over recent years and some thoughts on future challenges for the urban jail.

MODEST SUGGESTIONS TOWARD POSITIVE CHANGE

Within the previous chapter I outlined the relationship between the consent decree and the loosely coupled nonsystem of criminal justice within Cook County, net-widening associated with expansion, and contextual change within the jail environment. These three areas of dynamic change are not necessarily mutually exclusive. Net-widening within the Cook County Sheriff's Office is tethered to the limited involvement of other public institutions in serving the needs of residents who contribute the most to the local correctional population. For example, limited investment in mental health and drug addiction services within the particular geographies contributing the most to jail populations are associated with higher levels of public disorder calls for local police and in turn higher levels of jail admissions. Higher jail admissions create negative contextual changes in the jail environment. Internal attempts at addressing negative contextual changes have resulted in net-widening. Expansion of local pretrial correctional programming into the community has reinforced the general perspective that mental illness and drug addiction are not public health problems but criminal justice problems.

Community-based investment of social capital within neighborhoods and residents who contribute the greatest toward the local correctional population requires the inclusion of public institutions outside of the consent decree as full-time active problem solvers. Yet, the structure of the federal consent decree and the reluctance of outside public institutions to involve themselves within the federal legal arena continue to limit the inclusion of these parties from full participation. Without the inclusion of a wider array of public institutions, possible solutions to the social problems directly and indirectly contributing to overcrowding and conditions of confinement are relegated to a criminal justice agency ill-equipped to address wider ameliorative change. This conflation of public welfare and health issues with local criminal justice issues coupled with the possibility of court-ordered action by an overarching federal judiciary has limited the expansion of parties involved with this social problem, thereby pigeonholing the possibility of solutions.

INTERNAL CHANGES AND THE CONSENT DECREE DISPUTE

Internally, among the consent decree disputants, if the continuing social problem of jail overcrowding and conditions of confinement within the Cook County Department of Corrections is to be addressed in an ameliorative fashion there are numerous areas to focus upon. Within the current approaches being taken by the primary and secondary claims-makers, the first step would be for the federal judiciary to mandate baseline measures. Failure to agree upon baseline measures across the wider issue of counting overflow populations, as well as the more particular issues of access to law libraries, recreation, medical services and grievance procedures continues to limit the disputants in developing proactive problem-solving solutions. Agreement regarding main terms and base arguments associated with the definition of overcrowding has been documented within previous overcrowding research and has been especially problematic in regard to local jails.[1] Through judicially mandated baselines, the ongoing dispute has the capacity to break from the fetters of conversations and arguments rooted in legal maneuvering which has added to the action paralysis of the consent decree process.

In addition, as consistent baseline measures are integrated into the dispute, the opportunity for clear and concise evidence-based policy evaluation, measuring program success and failure, can be implemented. Combined with program and policy measurement, individual-level performance measures for midlevel management positions would create clear avenues of accountability between the executive-level leadership within the Cook County Sheriff's Office and the line-level custodial and professional staff. Between the years of 1993 and 2003, valid and reliable social science evaluation of jail overcrowding and conditions of confinement within Cook County has been weak to nonexistent. The need for a comprehensive approach to program and leadership planning, development, and evaluation within the Cook County Department of Corrections is vital in addressing this social problem.

Initiating a separate division of research and development within the Cook County Sheriff's Office that conducts ongoing internal evaluations of policy, programs and management on a rotating basis across the differing entities of CCDOC, CCDCSI, and CCDWJS would create the possibility of enhanced transparency and data-driven objective decision making. Leadership and management positions within a research and development division should be filled with trained social scientists with a track record of research associated with incarcerated populations and the comorbidity subject areas of drug abuse, mental illness and trauma-related issues. Trained and licensed attorneys, while useful in an adversarial system, are generally reticent and quite frankly ill-equipped to employ the social scientific methods necessary for objective data collection, measurement and analysis. In addition to an internal research and development division, the expansion of outside program and policy evaluation is necessary to provide a critical, independent and objective voice in assessing the problems and pitfalls of the institution in general and the differing subpopulations living and working within these facilities. A consistent and open policy of outside research application solicitation and review should be implemented. Merit-based blind review of research/policy analysis applications by a board of accredited social scientists should be implemented in an effort to control for the possibility of patronage and favoritism, as well as to ensure strong methodological evaluations. Outside and independent researcher access should be encouraged, not discouraged.

Physically, mentally and socially jails and jail populations are unhealthy. The application of internal and external social scientific inquiry that identifies individuals residing or working within these facilities who need to be marginalized from the correctional population is a good investment of time and resources. Identifying and exiting individuals working within these facilities and programs who are incapable of meeting the needs of an extremely challenging population will enhance the environment of the jail, the perspectives of correctional clientele and the morale of existing dedicated employees. In regard to correctional clientele, connecting appropriately identified incarcerated individuals with public health and housing providers prior to their exit from the institution may limit their continuous cycle between the jail and the community. Embracing a public health perspective, as opposed to a criminal justice perspective, for the drug addled, mentally ill and homeless populations continually cycling through the county criminal justice system is of the utmost importance not only for the Cook County Sheriff's Office and the Cook County Circuit Court, but also for the particular neighborhoods within Chicago most affected by the culture of control. Programs and policies should be evaluated based on the success of cessation from offending. Concentration upon trajectories of success that are correlated with desistance such as employment, housing, strengthening families and termination of drug use should be the focal point for all CCDOC programming not associated with identified high-rate and violent offenders.[2] While some of the current programming within CCDCSI and CCDWJS has implemented these program perspectives, further and expanded rigorous evaluation is needed.

RESEARCH METHODOLOGY AND JAIL RESEARCH

Out of frame activity, conversations and discussions surrounding conditions of confinement and overcrowding that are not included in court documents and media reports, more than likely have occurred.[3] Off-the-record conversations between consent decree disputants within judicial chambers, informal phone conversations between the John Howard Association and Cook County government officials and behind-the-scenes conversations between the Cook County Sheriff's Office, the Cook County state's attorney and County Board members all create validity limitations within this research.

In addition, the unique nature of Chicago, Cook County and state of Illinois politics creates further validity and generalizability limitations. For example, one of the Cook County Board members chairing the finance committee during the time period of this research was John Daley. His brother, Richard M. Daley, was the mayor of Chicago. The president of the Cook County Board of Commissioners during much of this time period was John Stroger, whose son, Todd Stroger, was an alderman on the Chicago City Council. These are just two of the unique oligarchic-style public service relationships that existed within Illinois during the time period of this research. It is safe to assume that informal conversations regarding public policy issues and strategies exist across city, county, and state agencies beyond the documentation used in this research. Executive level government positions filled by generations of family members within Chicago, Cook County and Illinois is a well-documented political and historical phenomenon. While these oligarchic relationships exist within other areas of the United States, they appear to be particularly magnified within this setting. Interestingly, while loose coupling between city, county and state officials occurs in regard to policy decision making, familial based tight coupling thrives among those same political figures who are making policy decisions.

While particular validity and generalizability limitations exist within this research, overall there has been very little research surrounding local-level jail overcrowding within large urban settings. Recent criminological literature positing explanations of the prison boom, imprisonment epidemic and incarceration binge has ignored the role that local-level criminal justice actors and politicians have played in the penal expansion movement.[4] As Wacquant argues, a major contributor to the growth of correctional systems in America was not only the volume of persons arrested by the police but also the "vastly enlarged role of the jail as a frontline dam of social disorders in cities."[5] Due to generalizability issues many researchers within the field of criminal justice have shied away from conducting extensive studies of county-level jails and jail facilities. Granted, access to local-level correctional facilities for research purposes can be quite challenging. Coupled with access issues, it appears the perspective of many criminal justice researchers seems to be that if there are generalizability challenges the subject matter does not rise to the level of further investigation. I would argue that the overt focus on generalizability by many in the social sciences has served to limit our understanding of these important public institutions. Each and every individual incarcerated within state penitentiary systems has passed through local-level jail incarceration. Research that expands our understanding of this criminal justice decision point and the unique nature of local-level incarceration has been sorely lacking within the criminological literature. In addition, the examination of interaction between the consent decree disputants that shapes local-level incarceration within Cook County has the capacity to provide insight for other urban jurisdictions that are currently facing overcrowding problems or that will face overcrowding problems in the future. Decisions by researchers to generally ignore the role of the jail or relegate jail findings as case study research of little value is tantamount to throwing out the baby with the bathwater.

While generalizability of this research across other jurisdictions is somewhat limited considering the unique nature of local-level politics, as well as jail population size variation, there are points of reference that can be applied in regard to the frames emanating from this research. For example, much of the previous overcrowding literature provides a narrative of the consent decree process whereby a wise sage within the federal judiciary serves as a protagonist in delivering a just incarceration process to an unjust local or state criminal justice system. Certainly this perspective of judicial activism was pronounced within the era when the southern plantation model of prisonization was dismantled through federal judicial decision making.[6] Yet, judicial activism is far from the reality emanating from the dominant frames produced within the Cook County consent decree process between 1993 and 2003. In addition, the other polemic within the overcrowding literature is that of an overt governmental cabal whereby the rights of the incarcerated are being further limited through legislative decision making such as the Prisoner Reform Litigation Act (1995) and legal rulings initiating a flexible standard of review in requests to modify consent decrees as outlined in *Rufo v. Inmates of the Suffolk County Jail* (1992).[7] While the proverbial pendulum swing toward a traditional view of the judiciary as dispute resolvers has affected specific jurisdictions, this is not entirely the case within Cook County. Instead what we have seen develop in Cook County is a conciliatory style of judicial decision making that has manifestly veered away from either of the polemics of reform or retreat. What continued federal judicial involvement has achieved seems to be more akin to an investment with a limited long-term positive return.

Regardless of these limitations, the data and analysis presented within this research provide an avenue of understanding how claims are framed by the consent decree disputants within formal court procedures and the media. In addition, a further understanding as to how these claims influence which frames become emergent, dominant and residual is revealed. Through this frame analysis a more advanced understanding of the complexity surrounding loose coupling and net-widening within a large urban criminal justice system is exposed. Finally, and arguably most important, the social reality of local-level jail incarceration within an overcrowded system is displayed and analyzed as changes under the mantra of reform were implemented over time.

RECENT DEVELOPMENTS AT CCDOC AND THE CONSENT DECREE DISPUTE

Within recent years CCDOC continues to change as emergent and residual frames rise and fall by the wayside. Across the parameters of conditions within CCDOC, population and space and expansion within the community, the jail consent decree dispute continues. During 2009, the average daily population within CCDOC was 9,043 inmates within an institution consisting of 9,884 available beds.[8] While classification issues can exacerbate bed availability within particular divisions the average overflow population during this time period was limited to sixteen inmates. In 2002, the average daily population within CCDOC was over 11,000 inmates with an overflow population of over 1,400 inmates. In general, the extent of overcrowding and institutional growth has dissipated in recent years. In addition and correlated, the number of jail admissions has fallen. Between 2001 and 2005 the average number of CCDOC booking admissions averaged over 101,000 per year. By 2009, the annual admissions were 86,067 new inmates.

In other words, forty-one fewer citizens were entering the jail on a daily basis in 2009 than entered the institution between 2001 and 2005. As beds remain available, due to lower admission and daily population numbers, the opportunity for the CCDOC to expand the scale of renovation projects within its facilities occurred.[9]

An overview of recent changes in jail conditions revealed generally positive incremental changes across the areas of environmental health, physical health and inmate services. According to the 2010 John Howard Association Monitoring Report, over 96 percent of cells remained available for use with fewer cells being closed for renovation and repair.[10] In addition, due to efforts by the Cook County Department of Facilities Management the "ceaseless damage" to CCDOC facilities had been stemmed by administrators and tradesmen.[11] Much of the proactive renovation and maintenance can be attributed to opportunities presented by lower inmate population levels between 2009 and 2011.

Yet, problems associated with overcrowding within specific jail divisions continue. Particularly problematic locations include Division XI, the Cermak Health Services division, and dormitory four within Division II. During 2007 and 2008 the lack of beds within Division XI was addressed through a method of shared beds whereby a small number of inmates slept in shifts. This approach to shared beds and shift sleeping known at CCDOC as hot-bunking is analogous to the approach the United States Navy has employed upon vessels at sea, which military personnel refer to as hot-racking. In addition small numbers of specific inmates within Division XI were also being housed outside the CCDOC facilities within nearby Kankakee and Jefferson County jails. These two particular approaches within Division XI dissipated as the number of inmates declined within the division.

Table Conclusion.1. Cook County Department of Corrections Annual Admissions/Bookings between 2004 and 2009

	Year	Month	Day
2004	105,641	8803.4	288.6
2005	101,112	8426.0	277.0
2006	99,109	8259.1	271.5
2007	96,737	8061.4	265.0
2008	92,031	7669.3	251.5
2009	86,067	7172.3	235.8

(John Howard Association, 2010:13)

Within Cermak Health Services, there are routinely a small number of inmates that exceed the number of available beds.[12] Yet, as in previous monitoring reports the conclusion to this ongoing problem is that the classification needs of physical and mental health trump the inmates' need for an assigned bed. In general, the overcrowded conditions within Cermak Health Services were found to be short-lived for any particular inmate as once individuals are medically stabilized they are soon transferred to divisions with assigned beds.[13]

More problematic then the short-lived issues in Division XI and Cermak Health Services are the issues within dormitory four of Division II. This area has been retrofitted from an old kitchen and a planned 300-person capacity dormitory to a 600-person capacity dormitory with the installation of bunk beds.[14] This area of warehoused low-level felons within an open dormitory poses specific challenges for the residents assigned, as well as the correctional officers working within the facility. Inmates and security staff have provided the court monitor with dozens of complaints regarding this particular dormitory.[15] In particular, due to staff shortages, inmates are receiving limited time outside of the overcrowded dormitory setting. In addition, staff shortages lead toward cross-watching by correctional officers. These types of security issues can become especially problematic in an open-dormitory setting whereby inmates have freedom of movement and limited supervision. The John Howard Association, while acknowledging recent increases in correctional officers at CCDOC, argued that without an increase of 542 new correctional officer positions, addressing the crowding problems within Division II would be difficult.[16]

Physical health parameters including food service, health care and personal hygiene issues were a large area of concentration for the consent decree disputants between 1993 and 2003. In recent years, frames surrounding food service complaints and personal hygiene have remained as residual frames of contestation. In fact, recent court monitor reports have referred to CCDOC staff as vigilant in providing personal hygiene items and upgrading mattresses and clothing items.[17] Remaining problems regarding personal hygiene frames have been attributed to inmate vandalism and individuals entering from the street to the receiving areas with infestations of lice and crabs.[18] Food service issue complaints have been minor. Most problematic and being thrust forward as a dominant frame have been issues associated with health care. Complaints regarding delayed medication rounds, accessibility and completeness of medical records to physicians, and difficulty seeing nurses and specialists by inmates are numerous.[19] In essence, while jail administrators and correctional officers have limited the number of complaints in transporting inmates to sick call, once inmates arrive at sick call the services they receive or do not receive are now the issues of complaint.

Frames of dispute regarding inmate services within the specific areas of law library visitation, inmate discipline and inmate grievance procedures have all vacillated between the emergent, dominant and residual frames of argument within previous years. In recent years, the area of law library visitation remains a focus of concern for the primary claims-makers within the consent decree. Specifically, the court monitors are concerned with a failure to retain a minimum level of law library visitation completion rate of 70 percent to 80 percent overall. While the maximum security divisions are many times meeting or exceeding these completion rates, over the past few years other divisions are mired in completion rates hovering at the 50 percent to 60 percent level.[20] This continues to be a violation of the consent decree.

Inmate disciplinary procedures are currently in compliance with the consent decree. According to the JHA during 2009, very few inmates have been held in segregation in violation of the consent decree, there were no complaints by inmates of untimely disciplinary hearings, inmates with psychiatric problems were being treated as nondisciplinary problems, and adjudications and injuries were on the decline.[21] In general, while the JHA continues to argue that inmates should receive copies of institutional rules sooner when entering the institution, this particular area has remained as a residual frame in recent years.

Frames regarding inmate grievances, in particular grievances associated with health care, have moved into the area of dominance in recent years. While the court monitor has applauded inmate utilization of the grievance process the context of recent grievances is revealing. Over 2,700 grievances were submitted by inmates during 2009. More than half (54.8 percent) of these grievances were related to medical treatment and complaints of unprofessional staff conduct by medical personnel.[22] Grievances regarding verbal and physical abuse initiated by security personnel during this same time period accounted for just over 10 percent of the complaints filed. Medical treatment and verbal disrespect by medical personnel grievances have accounted for the vast majority of inmate grievances between 2005 and 2009.[23]

Length of stay for inmates within CCDOC has also fluctuated within recent years. Overall, between 2003 and 2009 the length of stay for inmates has been reduced by more than fifty days. In May of 2003, the average length of stay was just over 216 days and by September of 2009 the length of stay had been reduced to just over 163 days.[24] In particular, this length of stay reduction has been most attributable to male inmates charged with less serious crimes. The length of stay for female inmates has increased slightly to about four and a half months and male inmates within the maximum security divisions length of stay has remained consistent at just over eleven months. As stated in previous discussions of length of stay within chapter 4, it is important to note that the average length for all inmates is inflated by the extended length of stay of individuals housed within the maximum security divisions. In addition, these averages do not include individuals booked who are released within one to two weeks after initial admission.

Alternative release mechanisms, which expanded during the late 1990s and early 2000s and were a large part of the dominant frames produced between 1993 and 2003, continue to be utilized, albeit less frequently. In addition, the Cook County judiciary has expanded its role in taking responsibility for court-ordered electronic monitoring and day reporting release.[25] This increased responsibility and lower jail admissions are somewhat attributable to the lowering usage of the Department of Community Supervision and Intervention programs of electronic monitoring and day reporting for male detainees. The CCDCSI electronic monitoring caseload has been reduced by more than 80 percent, from over 1,500 daily participants to 250 participants between 2003 and 2009. The CCDCSI day reporting caseload has been reduced by over 80 percent, from 485 daily participants to just over 150 participants during the same time period. Finally, the custodial Pre-Release Center has increased its caseload by over 30 percent to include a daily average of almost 450 inmates addressing drug and alcohol addiction problems in the incarcerated setting.[26]

The Department of Women's Justice Services has remained quite consistent in recent years in regard to program population totals. The Sheriff's Female Furlough Program, the rough equivalent of the male-based Day Reporting Program, continues to serve just over 100 individuals daily.[27] The Women's Justice Services Residential program, the equivalent of the male-based Pre-Release Center, has increased its capacity from 130 to 160 beds and in 2009 recorded a daily average population of 145 participants.[28]

One absolute change that has occurred as a result of the consent decree dispute process and the development of custodial and noncustodial release mechanisms initiated by the Sheriff's Office and CCDCSI is the exclusion of the use of unsupervised release by the executive branch of government within Cook County. In 1989, the Cook County Sheriff's Office issued 35,327 recognizance bonds to inmates admitted to the Cook County Jail. In 2005, after sixteen years of unprecedented growth, taxpayer dollars, building projects, political gamesmanship, mediation and conciliation, the Cook County Sheriff's Office issued its last I-bond.

THE FUTURE AND THE JAIL

Within recent years Cook County Jail admissions have been reduced, length of stay for some inmates has been reduced, overcrowding has been limited and overall conditions have continued to improve incrementally. The Department of Community Supervision and Intervention has been largely supplanted by a more tightly coupled Cook County justice system whereby the local judiciary has taken responsibility for noncustodial supervision which it had neglected to address in previous years.

In addition, while not fully embracing a public health perspective, the Cook County Sheriff's Office has acknowledged and worked to ameliorate specific problems associated with the physical and mental health challenges of the inmate population. Specific examples of compartmentalizing inmates with mental illness issues from disciplinary action connotes a positive trajectory in the service of a complex inmate population. A general acceptance of social scientific research findings associated with co-occurrence of mental health and addiction, psychiatric treatment needs, and their relationship to recidivism within particular populations is openly acknowledged by executive-level leaders within local corrections.[29] At the same time, inmate grievances related to health care and health-care services are problematic. Considering that the CCDOC is essentially a frontline public health provider for the specific geographies contributing the most to the jail population, failure within this area contributes to the overall decline of citizen health across the poorest neighborhoods in Chicago and Cook County. As the consent decree disputants grapple with these particular issues it seems apparent that a targeted approach linking community-based physical and mental health programming with city, county and state public health systems and the county criminal justice system as a continuum of service is essential.[30] Reliance on previous incarnations of community corrections initiatives without an expanded health-care component will produce limited success and continued failures for specific populations. Problematic with this venture is the desire of city of Chicago and state of Illinois public health agencies to include themselves within the necessary expansion of community-based health initiatives during a time of financial crisis and recession.[31]

Recent literature focusing upon the role of our current national economic crisis, its relation to our extremely high national incarceration rate, and the prison industry have led researchers to explore the perspectives of decarceration as an economic necessity and a silver lining to the recession.[32] While it is true that numerous states have been focusing on successfully limiting their incarcerated populations and lowering correctional costs as a newly realized fiduciary responsibility, it is not clear that the punitive ideology that helped established this industry will wane quickly. In fact, the local-level jail incarceration rate may actually begin a new resurgence as a result of the economic recession. Within California, a new focus on addressing unsustainable prison populations has led toward a state-level initiative of realignment whereby state prisoners are being relocated to their home counties to serve their remaining prison sentences.[33] This form of trickle-down incarceration will disproportionately transform local-level corrections within urban geographies in California.

The California initiative is being watched from a distance by other states grappling with similar financial shortfalls. Previous state of Illinois decision making in 2000 regarding parolees ignored local-level consequences related to their decision making and state prisoners.[34] If and when policies of correctional realignment are raised in Illinois, the dynamics of the consent decree will change once again. This type of approach while lowering prison-level populations will inevitably increase urban jail populations and increase the proportion of sentenced offenders within urban jails.

CONCLUSION

The primary contributions of this research are twofold. First, the research methodology applied within this analysis provided an opportunity to examine the disputing process within a loosely coupled criminal justice system. Moving beyond a purely descriptive approach to jail overcrowding, frame analysis of the consent decree dispute process unmasked the complexities of incarceration policy and subsequent organizational change that would otherwise be hidden from public view. As Smith argues in his analysis of overcrowding research, descriptive case studies become analytical as they investigate the day-to-day contextual changes and experiences prior to and as reform decisions are absorbed.[35] It is within this perspective that frame analysis of court documents is an important addition to criminological research methods. As frame analysis captures the emergent, dominant and residual frames, over time we can begin to analyze the structural-functional changes that are occurring and not occurring within organizations. In the case of analyzing overcrowded penal institutions, this methodological approach allows the researcher to move beyond an overt focus on the judicial role and instead begin to address larger issues revolving around organizational change, administrative, bureaucratic, and political control.

While qualitative frame analysis does not lead toward direct numerical interpretation, the application of this methodological approach provides the capacity for interpretive analysis and further theory building within the public policy arena of crime and justice. Areas of adversarial contest within federal, state and local jurisdictions produce a plethora of court documents across a wide variety of rights-based issues whereby analysis using this method would be fruitful. Recent examples of adversarial contest include terrorism and torture policies and programs, contested election results, and racial profiling cases. Frame analysis as a method provides an opportunity for analytic social scientific inquiry into some of our most pressing social problems, how those problems are discussed and how they are not discussed within the legal and public sphere.

Between 1993 and 2003 the federal judiciary overseeing the *Duran* consent decree attempted to provide pragmatic guidance while reacting to specific crisis situations. It is within this context that particular emerging frames became dominant frames. As crises occurred, solutions that fit within a perspective of acceptance, at least to some degree, by all of the claims-makers were adopted and steered toward dominance by a conciliatory federal judiciary. The result of this pragmatic style of leadership by the federal judiciary created incremental improvements in regard to conditions of confinement across a larger and larger inmate population. Similar to Welsh's jail analysis, none of the disputants were completely happy with the results of these incremental improvements.[36]

A further result of this approach was the functional growth and importance of the disputants within the broader Cook County governmental system. The active consent decree process provided political and budgetary leverage for the Cook County Sheriff's Office within the overall finite county budget system. Solutions deemed appropriate by the consent decree disputants, solutions which then became dominant frames within the dispute, drew larger portions of Cook County's political and financial capital throughout the ten-year period of this research. In addition to building and program funding, the John Howard Association and the plaintiffs' attorneys continued to submit billable hours as they fulfilled their functional roles within the disputing process. From a public policy perspective, the counterfactual to these developments may have been a better use of taxpayer funds and political energy.

NOTES

1. Bleich, "Politics of Prison Crowding," 1133 (see chap. 1, n. 87); Welsh, *Counties In Court*, 73–85 (see intro. n. 2).

2. Kleiman, *When Brute Force Fails*, 181–82 (see intro., n. 68).

3. Goffman, *Frame Analysis*, 201 (see intro., n. 39).

4. Marie Gottschalk, "Money and Mass Incarceration: The Bad, the Mad, and Penal Reform," *Criminology and Public Policy* 8, no. 1, (2009); William Spelman, "Crime, Cash and Limited Options: Explaining the Prison Boom," *Criminology and Public Policy* 8, no. 1, (2009).

5. Wacquant, "Class, Race and Hyperincarceration," 75 (see chap. 6, n. 36).

6. Feeley and Rubin, *Judicial Policymaking*, 367 (see intro., n. 2).

7. Palmer, *Constitutional Rights of Prisoners*, 389–410 (see chap. 1, n. 26); Rufo v. Inmates of the Suffolk County Jail, 502 U.S. 367 (1992).

8. John Howard Association, *Court monitoring report for Duran v. Brown et al. 74C 2949 Crowding and conditions of confinement at the Cook County Department of Corrections and compliance with the consent decree* (Chicago, 2010): 3.

9. John Howard Association, *Court Monitoring Report*, 2010, 45.

10. John Howard Association, *Court Monitoring Report*, 2010, 43.

11. John Howard Association, *Court Monitoring Report*, 2010, 45.

12. John Howard Association, *Court Monitoring Report*, 2010, 66.

13. John Howard Association, *Court Monitoring Report*, 2010, 66.

14. John Howard Association, *Court Monitoring Report*, 2010, 67.

15. John Howard Association, *Court Monitoring Report*, 2010, 67.

16. John Howard Association, *Court Monitoring Report*, 2010, 64.
17. John Howard Association, *Court Monitoring Report*, 2010, 54.
18. John Howard Association, *Court Monitoring Report*, 2010, 56.
19. John Howard Association, *Court Monitoring Report*, 2010, 76.
20. John Howard Association, *Court Monitoring Report*, 2010, 69.
21. John Howard Association, *Court Monitoring Report*, 2010, 86–92.
22. John Howard Association, *Court Monitoring Report*, 2010, 79.
23. John Howard Association, *Court Monitoring Report*, 2010, 82.
24. John Howard Association, *Court Monitoring Report*, 2010, 16.
25. John Howard Association, *Court Monitoring Report*, 2010, 41–42.
26. John Howard Association, *Court Monitoring Report*, 2010, 39.
27. John Howard Association, *Court Monitoring Report*, 2010, 21.
28. John Howard Association, *Court Monitoring Report*, 2010, 32.
29. Bridget O'Shea, "Psychiatric Patients with no Place to go but Jail," *New York Times,* February 18, 2012, http://www.nytimes.com/2012/02/19/health/in-chicago-mental-health-patients-have-no-place-to-go-html.
30. Arthur Lurigio, "MCJA Keynote Address: Responding to the Needs of People with Mental Illness in the Criminal Justice System: An Area Ripe for Research and Community Partnerships," *Journal of Crime and Justice* 35, no. 1 (2012): 9–10.
31. Bridget O'Shea, "Psychiatric Patients with no Place to go but Jail."
32. Marie Gottschalk, "Cell Blocks and Red Ink: Mass Incarceration, the Great Recession and Penal Reform," *Daedalus* 139, no. 3 (2010); Jonathan Simon. "Clearing the "Troubled Assets" of America's Punishment Bubble," *Daedalus* 139, no. 3 (2010); Christian Henrichson and Ruth Delaney. "The Price of Prisons; What Incarceration Costs Taxpayers," Vera Institute of Justice, (2012).
33. The impetus for California's realignment policy was the Supreme Court decision ruling the California prison system as unconstitutional under the 8th Amendment to the United States Constitution. See Brown v. Plata, 563 U.S. 131 (2011).
34. Cook County Board Report (see chap. 3, n. 39).
35. Smith, "Prison reform Litigation Era," 355 (see chap. 1, n. 46).
36. Welsh, *Counties in Court*, 206–11.

Appendix

Additional Methodological Notes

Reliability of the stakeholder textual analysis was strengthened through independent corroborative techniques. In addition, reliability of the stakeholder textual analysis was enhanced through detailed excerpts from the source data. Independent corroborative techniques consisted of the use of non-content analytic source material garnered from the wider justice and punishment literature related to incarceration in prisons and jails.[1] In addition, multiple independent examples for interpretations of dominant, emergent, and residual frames from the official source text were identified and included in the analysis.

Within the stakeholder data analysis face validity was established through the use of primary source documents which capture important social issues not readily available to the general public or for that matter the criminological research community. Rather than only using news media representations of the jail overcrowding dispute, the integration of source material provided closeness to the specific discourse surrounding the dispute. Content validity was established and strengthened through semantic validation. Semantic validation uses primary source quotations to verify interpretations made within the analysis. Semantic validity is considered to be allied largely with qualitative discourse analysis.[2] In addition, concurrent criterion-related validity was strengthened through the use of primary source material which represents the dominant, emergent and residual frames articulated throughout the ten years of data. The text presented within the source documents serve as an illustration of the particular frames of discourse as they have occurred in time throughout the ten year period of the dispute.

Reliability or coding stability within the media analysis was achieved by establishing a pilot test of coding across a small sample of the data population. Through a pilot test of the coding, instrument accuracy was evaluated. Inter-rater reliability measures were applied to the coding scheme. Through multiple observers who were trained to use the signature matrix/table of jail overcrowding issue packages, consistency of judgment was ascertained.[3] As Boyatzis argues, "Consistency of judgment among viewers is dependent on the access of the multiple coders to the raw information."[4] Two different graduate students were trained separately on the use of the coding scheme and jail overcrowding signature matrix. These graduate students then coded the same raw data excerpts (newsprint articles) randomly selected from the media data.

The two independent scorers applied presence and absence coding in regard to the four punishment packages stipulated within the jail signature matrix. Agreement between the independent coders was measured using the agreement coefficients of Scott's pi and Cohen's Kappa. Both of these inter-rater reliability measures are specific for categorical data whereby the percentage-of-agreement measure corrects for chance or random agreement.[5] These measures have been found to be appropriate in previous reliability testing of thematic and content analysis methods at the manifest level.[6] While the percentage agreement between the two coders revealed a score of .75, the more precise agreement coefficients revealed a Scott's pi score of .66 and a Cohen's Kappa of .67.

In addition to measuring consistency among viewers through the use of multiple observers, consistency over time was realized using a test — retest method. In essence, the multiple coders originally used for inter-rater reliability recoded the pretest raw data at a later date. Coefficients ranged between .65 and .66 on the Scott's pi score and .66 and .67 on the Cohen's Kappa score. The results of synchronic (inter-rater) as well as diachronic (test-retest) methods of reliability testing verify the efficacy of the coding scheme.

Within the media content analysis, face validity, construct validity, as well as criterion-related validity were strengthened through the implementation of a signature matrix that was adapted from previous research concerning ideological concepts of punishment.[7] Content validity of categories in implicit concept analysis, in particular, was achieved by using multiple classifiers documented within the signature matrix. Multiple catchphrases were searched for within the media data that are conceptually linked to the differing packages. For example, the root causes of arrest and incarceration package were coded from narratives that focus upon mental illness, as well as drug dependency and poverty. These classifiers provide a comprehensive representation of the theoretical tenets of incarceration. Using multiple classifiers, the concept categories were broadened to include differing linguistic word choices which are implicit of the ideological concepts.

In regard to external validity, it is imperative that one defines categories that accurately measure the specific ideas and behaviors or in this particular case the specific ideology. The use and strict adherence to a systematic and exhaustive coding scheme is essential for the replication of future research using this data as well as similar data in different settings.

Capturing individual-level and organizational-level interaction within the ongoing Cook County Jail dispute as related through textual communications emanating from the *Duran v. Sheahan* federal consent decree provided an opportunity to examine assumptions associated with incarcerated populations. How these themes and frames are discussed and not discussed within the jail dispute provided a narrative of promoted meaning by the differing disputants. As these narratives competed for preeminence the complexity of the social problem surrounding expanding incarceration at the local level was revealed. In addition, the data fully exposed a significant and ongoing public policy problem and its relation to a loosely coupled criminal justice system.

Strengths and Limitations

Basic strengths of a content analysis methodology are well documented within the literature.[8] Specific to this data, strengths include the ability to use a large amount of public records to assess the events and processes revolving around jail overcrowding and conditions of confinement within Cook County. Content analysis as an unobtrusive research method is a further strength within an ongoing consent decree whereby litigants are reluctant to provide interviews. In addition, content analysis can provide valuable historical/cultural insight into the process of incarceration in a large urban jail setting. This method allowed closeness to specific texts which can alternate between specific categories and relationships. Finally, this methodology was used to systematically examine texts for purposes of interpreting complex criminal justice systems, complex organizational thought processes and language within public decision-making territories not readily available to the general public.

Limitations of content analysis methodologies are also well documented within the social science literature.[9] Limitations include:

1. Causal inference between variables cannot be interpreted with this method.
2. Latent interpretations of text are subject to human error.
3. Content analysis is inherently reductive in nature.
4. Content analysis has the capacity to disregard the context that produced the text.

A specific limitation to this particular study was that a mixed methodological plan including intensive interviews and ethnographic field observations was not possible. These methods were unavailable to the researcher due to the fact that the *Duran v. Sheahan* consent decree is an ongoing federal court case. Any new data garnered through interviews and observations may be considered evidentiary by the judiciary. This being the case, disputants were apprehensive and precluded from making statements concerning jail conditions and overcrowding outside of the parameters of the federal court procedure.

Table Appendix. 1. Signature Jail Matrix

Package	Frame	Position
Order and Control	The issue is how to provide order, safety, control and respect for authority within the institution for all individuals incarcerated, working within and visiting the institution.	Failure to respect authority, law and order create dangerous circumstances for all those who live, work and reside within the institution.
Rights of the Accused	The issue is how to address the rights of the accused under the mantra of due process and civil rights.	The overt control within the institution violates individual civil rights for those who are innocent until proven guilty.
Root Causes of Arrest and Incarceration	The issue is social stratification and its relation to those individuals who are arrested and incarcerated.	The incarcerated population is largely the consequence of social conditions such as poverty, drug dependency, joblessness and mental illness.
Community Pursuit of Justice and Balanced Needs	The issue is the relationship between the community and the individuals who become incarcerated, those individuals imminent return to the community, victims' rights and restoration.	Incarcerated individuals need to maintain ties to their communities and families while addressing the reasons they entered into the criminal justice system.

Package	Exemplars	Catchphrases
Order and Control	Stories, incidents and data concerning individuals who violate authority and control thereby creating public and institutional safety problems.	Crime control. Public and institutional safety. Dangerous criminals and offenders. Gangs and gang members. Accountability to the public. Risk of flight. Violent histories.
Rights of the Accused	Stories, incidents and data in which the rights of the accused are violated.	Constitutional rights. Innocent until proven guilty. Charged with a crime. Defendant. Predicting failure to appear. Speedy trial. Due process. Democracy and democratic system. Civil rights.
Root Causes of Arrest and Incarceration	Stories, incidents and data focusing on the need to address social stratification problems and issues within the incarcerated population.	Drug dependent. Joblessness. Homelessness. Mental Illness. Poverty. Lack of opportunity. War on crime, poverty and drugs. Racism.
Community Pursuit of	Stories, incidents and data focusing on the relationship	Restoration. Balanced response. Pragmatism. Victim and

Justice and Balanced Needs	between the community and those individuals incarcerated and under the control of the criminal justice system	community needs. Participants and clients. Support systems outside the institution. Intervention and supervision. Therapeutic justice.	

Package	Depictions	Roots	Principles
Order and Control	Individuals at the CCDOC are dangerous criminals in need of surveillance. These inmates must be deterred from victimizing others in the community.	The root of the problem is the action of criminals. These individuals need to be processed through a justice system based on a crime control model. Approaches that attempt to justify criminal actions should be disparaged. Control and authority must be strong to provide specific deterrence to the individuals incarcerated at CCDOC and general deterrence to citizens in the community.	Respect for authority and fear of punishment are the basis of a correctional institution. Individuals must be held accountable for their actions.
Rights of the Accused	Individuals at CCDOC are accused defendants with constitutional rights who are many times victimized by the system and the individuals who work within the system in regards to their civil rights.	The root of the problem is a justice system that does not provide effective due process to the accused. A continued focus on civil liberties within correctional institutions and insurance to the accused that their rights will be addressed as they proceed through the system as a defendant.	Constitutional guarantees regarding due process and protection of the rights of the accused and incarcerated should be our most important consideration.
Root Causes of Arrest and Incarcerati on	Individuals at CCDOC are oppressed minorities who lack opportunity in mainstream capitalist society. As such, these individuals are	The root of the problem is social structural inequality within society and the criminalization of the	As a society or a government institution we have an obligation to

	sequestered within a criminal justice industry that fights symbolic wars on drugs crime and order.	underclass.	attack poverty, racism and structural inequality rather than punish its victims.
Community Pursuit of Justice and Balanced Needs	Individuals at CCDOC are clients and participants within a social service network that needs to identify and address problematic behaviors in an effort to create reparation between victims in the community and the client/ participant. Retaining community based ties between the accused and the community is essential.	The root of the problem is a lack of community and the inability of the criminal justice system to enhance community. Restoration and reparation through community linkage and acknowledgement of harm will provide balance and justice.	Maintaining a peaceful society requires acknowledgement of harm done by all parties through reparation, healing and restoration.

NOTES

1. Bruce Berg, *Qualitative Research Methods for the Social Sciences*, (Boston, MA: Allyn and Bacon, 1995): 176.

2. Klaus Krippendorf, *Content Analysis: An Introduction to its Methodology*, (Thousand Oaks, CA: Sage, 2004): 323–30.

3. Graduate students from the Department of Criminal Justice at Chicago State University were trained in the use of the signature jail matrix.

4. Richard Boyatzis, *Transforming Qualitative Information: Thematic Analysis and Code Development*, (Thousand Oaks, CA: Sage, 1998): 147.

5. Neuendorf, *Content Analysis Guidebook*, 154–55 (see intro., n. 59); Paul Vogt, *Dictionary of Statistics and Methodology*, (Thousand Oaks, CA: Sage, 1999): 44.

6. Shadd Maruna, *Making Good: How Ex-Convicts Reform and Rebuild Their Lives*, (Washington, DC: American Psychological Association, 2001): 170; Nuendorf, *Content Analysis*, 154.

7. Beckett, *Making Crime Pay*, 68–71 (see intro., n.43).

8. Berg, 1995; Neuendorf, 2002.

9. Berg, *Qualitative Research*, 193–95; Nuendorf, *Content Analysis*, 2002.

Bibliography

"A Sign of Hope at Cook County Jail," *Chicago Tribune,* September 27, 1993, sec A14.

Altheide, David. *Qualitative Media Analysis.* Thousand Oaks, CA: Sage, 1996.

Anderson, Lloyd. *Voices From a Southern Prison.* Athens, GA: University of Georgia Press, 2000.

Arrigo, Bruce and Dragon Milovanovic. *Revolution in Penology: Rethinking the Society of Captives.* Lanham, MD: Rowman & Littlefield Press, 2009.

Atterbury v. Ragen, 237 F.2d 953 (7th Cir. 1956).

Austin, James and Barry Krisberg. "NCCD Research Review: Wider, Stronger, and Different Nets: the Dialectics of Criminal Justice Reform," *Journal of Research in Crime and Delinquency* 18, (1981): 165–96.

Austin, James, Barry Krisberg and Paul Litsky. "Effectiveness of Supervised Pretrial Release," *Crime and Delinquency* 31, no.4 (1985): 519–37.

Backstrand, John, Don Gibbons, and Joseph Jones. "Who is in Jail? An Examination of the Rabble Hypothesis." *Crime and Delinquency* 38, no. 2 (1992): 219–29.

Baumer, Terry. "Reducing Lockup Crowding with Expedited Initial Processing of Minor Offenders." *Journal of Criminal Justice* 35, (2007): 273–81.

Baumer, Terry, and Kenneth Adams. "Controlling a Jail Population by Partially Closing the Front Door: An Evaluation of a 'summons in lieu of arrest' policy." *The Prison Journal* 86, no. 3 (2006): 386–402.

Beck, Allen. *Jail Population Growth: Sources of Growth and Stability.* Washington, DC: U.S. Department of Justice, Bureau of Justice Statistics, 2003.

Becker, Robert. "County's Politicians Make Bickering Their Way of Life." *Chicago Tribune,* November 2, 1999, sec B1.

Beckett, Katherine. "Media Depictions of Drug Abuse: The Impact of Official Sources." *Research in Political Sociology* 7, (1995):161–82.

Beckett, Katherine. *Making Crime Pay: Law and Order in Contemporary American Politics.* New York: Oxford University Press, 1997.

Beckett, Katherine, and Theodore Sasson. *The Politics of Injustice: Crime and Punishment in America.* Thousand Oaks, CA: Pine Forge Press, 2000.

Beckett, Katherine, and Bruce Western. "Governing Social Marginality: Welfare, Incarceration, and the Transformation of State Policy." *Punishment and Society* 3, (2001): 43–59.

Berg, Bruce. *Qualitative Research Methods for the Social Sciences.* Boston: Allyn and Bacon, 1995.

Best, Joel. "'Road Warriors' on 'Hair–Trigger Highways' cultural resources and media construction of the 1987 freeway shooting problem." *Sociological Inquiry* 61, no. 3 (1991): 327–45.

Best, Joel. "Constructionism in Context." In *Images of Issues* 2nd Ed., edited by Joel Best, 337–54. New York: Aldine DeGruyeter, 1995.

Best, Joel and Mary Hutchinson. "The Gang Initiation Rite as a Motif in Contemporary Crime Discourse." *Justice Quarterly* 13, no. 3 (1996): 383–404.

Bleich, Jeff. "The Politics of Prison Crowding." *California Law Review* 77, (1989): 1125–80.

Blumstein, Alfred, and Joel Wallman. *The Crime Drop in America.* New York: Cambridge Press, 2000.

Boyatzis, Richard. *Thematic Analysis and Code Development: Transforming Qualitative Information.* Thousand Oaks CA: Sage, 1998.

Brown v. Allen, 344 U.S. 443 (1953).

Brown v. Board of Education, 347 U.S. 483 (1954).

Brown v. Plata, 563 U.S. 131 (2011).

Bursik, Robert and Harold Grasmick. *Neighborhoods and Crime: The Dimensions of Effective Community Control*. San Francisco, CA: Lexington Books, 1993.

Byrne, James and Don Hummer. "The Nature and Extent of Prison Violence." In *The Culture of Prison Violence*, edited by James Byrne, Don Hummer, and Faye Taxman, 12–25. Boston: Pearson Publishing, 2008.

Cadigan, Timothy. "Electronic Monitoring in Federal Pretrial Release," *Federal Probation* 55, (1991): 26–30.

Carroll, Leo. *Lawful Order: A Case Study of Correctional Crises and Reform*. New York: Garland Press, 1998.

Center for Urban Research and Learning and The Human Relations Foundation/Jane Addams Policy Initiative, "*Minding the Gap: An Assessment of Racial Disparity in Metropolitan Chicago*" Center for Urban Research and Learning Publications and Other Works Paper 16. http://ecommons.luc.edu/curl_pubs/162011.

Center on Sentencing and Corrections, "Los Angeles County Jail: Overcrowding Reduction Project, Final Report: Revised," New York, NY: Vera Institute of Justice, September 2011.

Chermak, Steven. "The Presentation of Drugs in the News Media: The News Sources Involved in the Construction of Social Problems." *Justice Quarterly* 14, no. 4. (1997): 687–718.

Chermak, Steven. *Searching for a Demon: The Media Construction of the Militia Movement*. Boston: Northeastern University Press, 2002.

Chermak, Steven and Edmund McGarrell. "Problem Solving Approaches to Homicide: An Evaluation of the Indianapolis Violence Reduction Partnership." *Criminal Justice Policy Review* 15, no. 2 (2004):161–204.

Chilton, Bradley. *Prisons Under the Gavel: The Federal Court Takeover of Georgia Prisons*. Columbus: Ohio State University, 1991.

Chilton, Bradley and Susette Talarico. "Politics and Constitutional Interpretation in Prison Reform Litigation: The Case of *Guthrie v. Evans*." In *Courts, Corrections and the Constitution*, edited by John Dilulio, 115–37. New York: Oxford University Press, 1990.

Clear, Todd and George Cole. *History of Corrections in America*. Belmont, CA: Wadsworth, 1997.

Clemmer, Donald. *The Prison Community*. New York: Holt, Rinehart and Winston, 1958.

Conlin, John. *Why Crime Rates Fell*. Boston: Allyn & Bacon, 2003.

Cook County Board Report of the Committee on Law Enforcement and Corrections, The Board of Commissioners of Cook County (Chicago, 2001).

Cook County Board Report of the Committee on Law Enforcement and Corrections, The Board of Commissioners of Cook County (Chicago, 2002).

Cook County Board Report of the Committee on Law Enforcement and Corrections, The Board of Commissioners of Cook County (Chicago, 2003).

Cook County Judiciary Advisory Council, *Analysis of Cook County Jail Crowding and Costs Caused by New State Parole Enforcement Procedures* (Chicago, 2001).

Cook County Sheriff's Office, "Press Release: Overcrowding May Force Jail Inmates into 'Tent City.'" Chicago, May 9, 2002.

Cook County Sheriff's Office, "Cook County Sheriff's Office 2004 Annual Budget," (Chicago, 2004).

Cooper v. Pate, 378 U.S. 546 (1964).

Cooprider, Keith and John Kerby. "Practical Application of Electronic Monitoring at the Pretrial Stage," *Federal Probation* 54, (1991): 28–35.

Craddock, Amy and Laura Graham. "Recidivism as a Function of Day Reporting Center Participation." *Journal of Offender Rehabilitation*, 34, (2001): 81–100.

Crouch, Ben and James Marquart. "*Ruiz*: Intervention and Emergent Order in Texas Prisons." In *Courts, Corrections and the Constitution,* edited by John Dilulio, 94–114. New York: Oxford University Press, 1990.

Cullen, Francis, John Wright, and Brandon Applegate. "Control in the Community: The Limits of Reform? " In *Choosing Correctional Interventions that Work: Defining the Demand and Evaluating the Supply,* edited by Alan Harland, 69–116. Newbury Park, CA: Sage Publications, 1996.

Cunniff, Mark. *Jail Crowding: Understanding Jail Population Dynamics.* Washington, DC: U.S. Department of Justice, National Institute of Corrections, 2002. NIC Publication No.017209.

Currie, Elliott. *Crime and Punishment in America.* New York: Holt Publishing, 1998.

Cushman, Robert. *Preventing Jail Crowding: A Practical Guide.* Washington, DC: U.S. Department of Justice, National Institute of Corrections, 2002. NIC Publication No. 016720.

D'Alessio, Stewart and Lisa Stolzenberg. "The Effect of Available Capacity on Jail Incarceration: An Empirical Test of Parkinson's Law." *Journal of Criminal Justice* 25, no.4 (1997): 279–88.

Darrow, Clarence. *Crime and Criminals: Address to the Prisoners in the Cook County Jail and Other Writings on Crime and Punishment.* Chicago, IL: Charles H. Kerr, 2000.

Davis, Robert, Brandon Applegate, Charles Otto, Ray Surette, and Bernard McCarthy. "Roles and Responsibilities: Analyzing Local Leaders' Views on Jail Crowding From a Systems Perspective." *Crime and Delinquency* 50, no3. (2004): 458–82.

Debs, Eugene. *Walls and Bars.* Montclair, NJ: Patterson Smith, 1973.

"Defendants' Status Report," in *the United States District Court for the Northern District of Illinois Eastern Division, Dan Duran, et al., Plaintiffs v. Michael F. Sheahan, Sheriff of Cook County, et al., Defendants. 74 C 2949, Judge George M. Marovich,* (1992).

"Defendants' Status Report," in *the United States District Court for the Northern District of Illinois Eastern Division, Dan Duran, et al., Plaintiffs v. Michael F. Sheahan, Sheriff of Cook County, et al., Defendants. 74 C 2949, Judge George M. Marovich,* (1993).

"Defendants' Status Report," in *the United States District Court for the Northern District of Illinois Eastern Division, Dan Duran, et al., Plaintiffs v. Michael F. Sheahan, Sheriff of Cook County, et al., Defendants. 74 C 2949, Judge George M. Marovich,* (1994).

"Defendants' Status Report," in *the United States District Court for the Northern District of Illinois Eastern Division, Dan Duran, et al., Plaintiffs v. Michael F. Sheahan, Sheriff of Cook County, et al., Defendants. 74 C 2949, Judge George M. Marovich,* (1995).

"Defendants' Status Report," in *the United States District Court for the Northern District of Illinois Eastern Division, Dan Duran, et al., Plaintiffs v. Michael F. Sheahan, Sheriff of Cook County, et al., Defendants. 74 C 2949, Judge George M. Marovich,* (1996).

"Defendants' Status Report," in *the United States District Court for the Northern District of Illinois Eastern Division, Dan Duran, et al., Plaintiffs v. Michael F. Sheahan, Sheriff of Cook County, et al., Defendants. 74 C 2949, Judge George M. Marovich,* (1997).

"Defendants' Status Report," in *the United States District Court for the Northern District of Illinois Eastern Division, Dan Duran, et al., Plaintiffs v. Michael F. Sheahan, Sheriff of Cook County, et al., Defendants. 74 C 2949, Judge George M. Marovich,* (1998).

"Defendants' Status Report," in *the United States District Court for the NorthernDistrict of Illinois Eastern Division, Dan Duran, et al., Plaintiffs v. Michael F. Sheahan, Sheriff of Cook County, et al., Defendants. 74 C 2949, Judge George M. Marovich,* (1999).

"Defendants' Status Report," in *the United States District Court for the Northern District of Illinois Eastern Division, Dan Duran, et al., Plaintiffs v. Michael F. Sheahan, Sheriff of Cook County, et al., Defendants. 74 C 2949, Judge George M. Marovich,* (2000).

"Defendants' Status Report," *In the United States District Court for the Northern District of Illinois Eastern Division, Dan Duran, et al., Plaintiffs v. Michael F. Sheahan, Sheriff of Cook County, et al., Defendants. 74 C 2949, Judge George M. Marovich,* (2001).

"Defendants' Status Report," in *the United States District Court for the Northern District of Illinois Eastern Division, Dan Duran, et al., Plaintiffs v. Michael F. Sheahan, Sheriff of Cook County, et al., Defendants. 74 C 2949, Judge George M. Marovich,* (2003).

"Defendants' Supplemental Status Report," in *the United States District Court for the Northern District of Illinois Eastern Division, Dan Duran, et al., Plaintiffs v. Michael F. Sheahan, Sheriff of Cook County, et al., Defendants. 74 C 2949, Judge George M. Marovich,* (1993).

Dilulio, John. "The Old Regime and the *Ruiz* Revolution: The Impact of Judicial Intervention on Prisons and Jails on Texas Prisons." In *Courts, Corrections and the Constitution,* edited by John Dilulio, 51–72. New York: Oxford University Press, 1990.

Duffee, David. *Explaining Criminal Justice: Community Theory and Criminal Justice Reform.* Cambridge, MA: Oelgeschlager, Gunn & Hain, 1980.

Duncombe, William and Jeffery Straussman. "Judicial Intervention and Local Spending." *Policy Studies Journal* 22, no. 4 (1994): 604–14.

Duran v. Sheahan et al., 74 C 2949, U. S. District Court, Northern District of Illinois.

Edelstein, Charles, John Case, Alvin Cohn, Norman Early Jr., George Gish, D. Alan Henry, Sterling Johnson Jr., Leon Leiberg and Joseph Trotter Jr. *An Assessment of the Felony Case Process in Cook County, Illinois and Its Impact on Jail Crowding.* Washington, DC: The American University, School of Public Affairs, 1989.

Eisenstein, James, Roy Fleming, and Peter Nardulli. *The Contours of Justice: Communities and Their Courts.* Lanham, MD: University Press of America, 1999.

Eisenstein, James and Herbert Jacob. *Felony Justice: An Organizational Analysis of the Criminal Courts.* Boston: Little Brown Company, 1977.

Ekland-Olson, Sheldon and Steve Martin. "Organizational Compliance with Court-Ordered Reform." *Law and Society Review* 22, (1988): 359–83.

Elsner, Alan. *Gates of Injustice: The Crises in America's Prisons.* Upper Saddle River, NJ: Prentice Hall, 2006.

Fasano, Charles and Suzanne MacKinnon. "The Impact of Litigation on the Cook County Department of Corrections," *Corrections Management Quarterly* 3, no. 2 (1999): 35–42.

Feeley, Malcolm. *The Process is the Punishment.* New York: Russell Sage Foundation, 1979.

Feeley, Malcolm. "The Significance of Prison Conditions Cases: Budgets and Reasons," *Law and Society Review* 23, no.2 (1989): 273–81.

Feeley, Malcolm and Roger Hanson. "The Impact of Judicial Intervention on Prisions and Jails: A Framework for Analysis and Review of the Literature." In *Courts, Corrections and the Constitution,* edited by John Dilulio, 12–46. New York: Oxford University Press, 1990.

Feeley, Malcolm and Edward Rubin. *Judicial Policymaking and the Modern State: How the Courts Reformed America's Prisons.* Cambridge: Cambridge University Press, 2000.

Fegelman, Andrew. "150-Patient Jail Hospital to Be Built." *Chicago Tribune,* July 8, 1993, sec. B2.

Fegelman, Andrew. "County Board's Decision Leaves Boot Camp Marching in Place." *Chicago Tribune,* May 23, 1994, sec. B2.

Fegelman, Andrew. "Lack of Manpower Creates Safety Risks, Jail Watchdog Group Says." *Chicago Tribune,* November 9, 1994, sec. B2.

Fieweger, Michael. "Consent Decrees in Prison and Jail Reform: Relaxed Standard of Reviewf for Government Motions to Modify Consent Decrees." *The Journal of Criminal Law and Criminology* 83, no. 4 (1993): 1024–54.

Fiss, Owen. "Foreword: The Forms of Justice." *Harvard Law Review* 93, (1979): 1–58.

Forte, Lorraine. "New Hospital to Save Jail Cash," *Chicago Sun-Times,* July 18, 1997: 57.

Foucault, Michel. *Discipline and Punish: The Birth of the Prison.* New York: Vintage, 1977.

Friedman, Lawrence. *Crime and Punishment in American History.* New York: Basic Books, 1993.

Frow, John. *Cultural Studies and Cultural Value.* Oxford: Clarendon Press, 1995.

Fuller, Lon. "The Forms and Limits of Adjudication." *Harvard Law Review* 92, (1978): 353–409.

Garafalo, James and Richard Clarke. "The Inmate Subculture in Jails." *Criminal Justice and Behavior* 12, 1985: 415–34.

Gamson, William. "Goffman's Legacy to Political Sociology." *Theory and Society* 14, (1985): 605–22.

Gamson, William. *Talking Politics*. Cambridge: Cambridge University Press, 1992.

Gamson, William and David Stuart. "Media Discourse as a Symbolic Contest: The Bomb in Political Cartoons." *Sociological Forum* 7, no. 1 (1992): 55–86.

Gaes, Gerald. "The Effects of Overcrowding in Prison." In *Crime and Justice An Annual Review of Research Vol. 6*, edited by Michael Tonry and Norval Morris, 95–146. Chicago: University of Chicago Press, 1985.

Gaes, Gerald. "The Effects of Overcrowding in Prison." *Crime and Justice* 6, (1985): 95–146.

Garland, David. *The Culture of Control: Crime and Social Order in Contemporary Society*. Chicago, IL: University of Chicago Press, 2001.

Geertz, Clifford. *Local Knowledge*. New York: Basic Books, 1983.

Geertz, Clifford. "Deep Play: Notes on Balinese Cockfight." In *Interpretive Social Science: A Second Look*, edited by Paul Rabinow and William Sullivan, 195–240. Berkeley, CA: University of California Press, 1987.

Gibbs, John. "Disruption and Distress: Going From Street to Jail." In *Coping with Imprisonment*, edited by Nicolette Parisi, 29–44. Beverly Hills, CA: Sage Publications, 1982.

Glaser, Barney and Anslem Strauss. *The Discovery of Grounded Theory: Strategies for Qualitative Research*. Chicago: Aldine, 1967.

Goffman, Erving. *Frame Analysis: An Essay on the Organization of Experience*. Cambridge: Harvard University Press, 1974.

Goldfarb, Ronald. *Jails: The Ultimate Ghetto of the Criminal Justice System*. Garden City, NY: Anchor Press, 1975.

Gottschalk, Marie. "Money, and Mass Incarceration: The Bad, the Mad, and Penal Reform." *Criminology and Public Policy* 8, no.1 (2009): 97–109.

Gottschalk, Marie. "Cell Blocks and Red Ink: Mass Incarceration, the Great Recession and Penal Reform." *Daedalus* 139, no. 3 (2010): 62–73.

Hagan, John. "Why is There So Little Criminal Justice Theory? Neglected Macro- and Micro-Level Links Between Organization and Power." *Journal of Research in Crime and Delinquency* 26, no. 2 (1989):116–35.

Hall, Stuart. "Cultural Studies: Two Paradigms," *Media Culture and Society* 2, no.1 (1980): 57–72.

Harland, Alan. "Jail Crowding and the Process of Criminal Justice Policymaking." *The Prison Journal* 71, (1991): 77–92.

Harrington v. Kiley et al., 74 C 3290, U.S. District Court, Northern District of Illinois.

Harrison, Paige and Allen Beck, *Prison and Jail Inmates at Midyear 2005*. Washington, DC: U.S. Department of Justice, Office of Justice Programs, 2006. NCJ Publication No. 21–3133.

Harrison, Paige and Jennifer Karberg. *Prison and Jail Inmates at Midyear 2003*. (Washington, DC: U.S. Department of Justice, Office of Justice Programs, 2003), NCJ Publication No. 20–3947.

Hassine, Victor. *Life Without Parole: Living in Prison Today*. New York: Oxford University Press, 2009.

Hayward, Keith and Jock Young. "Cultural Criminology: Some Notes on the Script," *Theoretical Criminology*, 8 (2004): 259–73.

Heinz, John and Peter Manikas. "Networks among Elites in a Local Criminal Justice System," *Law and Society Review*, 26, no. 4, (1992): 831–855.

Henrichson, Christian and Ruth Delaney. "The Price of Prisons: What Incarceration Costs Taxpayers," New York: Vera Institute of Justice, 2012.

Henry, Gary. *Practical Sampling*. Newbury Park CA: Sage, 1990.

Hunter, Albert. "Private, Parochial and Public School Orders: The Problem of Crime and Incivility in Urban Communities." In *The Challenge of Social Control: Citizenship and Institutions Building in Modern Society,* edited by Gerald Suttles and Mayer Zald, 230–242. Norwood NJ: Ablex Publishing, 1985.

Irwin, John. *The Felon.* Berkeley, CA: University of California Press, 1970.

Irwin, John. *The Jail: Managing the Underclass in American Society.* Berkeley, CA: University of California Press, 1985.

Irwin, John. *The Warehouse Prison: Disposal of the New Dangerous Class.* Los Angeles CA: Roxbury Publishing, 2005.

Irwin, John and James Austin. *It's About Time: America's Imprisonment Binge.* Belmont, CA: Wadsworth Publishing, 1994.

Irwin, John and Donald Cressey. "Thieves, Convicts, and Inmate Culture," *Social Problems* 10, (1962): 142–55.

James, William. *Principles of Psychology: Vol. 2.* New York: Dover, 1950.

Jacob, Herbert. The Governance of Trial Judges. *Law and Society Review* 31, no.1. (1997): 3–30.

Jacobs, James. *Statesville: The Penitentiary in Mass Society.* Chicago: University of Chicago Press, 1977.

Jenkins, Phillip. "'The Ice Age' The Social Construction of a Drug Panic," *Justice Quarterly* 11, no.1 (1994): 7–31.

John Howard Association, *Court Monitoring Report for Duran v. Sheahan et al.* 74 C 2949 *Crowding and Conditions of Confinement at the Cook County Department of Corrections and Compliance with the Consent Decree* (Chicago, 1989).

John Howard Association, *Court monitoring report for Duran v. Sheahan et al. 74 C 2949: Crowding and conditions of confinement at the Cook County Department of Corrections and compliance with the consent decree* (Chicago, 1994).

John Howard Association, *Court monitoring report for Duran v. Sheahan et al. 74 C 2949: Crowding and conditions of confinement at the Cook County Department of Corrections and compliance with the consent decree* (Chicago, 1995).

John Howard Association, *Court monitoring report for Duran v. Sheahan et al. 74 C 2949: Crowding and conditions of confinement at the Cook County Department of Corrections and compliance with the consent decree* (Chicago, 1996).

John Howard Association, *Court monitoring report for Duran v. Sheahan et al. 74 C 2949: Crowding and conditions of confinement at the Cook County Department of Corrections and compliance with the consent decree* (Chicago, 1997).

John Howard Association, *Court monitoring report for Duran v. Sheahan et al. 74 C 2949: Crowding and conditions of confinement at the Cook County Department of Corrections and compliance with the consent decree* (Chicago, 1998).

John Howard Association, *Court monitoring report for Duran v. Sheahan et al. 74 C 2949: Crowding and conditions of confinement at the Cook County Department of Corrections and compliance with the consent decree* (Chicago, 1999).

John Howard Association, *Court monitoring report for Duran v. Sheahan et al. 74 C 2949: Crowding and conditions of confinement at the Cook County Department of Corrections and compliance with the consent decree* (Chicago, 2000).

John Howard Association, *Court monitoring report for Duran v. Sheahan et al. 74 C 2949: Crowding and conditions of confinement at the Cook County Department of Corrections and compliance with the consent decree* (Chicago, 2001).

John Howard Association, *Court monitoring report for Duran v. Sheahan et al. 74 C 2949: Crowding and conditions of confinement at the Cook County Department of Corrections and compliance with the consent decree* (Chicago, 2002).

John Howard Association, *Court monitoring report for Duran v. Sheahan et al. 74 C 2949: Crowding and conditions of confinement at the Cook County Department of Corrections and compliance with the consent decree* (Chicago, 2003).

John Howard Association, *Court Monitoring Report for Duran v. Sheahan et. al. 74 C2949: Crowding and Conditions of Confinement at the Cook County Department of Corrections and Compliance with the Consent Decree,* (Chicago, 2004).

John Howard Association, *Court Monitoring Report for Duran v. Brown et. al. 74 C2949: Crowding and Conditions of Confinement at the Cook County Department of Corrections and Compliance with the Consent Decree,* (Chicago, 2010).

John Howard Association, *Review of the Inmate Grievance Procedure at the Cook County Department of Corrections, Duran v. Sheahan et al. 74 C 2949* (Chicago, 1997).

Johnson v. Dye, 338 U.S. 864 (1949).

Juszkiewicz, Jolanta. "Dealing Effectively with Crowded Jails: The Judge's Role." *Policy Studies Review* 7, no.3 (1988): 581–91.

Kennedy, David, Anthony Braga, Anne Piehl, and Elin Waring. *Reducing Gun Violence: The Boston Gun Project's Operation Ceasefire.* Washington, DC: U.S. Department of Justice, National Institute of Justice, 2001.

Kinkade, Patrick, Matthew Leone and Scott Semond. "The Consequences of Jail Crowding." *Crime and Delinquency* 41, no.1 (1995): 150–61.

Kitsuse, John and Malcolm Spector. "Toward a Sociology of Social Problems: Social Conditions, Value-Judgment and Social Problems." *Social Problems, 20,* (1973): 407–19.

Kleiman, Mark. *When Brute Force Fails: How to Have Less Crime and Less Punishment.* Princeton, NJ: Princeton University Press, 2009.

Klinger, David. "Demeanor or Crime? Why Hostile Citizens Are More Likely to be Arrested." *Criminology* 32, (1994): 475–93.

Klofas, John. "Measuring Jail Use: A Comparative Analysis of Local Corrections." *Journal of Research in Crime and Delinquency* 27, no. 3 (1990a): 295–317.

Klofas, John. "The Jail and the Community." *Justice Quarterly* 7, no.1 (1990b): 69–101.

Klofas, John, Stan Stojkovic and David Kalinich. "The Meaning of Correctional Crowding: Steps Toward an Index of Severity," *Crime and Delinquency* 38, no.2 (1992): 171–88.

Krippendorff, Klaus. *Content analysis: An Introduction to its Methodology.* Thousand Oaks CA: Sage, 2004.

Kuczka, Susan. "Female Jail Officers Fight Back Against Harassment." *Chicago Tribune,* October 15, 1993, Sec. B1.

Kyckelhahn, Tracey and Thomas Cohen. *Felony Defendants in Large Urban Counties 2004* (NCJ Publication No. 22–1152). Washington, DC: U.S. Department of Justice, Office of Justice Programs, 2008.

La Vigne, Nancy, Cynthia Mamalian, Jeremy Travis, and Christy Visher. *A Portrait of Prisoner Reentry in Illinois* (NCJ Publication No. 207536). Washington, DC: The Urban Institute, 2003.

Lurigio, Arthur. "MCJA Keynote Address: Responding to the Needs of People with Mental Illness in the Criminal Justice System: An Area Ripe for Research and Community Partnerships," *Journal of Crime and Justice* 35, no. 1 (2012): 1–12.

Lurigio, Arthur, David Olson and Katrina Sifferd. "A Study of the Cook County Day Reporting Center," *Journal of Offender Monitoring* 12, (1999): 5–12.

MacKenzie, Doris Layton. "Reducing the Criminal Activities of Known Offenders and Delinquents: Crime Prevention in the Courts and Corrections." In *Evidence Based Crime Prevention: Revised Edition,* edited by Lawrence Sherman, David Farrington, Brandon Welsh and Doris Layton MacKenzie, 330–404. New York: Routledge, 2002.

MacKenzie, Doris Layton and Claire Souryal. *Multi-Site Evaluation of Shock Incarceration.* National Institute of Justice Research Report (NCJ 150062). Washington DC: U.S. Department of Justice, 1994.

Main, Frank and Carlos Sadovi. "County Jail to Return Convicts to Prison." *Chicago Sun-Times,* March 26, 2002, p. 7.

Manikas, P. M. *Criminal Justice Policymaking: Boundaries and Borderlands, Final Report of the Criminal Justice Project.* Evanston, IL: Northwestern University, Center for Urban Affairs and Policy Research. 1990.

Manning, Peter. *Police Work: The Social Organization of Policing* (2nd ed.). Prospect Heights, IL: Waveland Press, 1997.

Marquardt, James and Ben Crouch. "Judicial Reform and Prisoner Control: The Impact of *Ruiz v. Estelle* on a Texas Penitentiary," *Law and Society Review* 19, (1985): 557–86.

Martin, Christine. *Cook County Pretrial Release Study*. Chicago, IL: Illinois Criminal Justice Information Authority, 1992.

Martin, Christine, David Olson, and Arthur Lurigio. *An Evaluation of the Cook County Sheriff's Day Reporting Center Program: Rearrest and Reincarceration After Discharge*. Chicago, IL: Illinois Criminal Justice Information Authority, 2000.

Maruna, Shadd. *Making Good: How Ex-Convicts Reform and Rebuild Their Lives*. Washington, DC: The American Psychological Association, 2001.

Mather, Lynn and Barbara Yngvesson. "Language, Audience, and the Transformation of Disputes." *Law and Society Review 15*, (1980–81): 775–821.

Mattick, Hans. "The Contemporary Jails of the United States: An Unknown and Neglected Area of Justice." In *Handbook of Criminology*, edited by Daniel Glaser, 777–848. Chicago: Rand McNally, 1974.

Mauer, Marc. *Race to Incarcerate*. New York: The New Press, 2006.

McCarthy, Belinda and Bernard McCarthy. *Community-Based Corrections*. Belmont, CA: Wadsworth Publishing, 1991.

McConville, Sean. "Local Justice: The Jail." In *The Oxford History of the Prison: The Practice of Punishment in Western Society*, edited by Norval Morris and David Rothman, 266–94. New York: Oxford University Press, 1998.

McLuhan, Marshall. *Understanding Media: The Extension of Man*. Corte Madera, CA: Gingko Press, 2003.

Melde, Chris. "Penal Reform and the Stability of Prison Adaptive Modes." *Journal of Crime and Justice* 31, (2008): 59–80.

Monroe v. Pape, 365 U.S. 167 (1961).

Morris, Norval and Michael Tonry. *Between Prison and Probation: Intermediate Punishments in a Rational Sentencing System*. New York: Oxford University Press, 1990.

Neuendorf, Kimberly. *The Content Analysis Guidebook*. Thousand Oaks, CA: Sage Publications, 2002.

Ohlin, Lloyd and Frank Remington. *Discretion in Criminal Justice: The Tension Between Individualization and Uniformity*. New York: State University of New York Press, 1993.

O'Shea, Bridget. "Psychiatric patients with no Place to go but Jail," *New York Times*, February 18, 2012, http://www.nytimes.com/2012/02/19/health/in-chicago-mental-healthpatients-have-no-place-to-go-html.

Oshinsky, David. *Worse Than Slavery: Parchman Farm and the Ordeal of Jim Crow Justice*. New York: Simon and Schuster, 1996.

Padgett, Kathy, William Bales, and Thomas Blomberg. "Under Surveillance: An Empirical Test of the Effectiveness and Consequences of Electronic Monitoring." *Criminology and Public Policy* 5, no.1, (2006): 61–92.

Pallasch, Abdon. "Longtime Cop Vies for Sherriff's Badge," *Chicago Tribune*, October 7, 1998, p. 10.

Palmer, John. *Constitutional Rights of Prisoners*, 8th ed. New York: Anderson Publishing, 2006.

Papachristos, Andrew, Tracey Meares, and Jeffery Fagan. "Attention Felons: Evaluating Project Safe Neighborhood in Chicago." *Journal of Empirical Legal Studies* 4, no.2, (2007): 223–72.

Petersilia, Joan and Susan Turner. "Comparing Intensive and Regular Supervision for High Risk Probationers." *Crime and Delinquency* 36, (1990): 87–111.

"Plaintiffs' Response to Defendant's Status Report and to John Howard Association Monitoring Report," in *the United States District Court for the Northern District of Illinois Eastern Division, Dan Duran, et al., Plaintiffs v. Michael F. Sheahan, Sheriff of Cook County, et al., Defendants. 74 C 2949, Judge George M. Marovich*, (1995).

"Plaintiffs' Response to Defendant's Status Report and to John Howard Association Monitoring Report," in *the United States District Court for the Northern District of*

Illinois Eastern Division, Dan Duran, et al., Plaintiffs v. Michael F. Sheahan, Sheriff of Cook County, et al., Defendants. 74 C 2949, Judge George M. Marovich, (1997).

"Plaintiffs' Response to Defendant's Status Report and to John Howard Association Monitoring Report," in *the United States District Court for the Northern District of Illinois Eastern Division, Dan Duran, et al., Plaintiffs v. Michael F. Sheahan, Sheriff of Cook County, et al., Defendants.* 74 C 2949, Judge George M. Marovich, (1998).

"Plaintiffs' Response to Defendant's Status Report and to John Howard Association Monitoring Report," in *the United States District Court for the Northern District of Illinois Eastern Division, Dan Duran, et al., Plaintiffs v. Michael F. Sheahan, Sheriff of Cook County, et al., Defendants.* 74 C 2949, Judge George M. Marovich, (1999).

"Plaintiffs' Response to Defendant's Status Report and to John Howard Association Monitoring Report," in *the United States District Court for the Northern District of Illinois Eastern Division, Dan Duran, et al., Plaintiffs v. Michael F. Sheahan, Sheriff of Cook County, et al., Defendants.* 74 C 2949, Judge George M. Marovich, (2000).

"Plaintiffs' Response to Defendant's Status Report and to John Howard Association Monitoring Report," in *the United States District Court for the Northern District of Illinois Eastern Division, Dan Duran, et al., Plaintiffs v. Michael F. Sheahan, Sheriff of Cook County, et al., Defendants.* 74 C 2949, Judge George M. Marovich, (2001).

Pogrebin, Mark. "Scarce Resources and Jail Management." *International Journal of Offender Therapy and Comparative Criminology* 26, (1982): 263–74.

Pontell, Henry and Wayne Welsh. "Incarceration as a Deviant Form of Social Control: Jail Overcrowding in California," *Crime and Delinquency* 40, no.1 (1994):18–36.

Possley, Maurice and Steve Mills. "Former Guard Allege 2nd Mass Beating." *Chicago Tribune,* February 28, 2003, sec. A1.

Pretrial Services Resource Center. *A Second Look at Alleviating Jail Crowding: A Systems Perspective,* Washington, DC: U.S. Department of Justice, Office of Justice Programs, Bureau of Justice Assistance, 2000. NCJ Publication No. 182507.

Raspberry, William. "Inmates Have the Power to Change Their Destinies." *Chicago Tribune,* December 30, 1994, p. 19.

Renzama, Marc and Evan Mayo-Wilson. "Can Electronic Monitoring Reduce Crime for Moderate to High-Risk Offenders?" *Journal of Experimental Criminology* 1, (2005): 215–37.

Resolution Cook County Board of Commissioners. *Resolution sponsored by the Honorable John H. Stroger, Jr. President of the Cook County Board of Commissioners,* April 9, 2002 meeting, (Chicago, 2002).

Rhine, Edward. "The Rule of Law, Disciplinary Practices, and Rahway State Prision: A Case Study in Judicial Intervention and Social Control." In *Courts, Corrections and the Constitution,* edited by John Dilulio, 173–222. New York: Oxford University Press, 1990.

Rhodes v. Chapman, 452 U.S. 337 (1981).

Robinson v. California, 370 U.S. 660 (1962).

Rose, Dina and Todd Clear. "Incarceration, Social Capital, and Crime: Implications for Social Disorganization Theory," *Criminology* 36, (1998): 441–480.

Rothman, David. *Conscience and Convenience: The Asylum and Its Alternatives in Progressive America.* Boston: Little Brown, 1980.

Rothman, David. *The Discovery of Asylum: Social Order and Disorder in the New Republic.* Boston: Little Brown, 1990.

Rottman, David and John Kimberly. "The Social Context of Jails." In *Correctional Institutions* 3rd ed., edited by Robert Carter, Daniel Glaser and Leslie T. Wilkins, 125–39. New York: Harper Row, 1985.

Rubin, Herbert and Irene Rubin. *Qualitative Interviewing: The Art of Hearing Data.* Thousand Oaks CA: Sage, 1995.

Ruffo v. Inmates of the Suffolk County Jail, 112 U.S. 748 (1992).

Sabol, William and Todd Minton. *Jail Inmates at Midyear 2007.* Washington, DC: U.S. Department of Justice, Office of Justice Programs, 2008. NCJ Publication No. 221945.

Sahlins, Marshall. *Historical Metaphors and Mythical Realities: Structure in the Early History of the Sandwich Islands Kingdom.* Ann Arbor, MI: University of Michigan Press, 2000.

Sampson, Robert. *Great American City: Chicago and the Enduring Neighborhood Effect.* Chicago IL: University of Chicago Press, 2011. *Daedalus* 139, no. 3, (2010): 20–31.

Sampson, Robert and Charles Loeffler. "Punishment's Place: The Local Concentration of Mass Incarceration."

Sandovi, Carlos. "Jail Program Helps Moms Learn Skill of Parenting." *Chicago Sun-Times,* January 1, 2001, p. 12.

Scheingold, Stuart. *The Politics of Street Crime: Criminal Process Cultural Obsession.* Philadelphia: Temple University Press, 1991.

Scheufele, Dietram. "Framing as a Theory of Media Effects." *Journal of Communication* Winter, (1999): 103–22.

Schlanger, Margo. "Beyond the Hero Judge: Institutional Reform Litigation as Litigation," *Michigan Law Review* 97, (1999): 1994–2036.

Schmid, Thomas and Richard Jones. "Prison Adaptation Strategies of First-time, Short-term Inmates," *Journal of Contemporary Ethnography* 21, (1993): 439–63.

Sechrest, Dale. "The Effects of Density on Jail Assaults," *Journal of Criminal Justice* 19, (1991): 211–23.

Selke, William. *Prisons in Crises.* Bloomington, IN: Indiana University Press, 1993.

Shelden, Randall and William Brown. "Correlates of Jail Overcrowding." *Crime and Delinquency* 37, no.3 (1991): 347–62.

Sherman, Lawrence, David Farrington, Brandon Welsh and Doris Layton MacKenzie. *Evidence-Based Crime Prevention: Revised Edition.* New York: Routledge, 2002.

Sigmon, Jane, M. Elaine Nugent, John Goerdt and Scott Wallace. *Key Elements of Successful Adjudication Partnerships,* Washington, DC: U.S., Department of Justice, Office of Justice Programs, Bureau of Justice Assistance, 1999. NCJ Publication No. 173949.

Simon, Jonathan. ""Clearing the 'Troubled Assets" of America's Punishment Bubble," *Daedalus* 139, no. 3 (2010): 91–101.

Smith, Christopher. "The Prison Reform Litigation Era: Book Length Studies and Lingering Research Issues." *The Prison Journal* 83, no.3 (2003): 337–58.

Smylka, John and William Selke. *Intermediate Sanctions.* Cincinnati, OH: Anderson Publishing, 1995.

Spelman, William. "Crime, Cash, and Limited Options: Explaining the Prison Boom." *Criminology and Public Policy* 8, no.1 (2009): 29–77.

"Status Report of Proceedings before the Honorable George M. Marovich," *In the United States District Court for the Northern District of Illinois Eastern Division, Dan Duran, et al., Plaintiffs v. Michael F. Sheahan, Sheriff of Cook County, et al., Defendants. 74 C 2949, Judge George M. Marovich,* (1996).

"Status Report of Proceedings before the Honorable George M. Marovich," *In the United States District Court for the Northern District of Illinois Eastern Division, Dan Duran, et al., Plaintiffs v. Michael F. Sheahan, Sheriff of Cook County, et al., Defendants. 74 C 2949, Judge George M. Marovich.* (1999).

Stojkovich, Stan and John Klofas, "Crowding and Correctional Change." In *Turnstile Justice: Issues in American Corrections,* edited by Ted Alleman and Rosemary Gido, 90–109. Upper Saddle River, NJ: Prentice Hall, 1997.

Stokols, Daniel. "On the Distinction Between Density and Crowding: Some Implications for Future Research," *Psychological Review* 79, (1972): 275–77.

Storey, Ted. "When Intervention Works: Judge Morris E. Lasker and New York City Jails." In *Courts, Corrections and the Constitution,* edited by John Dilulio, 138–172. New York: Oxford University Press, 1990.

Stowell, Jacob and James Byrne. "Does What Happens in Prison Stay in Prison? Examining the Reciprocal Relationship Between Community and Prison Culture." In *The Culture of Prison Violence,* edited by James Byrne, Don Hummer, and Faye Taxman, 27–39. Boston: Pearson Publishing, 2008.

"Strip-Searching Women in Jail," *Chicago Tribune,* April 8, 2001, sec A18.

Sullivan, Dennis and Larry Tift. "Court Intervention in Corrections: Roots of Resistance and Problems of Compliance," *Crime and Delinquency* July, (1975): 213–22.

Sykes, Gresham. *The Society of Captives: A Study of Maximum Security Prison.* Princeton, NJ: Princeton University Press, 1958.

Taggart, William. "Redefining the Power of the Federal Judiciary: The Impact of Court-Ordered Prison Reform on State Expenditures for Corrections." *Law and Society Review* 23, no.2 (1989): 241–71.

Tartaro, Christine. "The Impact of Density on Jail Violence," *Journal of Criminal Justice* 30, (2002): 499–510.

Toch, Hans. *Living in Prison: The Ecology of Survival.* New York: Free Press, 1977.

Tonry, Michael. "Stated and Latent Functions of ISP." *Crime and Delinquency* 36, (1990): 174–91.

Tonry, Michael. "Racial Politics, Racial Disparities, and War on Crime," *Crime and Delinquency 40,* (1994): 475–97.

Tonry, Michael and Mary Lynch. "Intermediate Sanctions." In *Crime and Justice* vol. 20, edited by Michael Tonry, 99–144. Chicago: University of Chicago Press, 1996.

Tonry, Michael. *Thinking About Crime: Sense and Sensibility in American Penal Culture.* Oxford; Oxford University Press, 2004.

Useem, Bert. "Crain: Non-Reformist Prison Reform." In *Courts, Corrections and the Constitution,* edited by John Dilulio, 223–48. New York: Oxford University Press, 1990.

Vogt, Paul. *Dictionary of Statistics and Methodology: A Nontechnical Guide for the Social Sciences.* Thousand Oaks CA: Sage, 1999.

Wacquant, Loic. "Class, Race and Hyperincarceration in Revanchist America." *Daedalus* 139, no. 3, (2010): 74–90.

Weisheit, Ralph and John Klofas. "The Impact of Jail: Collateral Cost and Affective Response." *Journal of Offender Counseling, Services and Rehabilitation* 14, (1989): 51–65.

Welch, Michael. "Jail Overcrowding: Social Sanitation and Warehousing of the Urban Underclass." In *Crime and Justice in America: Present Realities and Future Prospects,* edited by Paul Cromwell and Roger Dunham, 263–284. Upper Saddle River, NJ: Prentice–Hall, 1997.

Welsh, Wayne. "The Dynamics of Jail Reform Litigation: A Comparative Analysis of Litigation in California Counties." *Law and Society Review 26,* no. 3, (1992): 591–625.

Welsh, Wayne. "Changes in Arrest Policies as a Result of Court Orders Against County Jails." *Justice Quarterly* 10, no.1 (1993): 89–120.

Welsh, Wayne. *Counties in Court: Jail Overcrowding and Court–Ordered Reform.* Philadelphia: Temple University, 1995.

Welsh, Wayne and Henry Pontell. "Counties in Court: Interorganizational Adaptions to Jail Litigation in California," *Law and Society Review* 24, no.1 (1991): 73–101.

Welsh, Wayne, Henry Pontell, Matthew Leone and Patrick Kinkade. "Jail Overcrowding: An Analysis of Policymakers' Perceptions," *Justice Quarterly* 7, no.2 (1990): 341–370.

West, Cornell. *Democracy Matters: Winning the Fight Against Imperialism.* New York: Penguin Press, 2004.

West, Heather, William Sabol, and Sarah Greenman. Prisoners in 2009. Washington, DC: U.S. Department of Justice, Office of Justice Programs, 2010. NCJ Publication No. 231675.

Williams, Raymond. *Marxism and Literature.* New York: Oxford University Press, 1977.

Wilson v. Seiter, 501 U.S. 294 (1991).

Wilson, Terry. "Jail Menu Has Strike Against It." *Chicago Tribune,* April 14, 1993, sec. B8.

Wolff v. McDonald, 418 U.S. 539 (1974).

Wright, Kevin. "The Desirability of Goal Conflict Within the Criminal Justice System." *Journal of Criminal Justice* 9, (1980): 19–31.

Yackle, Larry. *Reform and Regret: The Story of Federal Judicial Involvement in the Alabama Prison System*. New York: Oxford University Press, 1989.

Young, Alison. *Imagining Crime*. London: Sage, 1996.

Zaitzow, Barbara and Jim Thomas. *Women in Prison: Gender and Social Control*. Boulder, CO: Lynne Rienner Publishers, 2003.

Zimring, Franklin. *The Great American Crime Decline*. New York, NY: Oxford University Press, 2007.

Zimring, Franklin and Gordon Hawkins. *The Scale of Imprisonment*. Chicago: University of Chicago Press, 1991.

Zimring, Franklin and Gordon Hawkins. *The Search for Rational Drug Control*. Cambridge: University of Cambridge Press, 1992.

Zwecker, Bill. "Morris Barges in with Jail Plan." *Chicago Sun-Times*, August 9, 1994, p.18.

Index